SUDDEN INFANT DEATH
Patterns, Puzzles and Problems

Jean Golding, Sylvia Limerick and
Aidan Macfarlane

Open Books

First published 1985 by Open Books Publishing Ltd,
West Compton House, Near Shepton Mallet, Somerset, England

© Jean Golding, Sylvia Limerick and Aidan Macfarlane

Hardback ISBN: 0 7291 0198 3
Paperback ISBN: 0 7291 0193 2

Set by V & M Graphics Ltd, Aylesbury and
printed by A. Wheaton & Co Ltd, Exeter.

Contents

Acknowledgements   vii

PART I: *Setting the Scene*

Chapter   1 Introduction   3

Chapter   2 A Perspective of Infant Deaths   5

Chapter   3 Case Histories   10

PART II: *Epidemiological Studies*

Chapter   4 Introduction to Epidemiological Methods   18

Chapter   5 Variation of Incidence with Time, Place and Age
             of Infant   22

Chapter   6 Characteristics of the Parents   43

Chapter   7 Characteristics of the Pregnancy   53

Chapter   8 Labour and Delivery   63

Chapter   9 Characteristics of the Infant in the Early Neonatal
             Period   67

Chapter 10 Characteristics of the Older Infant   77

Chapter 11 Medical History of the Siblings and the Mothers   87

Chapter 12 Summary of the Epidemiological Findings   94

PART III: *Possible Causes of Sudden Infant Death*

Chapter 13 Methods of Generating and Testing Hypotheses   104

Chapter 14 Excesses and Deficiencies   108

Chapter 15 Sleeping, Breathing and Heart Rate 119
Chapter 16 Infections and the Immune System 128

PART IV: *Reaction to Death*
Chapter 17 Bereavement 136
Chapter 18 Management Immediately after the Death 141
Chapter 19 The Coroner's Investigation 148
Chapter 20 Funerals and Administrative Problems 160
Chapter 21 Support for Parents 166
Chapter 22 Children's Reactions to Death 183

PART V: *The Way Ahead?*
Chapter 23 Prediction 190
Chapter 24 Prevention 196
Chapter 25 Amelioration 204
Chapter 26 The Unsolved Mystery 216
Appendix 1 Sudden Infant Deaths in Oxfordshire and West
           Berkshire 1971–75 224
Appendix 2 Retrospective Study of Parents: Foundation for the
           Study of Infant Deaths 226
Glossary 228
References 230
Index 256

Acknowledgements

We are, all three, grateful for the understanding and tolerance shown by our families during the difficult time when we were writing this book.

In relation to the surveys that were carried out, we acknowledge with gratitude the help and co-operation in undertaking the Foundation survey of Janet Beckley, secretary to the Foundation for the Study of Infant Deaths who corresponded with newly bereaved parents inviting them to complete the questionnaire, to Angela Gardner, statistician at the London School of Hygiene and Tropical Medicine for assistance in programming the computer for analysis of the 1980-1 questionnaires (the 1974-9 were analysed manually), to Dr. D. R. Chambers, HM Coroner for Inner North London, and Miss R. Cobb, HM Coroner for SE Kent, for advice on the Coroners' Rules, to Dr. Marie Lindsay at the Child Guidance Clinic, Aylesbury, for commenting on child reactions to death, and to Professor J. L. Emery for reading and commenting on the survey manuscript.

In addition, we are extremely grateful to the late John Baldwin and now Dr. Michael Goldacre, Directors of the Oxford Record Linkage Study for permission to carry out the survey and publish the results. This study is an ongoing study funded by the Department of Health and Social Security. The data were abstracted from clinical case notes by Mrs. Bettine Sutton and Mrs Jean Lawrie to whom we are especially grateful. We are also very grateful to Dr. Jean Keeling for assessing all the post-neonatal deaths, and defining those which were sudden infant deaths according to Beckwith's definition.

The actual manuscript could not have been prepared without the active participation of Jean Lawrie, Yasmin Iles, Mary Paterson, Tim Sladden, Clare Taylor, Jill Howse and Michael Mack to whom we are especially grateful.

Part I
Setting the Scene

Chapter 1

Introduction

Finality shocks us. The sudden cessation of a complex social and physical presence within a group of people is often accompanied by far reaching and long standing psychological, emotional and physical changes in those involved. This is perhaps never more true than with the sudden and totally unexpected death of a baby. Above all, being unexplained it seems especially unjust – 'Why my child?' – 'Why us?'.

Death comes to us all, our very existence as individual human beings within a society depends on the millions of births and deaths that preceded us. It is objectively unthinkable that death should not exist, and yet we have extreme difficulty as individuals in coming to terms in our personal lives with the facts that our deaths, and the deaths of our relatives, and those other people that we know, are inevitable.

The immediate and irredeemable loss in most cases needs to be shared. The physical facts of death will involve not only the parents, the child's grandparents and siblings, but friends, other relatives, neighbours, passing strangers, switchboard operators, ambulance men, hospital casualty staff, policemen, doctors, coroners, coroners' officers, pathologists, health visitors, priests and many others, each with general and specific roles to play in supporting others. They also have a role to play in the search to understand why the child should have died, and to gain knowledge that may help prevent others from doing so. It is for everyone that has been, is or may be involved that this book is written.

All babies dying must die for a reason – there may be one major disorder, or several minor abnormalities that in combination lead to the death of the child. By detailed research in many different areas, such as epidemiology, clinical medicine, genetics, etc – the causes of most deaths in childhood have been identified. Sudden unexpected deaths in young children may be due to causes similar to those already discovered, although the exact nature of these have not yet been identified. This may be because our understanding of normal physiological processes and the techniques that have been developed in post-mortem examination have not yet reached the stage of delicacy or discernment that is required. There is in this search a law of diminishing returns – vast inroads have been made into the causes of death since the processes of infection and malnutrition have been understood. With understanding has come prevention. There remains, however, a small but important group of deaths that are still unexplained.

In order to try to give what we hope is a balanced picture, and in an attempt to demystify 'sudden infant deaths' this book is divided into five sections. This first introductory section is a perspective on infant deaths in general and includes a brief outline of historical and social attitudes. The second and third sections contain a review of the hundreds of scientific articles and books written in the last 50 years or so on the subject. Previously unpublished information collected in a large epidemiological study is also included. The epidemiological results are described first. They use information from a population to show, for example, statistical associations between smoking in pregnancy and sudden infant death. This method of research can be a valuable background against which hypotheses can be produced as to the causes of sudden infant death. Then we deal with detailed clinical medical research and examine the evidence for the various hypotheses that have been suggested.

The fourth section is concerned with the practical response to the death. A considerable amount is known about counselling parents in bereavement, much of which is common sense but needs remembering at the relevant time. The experiences of some 700 parents in the weeks and months after the death are reported here for the first time. Their difficulties are of especial importance to the large number of people involved in the emotional trauma of these deaths.

The final section of the book concerns prevention and tries to provide answers to the question – 'Given what we know at present about factors associated with sudden infant death, can one give any advice to parents and others concerned about how to prevent it?' There is a short concluding statement with suggestions as to the lines that future research might take in continuing to unravel the complex problems involved.

We have called this book *Sudden Infant Death: Patterns, Puzzles and Problems*. It is a mystery story, but we are not able to offer the solution. What we have tried to do is describe the clues, show what we think are red herrings and discuss some of the theories that may contain the final answer.

Chapter 2

A Perspective of Infant Deaths

Fifty years ago in the Western World, sudden infant death was probably very much like the present picture of sudden infant deaths in the Third World areas, such as parts of Africa, Asia or South America. We know very little, at present, about infants dying suddenly and unexpectedly in these places because they are swamped numerically by the very large numbers of children dying as a result of infection and malnutrition.

Only one hundred years ago in England, out of every 1,000 babies born alive, 150 children would die before the end of the first year of life. It is likely that only 2 of these deaths would have been sudden infant deaths as discussed in this book. About 110 would have been due to problems associated with infection and malnutrition. A few deaths would be due to congenital malformations and tumours, much as they are now, and about 30 would have been associated with complications of birth.

In the early 1980's in England and America, out of every 1,000 babies born alive approximately 990 survive to their first birthday. Of the 10 that die, 6 do so in the first month of life due mainly to a low birthweight or congenital defect. Very occasionally one of these deaths is due to infection. The remaining 4 babies (out of the 1,000 births) that die, do so between the ages of one month and one year. Of these postneonatal deaths almost half will usually occur in hospital, due to obvious congenital abnormalities, or to an infection such as meningitis, gastro-enteritis or pneumonia that has not responded to treatment. A very small proportion will also be due to degenerative disorders or tumours.

The remaining half of the deaths will have occurred suddenly and unexpectedly. The great majority of deaths in this category will have occurred at home, or en route to hospital. Detailed post-mortem examination may show that some of these infants had died from an unsuspected congenital abnormality or an unrecognised infection or rare disorder or injury. In the remainder, there may be (a) no signs of any abnormality at all, (b) minor abnormalities, but no indication of a specific disease process, (c) evidence of disease but not thought to be severe enough to have caused death. Deaths falling into any of these three categories will be referred to as *sudden infant deaths*. The official definition was first given by Beckwith in 1969. 'The sudden death of any infant or young child which is unexpected by history and in whom a thorough necropsy examination fails to demonstrate an adequate cause of death'. This definition highlights the essential need to have a detailed post-mortem examination of every child that dies suddenly and unexpectedly and to enquire into the history of the baby. Numerically, sudden infant deaths account for over 1,500 deaths in the U.K. and about 8,000 in the U.S.A.

Historical Perspectives

Although, until recently, sudden infant deaths formed a relatively small proportion of all infant deaths – they were occasionally recognised as a distinct entity. From pre-Christian times until the 19th century, children found dead in their parents' bed were assumed to have been 'overlaid'. These were children thought to have died due to accidental smothering occurring when their parents rolled over on top of them whilst asleep. The earliest reference to such overlaying dates back to Kings I, Chapter 3, Verse xix. However, during the time when this theory was most prevalent, infanticide was also extremely common and little attempt was made to distinguish between overlaying and deliberate suffocation.

In medieval times cases of overlaying were dealt with by the ecclesiastical courts rather than secular ones, and it was accepted as being due to negligence or callousness on the part of the parents. In meting out punishment it appeared that these courts were less concerned with the protection of children's lives, than they were for providing punishment for what they considered to be a sin.

In England it was not until the 17th and 18th centuries that sudden unexpected deaths in infants became the concern of the police and the secular courts. By the early 19th century, civil and coroners' courts were investigating cases of overlaying and smothering to try to determine specific causes of death.

At the turn of the century overlaying was still a strong contender in England and Scotland as a cause of sudden infant death and the surgeon of police of Dundee, Scotland, in 1892 wrote:

'The principle causes producing this great mortality over overlaying are:

1. Ignorance and carelessness of mothers;
2. Drunkenness
3. Overcrowding
4. According to some observers, illegitimacy and the (life) insurance of infants'.

He strongly advocated a law prohibiting parents from having their infants in bed with them and also suggested the strenuous prosecution of parents whose children died in these circumstances.

Savitt showed that overlaying was largely the equivalent of what we now choose to call sudden infant death when he examined the age distribution of 266 cases of overlaying or smothering in Virginia slave children between 1853 and 1860. The peak incidence of the post-neonatal deaths was in the third month of life – an identical pattern to that now found for sudden infant deaths.

In the mid nineteenth century, authors in France were claiming that these deaths were not due to overlaying, but that the lungs showed specific respiratory changes. They claimed that in:

'what is called "Capillary Bronchitis" or "Suffocating Catarrh in children" (Laennec), intense congestion now and then occurs, which places the child's life in jeopardy for several hours. When the child is strong, is more than 7 or 8 months old, it seldom dies at the first attack of congestion. When the age is less than 6 months, death may occur in the first attack.'

At this time, post mortem examinations were not regularly carried out on such cases. However at the turn of the 19th century the thymus – a gland in the neck and upper chest – was thought to be enlarged in cases of children who were considered to have been overlaid. Obstruction of the upper airways by the thymus gland was proposed as an alternative cause, as the story of a German girl in the 1880's indicates:

'a case in which a servant girl was entrusted with the care of an infant who was sleeping in its cradle near her. In the morning the previously healthy baby was found dead in the cradle. The girl was imprisoned and the authorities ordered an autopsy, which was performed by Limman and Grawitz. Limman was unable to disprove Grawitz's contention that death was attributable to a colossally enlarged thymus pressing on trachea, bronchi and vessels. The magistrate released the woman ...'.

In spite of later evidence to the contrary, the theory of death being due to thymus enlargement, continued to hold sway for more than 50 years. However, the only other autopsy specimens available to the pathologists at that time were those from deaths due to malnutrition or infection, in both of which the thymus becomes involuted and small. Thus the apparently enlarged thymus in children dying from overlaying was in fact the normal size gland. This fact took a long time to be accepted by the medical profession. The following extract from a 1905 issue of the British Medical Journal is typical:

'enlargement of the gland is a recognised cause of sudden death in infants, owing either to direct pressure on the trachea, or to its pressure on the pneumogastric (vagus nerve) causing spasm of the glottis.'

During the 1920's there was a gradual return to the view in England that these children were dying due to external mechanical smothering. Shortly thereafter there was a change in the coroner's law, which made autopsies on infants dying suddenly almost mandatory. Following this change in the law, pneumonia was frequently given as the cause of death even when there were minimal changes in the pathology of the lungs at post-mortem. There may be several reasons for this, one of which was that there were still no good normal standards against which pathologists performing the examinations could judge their findings; in addition 'cause unknown' was unacceptable to the Registrar of Births and Deaths. In order to avoid further distress to the parents it was convenient to report natural causes of death in such cases. This misleading reporting led investigators to think that infection was the usual cause of death. The position was hardly challenged until the 1940's. The infective theory nevertheless has recently become popular again, owing to viruses occasionally being isolated. We shall discuss this more fully in Chapter 16.

It wasn't until the 1960's that the great expansion in research and accompanying theories of the causes of sudden infant death really began. The first of the major new theories was of 'allergy to milk protein', it being supposed that the majority of cases of sudden infant death were due to inhalation and regurgitation of milk into the lungs, with death resulting from anaphylactoid shock because the children were hypersensitised to cows' milk proteins.

The first major international conferences on the subject of sudden unexpected infant death were held in 1963 and 1969 in Seattle (Washington, USA) where many aetiological theories (possible causes) were discussed. Aetiology was again discussed at international symposiums held at Cambridge, England in 1970, Toronto in 1974 and Baltimore in 1982. They included discussion on various aspects of epidemiology, immunology, inborn errors of metabolism and upper airways obstruction. In spite of much research, no one has yet been able to show exact mechanisms, although hypotheses have continued to proliferate.

As the hypotheses have multiplied so has the nomenclature. This group of deaths are popularly known as 'cot' deaths in Britain, as 'crib' deaths in North America. Among the scientific community: sudden unexpected infant death (SUID), sudden unexpected death in infancy (SUDI), sudden infant death syndrome (SIDS) and other permutations and combinations of the words 'sudden', 'infant', 'unexpected', 'syndrome' and 'death' have been used. In this book we shall generally use the phrase 'sudden infant death'.

Chapter 3

Case Histories

Given below are five cases as examples of sudden infant death encountered by us. Minor details have been altered so that direct identification of parents is impossible.

Baby David
His mother had been a nurse. She was in her early thirties and had given up working after the birth of her first child. Her husband was a doctor at the local hospital. They had been happily married for eight years and had two children, a boy and girl aged 7 and 3 respectively. The present child was planned and antenatal care had been supervised by the Family Doctor. The Mother did not smoke and did not take any medication during pregnancy. Delivery was in the general practitioner unit at the local maternity hospital at 41 weeks gestation. The mother had gone into labour spontaneously, and the baby boy weighed 3,760 grams (8lbs). No resuscitation was needed and there were no problems in the days immediately after birth. Initial physical examination showed that the child was entirely normal, and the mother was discharged after two days in hospital, breast feeding her infant. Once home, the child fed normally and was well accepted by the other children in the family. The mother was visited at home by the community midwife and later by her health visitor. There was no need to take the child to see the general practitioner at any time. The baby was taken to the local child health clinic at 2 months of age for the normal screening examinations. These showed no abnormality at all. One day when the child was nearly three months old and shortly before he was due to have his first immunisation, he was put down at 2 p.m. in his own cot for his usual afternoon sleep. The room was centrally heated and the child was wearing a vest, nappies, a stretch suit, cardigan and covered by a sheet and two light blankets. He appeared to go straight to sleep and his mother went downstairs with

the 3 year old to do the washing up, leaving the baby's door open. She heard no sound from the baby and went up to check the child after 30 minutes. At that time she noticed he was lying on his stomach with his head turned on one side. He looked very pale and when she picked him up he was floppy and there was blood tinged froth around the mouth. He was still warm. The mother immediately tried to clear the baby's mouth and attempted mouth-to-mouth resuscitation after dialling 999 for an ambulance. This arrived in 5 minutes and the ambulance men took over attempts at resuscitation. The child arrived at the hospital within 10 minutes. At that time no heart beat and no signs of breathing were noted and further attempts at resuscitation were abandoned after an hour.

Later the same day a police officer arrived and took a statement from the mother and at the same time took the child's blankets and pillow, explaining that they were for examination by the coroner. The parents were informed that since the child had died suddenly and unexpectedly the death certificate had to be signed by the coroner after a post-mortem by the hospital pathologist.

Two days later the parents were contacted by the hospital pathologist who explained that the post-mortem examination showed that their child had been completely normal except that some vomit had been found in the baby's mouth and upper airways. There was some slight reddening of the upper airways and signs of mild infection in the lungs. They were also informed that more detailed results of the post mortem would be available later. On the same day the coroner's officer rang to explain that the death certificate had been signed by the coroner and no further enquiry was to be held. The parents subsequently collected the child from the hospital and arranged burial although they had been informed that this could be arranged by the hospital. Both parents were seen by the paediatrician responsible for the attempts at resuscitation of the baby, and further post mortem results were given. These did not indicate any further abnormalities.

The parents arranged to take the 7 year old and 3 year old siblings regularly to see the grave where the baby was buried and explained to them that their new brother had died. Both children asked many questions as to where he had gone and appeared to be reassured by the straightforward answers that the parents gave. However, three months later the three year old began showing aggressive behaviour to her parents, she began to wet herself and had to go back into nappies. This behaviour continued for a further nine months causing considerable distress to the parents. However, at this time, when questioned by her mother directly as to whether she was worried about her younger brother having died, the child explained that she had gone into the child's bedroom before the mother found the child dead and had tried to wake the baby up herself and had been unable to do so. She then frankly explained that she thought that she might have been responsible for whatever had happened to the baby. After considerable reassurance from the parents that the baby's death had nothing to do with her, the child ceased to show any behaviour problems.

Baby Sarah

The Mother was in her early twenties and continued to work throughout her pregnancy as a hairdressing assistant. The father was a butcher aged 24 who had been married previously but had no children by that marriage. The marriage was thought to be unstable from the start, as the father drank heavily and disappeared from the home from time to time. This was the mother's first pregnancy. She reported for antenatal care 16 weeks after her last menstrual period, and at 20 weeks of pregnancy was admitted to hospital with bleeding. She was treated with bed rest and sedatives; subsequently the bleeding stopped and she was discharged home. Throughout the whole of the pregnancy the mother smoked 25 cigarettes a day and father smoked 20 cigarettes a day. The mother had a history of asthma.

She was admitted to the maternity hospital at 39 weeks of pregnancy with further bleeding and labour was induced resulting in the uneventful delivery of a girl weighing 3,510 grams (7lb 12oz). On examination the child appeared completely normal, and was breast fed for the first two weeks then changed to bottle feeding because the mother felt that she did not have an adequate amount of milk.

The parents lived in a damp flat. There were outstanding arrears in the payment for electricity and rent. To add to the difficulties, the father became unemployed and was subsequently charged with theft, gross bodily harm and indecent assault. The mother became depressed and was put on anti-depressants by the general practitioner. At one month of age the child was put on the social services 'at risk' register and was seen frequently at home by the health visitor because of screaming and feeding problems.

At two months of age the child developed eczema, which was treated with a hydrocortisone ointment and at four months of age developed 'wheezy bronchitis' which was treated with antibiotics. When the child was six months old she spent a week in hospital with severe bronchiolitis and shortly after discharge from hospital she was fostered for two weeks, as the mother was ill and the father had left home. It was stated by the social services at this time that there was never any question of any physical abuse of the child by the parents.

However, in the first six months the health visitor had needed to visit the home 19 times.

One evening when the child was eight months old, she was put to bed as normal, at 7 p.m. At midnight the mother fed the child as usual – a bottle of cows' milk. Although the child usually awoke for a further feed at 6.30 a.m., that morning she failed to do so and the mother slept on. At 8.30 a.m. the mother went to wake the baby up and found her lying head downwards under her bed clothes at the bottom of the bed. When the mother pulled back the bed clothes the child was grey, cold and lifeless. There was vomit on the sheet and around her mouth.

Baby Rory

The mother was in her thirties and had been a barmaid before marriage. She had ceased to work after the birth of her first child. The father was a farmer aged 36 and they had one normal boy aged 6. Their second child was also a boy who had died suddenly and unexpectedly at home at three months of age. The present pregnancy was her third. The parents lived in a farm house, with central heating, in an isolated area. They had lived there for 5 years.

The present pregnancy was planned although they had waited for two years after the previous pregnancy on the advice of their family doctor, so that they could fully mourn the loss of their previous child. During the pregnancy the mother had a threatened miscarriage and was given the drug Primulot. She went into spontaneous labour at 38 weeks and delivered a normal boy weighing 3,125 grams (6lb 14oz).

In the hospital where the child was delivered studies were being undertaken of babies born to parents who had already had a sudden infant death. The paediatrician concerned with this study saw the parents 5 days after delivery and asked whether he might record the baby's breathing patterns and heart patterns the following day. The parents both agreed. The following day the mother breast fed her baby at midday and put the baby in its cot with three other babies in a side room next to the main ward. She then went to talk to her friends. About 20 minutes later a nurse checking on the babies, found the baby grey and lifeless and without a heart beat. Attempts at resuscitation failed. Post mortem examination showed no abnormality.

Baby Thomas

The father was a builder's labourer and the mother a factory worker aged 21. The couple had been married for 5 years and already had two boys aged 4 and 1. At four months of pregnancy the mother developed influenza which lasted for a week. There were no other abnormalities until at six and a half months of pregnancy, an ultrasound examination showed twins. No medicines, other than iron, had been taken during the pregnancy. At seven months of pregnancy the mother was admitted to hospital because of increased blood pressure and ankle swelling. At 32 weeks gestation she went into labour and delivered twins. The twin boys weighed 2,030 grams (4lb 8oz) and 1,823 grams (4lb) respectively. They were admitted to special care where the smaller second twin developed severe respiratory distress and needed artificial ventilation for four days. The other twin had an uneventful course in the special care baby unit, and both babies were sent home at 6 weeks of age.

They left hospital feeding on one type of dried milk but subsequently were changed to another two weeks after discharge home. Cereals were introduced at 3 months of age to both twins. The second twin was seen by the family doctor four times in the first four months: twice for upper respiratory tract infections, once with diarrhoea and once with a severe nappy rash. The baby had two courses of antibiotics and one course of nose drops. At age four months he developed mild snuffles but was otherwise well. The doctor and health visitor were not contacted as the child did not appear ill. Three days after the attack of snuffles the twins were put to bed; both appeared normal. They went to sleep at approximately 9 p.m. Father checked the children before going to bed at 1 a.m. at which time both children were asleep.

The mother fed both twins at 5 a.m. The second twin fed slowly, but otherwise appeared normal. At 7.30 a.m. their mother went in to see the twins again; twin 1 woke normally but twin 2 was grey, floppy and unresponsive. The mother tried to feed the child again, but he would make no effort at feeding. The father had already left for work and as her own phone was out of order, she ran next door to use the neighbour's phone to contact her family doctor. When she returned to the house twin 2 was dead.

On post mortem examination there were signs of mild infection in the child's lung and respiratory syncytial virus was identified from the tissue. Three days after twin 2 died, twin 1 was admitted as an emergency to hospital having suddenly become pale, drowsy and difficult to feed. Chest X-ray showed changes suggestive of pneumonia, and respiratory syncytial virus was subsequently isolated from swabs. He recovered after being severely ill for 5 days.

Baby Corah

The mother was a West Indian catering manageress aged 19. She was unmarried. The father of the child was unemployed. The pregnancy was unplanned. The mother was living in a small cold flat with two cats. She did not smoke. She had had a termination of a previous pregnancy three months before the present conception. During this pregnancy she developed a urinary tract infection at four months and a vaginal infection at six months. At 38 weeks she went into spontaneous labour and delivered a girl weighing 2,325 grams (5lb 2oz). The baby was given a vaccination against tuberculosis, but appeared healthy. She was breast fed.

She was subsequently a regular attender at the child health clinic. At two months of age, the baby had an episode when she became blue and lifeless – the episode lasted for about a minute and the family doctor who was called could find nothing abnormal. At three months of age the child was taken for the first vaccination (against diphtheria, tetanus, pertussis and polio). Twenty four hours after the vaccination the child appeared to be rather grizzly and ran a mild fever. Two days later she was left with a child-minder as usual during the day, whilst the mother went out to work. The child-minder looked after three other children. The baby was put to sleep in a pram outside the kitchen window in the November afternoon. In the pram the child was wearing two vests, nappies, tights, a stretch suit, a cardigan, zip-up sleeping bag, four blankets and a quilt. When the baby minder went to see the child an hour and a half later the child was dead. She immediately called an ambulance. On admission to the mortuary one hour later the child's temperature was 102° F. No specific cause for the child's death was found on post mortem examination.

These case histories have been presented to show how complex and yet how normal the events preceding a death may appear. Nevertheless, there was no obvious pattern running through the five stories described. The weight that should be put on various facets of these histories can only be estimated if one knows the background of those thousands of infants who do not die. The discipline of epidemiology comes to the fore at this point.

Part II
Epidemiological Studies

Chapter 4

Introduction to Epidemiological Methods

Epidemiological methods were first developed to study epidemics of infectious diseases in the nineteenth century. These methods have been further developed and refined to include the study of most aspects of health and disease. A variety of techniques are used, the aim of basic studies being to assess the frequency with which a disorder occurs within a specified population, and the ways in which the frequency varies with different social, biological and environmental factors.

The essence of a good epidemiological study lies in: (a) accurate information concerning which persons do and do not have the disorder; (b) identical definitions of social, biological and environmental factors in persons both with and without the disorder; (c) if sub-populations of persons without the disorder are compared with persons with the disorder, there should be no bias in their selection.

Where the condition studied is relatively rare, such as sudden infant death, there are major difficulties in obtaining sufficient numbers of cases for valid interpretation. Even when the study is large enough, a determination of a statistic as apparently simple as the *frequency* or *incidence* is fraught with difficulty. The first essential is to define the *population* which is being studied. This might consist of all babies *born* in a certain area within a given time period, or it might be all infants *living* in a certain area within a time period. In either instance it is essential to know the number of children in the population chosen and to be absolutely certain of identifying all deaths to those children. In any study, it is important that each death be examined to ensure whether it could be a case of sudden infant death. Major errors can occur unless this rigorous approach is undertaken. For example, because the syndrome most frequently occurs while the child is asleep at home, some investigators have restricted their attention to deaths registered as having occurred at home. As we shall show later, if we had used such an approach in one of our studies we would have underestimated the frequency by 35%.

Another major cause of inaccuracy can be found in any study relying on statements concerning cause of death as written on death certificates. Such statements reflect the biases and habits of the certifying coroner or doctor rather than objective facts. The term sudden infant death syndrome or equivalent was first accepted as a natural registrable cause of death by the Registrar General and Coroner's Society of England and Wales in 1971, and the deaths were classified as 'Sudden Death cause unknown' (ICD 795 in the 8th revision of the International Classification of Diseases). The term Sudden Infant Death Syndrome was first included in the International Classification of Diseases in the 9th revision in 1979, since when it has been an acceptable natural registrable cause of death internationally.

In spite of the fact that sudden infant deaths can be registered as such, they are still often recorded as having been due to pneumonia, bronchitis, inhalation of vomit or asphyxia even though the pathological evidence may be minimal. Certainly, at one time in Britain it was thought that parents would be more worried by a death certificate with the words 'sudden unexpected infant death' or 'cause unknown' rather than by 'bronchopneumonia'. The pendulum has now swung, and the proportion of sudden infant deaths which are recorded as such on death certificates has increased, although it has still not reached 100%. We shall show in Chapter 19 that there is increasing evidence that many parents are now less worried by the term sudden infant death on the death certificate than by a cause such as pneumonia.

Another major source of bias lies in the actual definition of the cases, as this relies on the techniques, experience and assiduousness with which the pathologist has carried out the post-mortem and recorded the results. It must be stressed that a diagnosis of sudden infant death should never be accepted in the absence of a thorough post-mortem examination. Another major problem is found in interpreting the results of the post-mortem examination.

John Emery has shown that, from his examination of the history and the post-mortems of a population of children dying suddenly and unexpectedly, he can identify major lesions in over 40%, minor lesions in a third and no lesions at all in only a quarter of the deaths. The interpretation of such findings is however, subjective. They are impossible to evaluate without details of the lesions that would be found in a normal child of the same age. The only way of obtaining such control information would be to study a group of children who had died suddenly for defined reasons (e.g. a road traffic accident), yet such deaths are very rare in the age group at which sudden infant deaths occur. The dangers associated with inappropriate controls have already been pointed out in the introduction when we discussed the previously widely held belief that the deaths were thought to be due to a large thymus.

Careful interpretation of any findings by the pathologist is of great importance. For example, not infrequently there is evidence from the post-mortem that the infant has inhaled his own vomit. Now it is conceivable that such an occurrence could actually kill a baby, but it is much more likely that the infant vomited during his final struggle (his death throes), and the inhalation was merely a natural consequence of the mode in which he died or the result of attempted resuscitation. Another frequent finding is of some minor inflammation of the lungs or bronchi, indicating the presence of a chest infection. The significance of this could only be validly assessed if one knew how many normal live children also showed such signs – especially during the winter months.

Other ways in which studies may be misleading can be detected using statistical tests. Consider a simple example: suppose a study was being carried out into the genetic make-up of mothers of sudden infant deaths. The scientists interviewed six mothers and noted that they all had blue eyes. They knew that only half the women in the area had blue eyes. Would they be justified in saying either that (a) women with blue eyes are more likely to have sudden infant deaths, or (b) women with blue eyes are not more likely than other women to have an infant who dies suddenly and unexpectedly. A statistical test will assess which of these statements is more likely to be true, given the numbers involved. Note that the test cannot say which *is true*, it can only deal in probabilities. When the results are strong, they are said to be statistically significant – but there is always a chance that they may be misleading.

In this section, we have illustrated only results that are statistically significant. The two new studies presented for the first time in this book were undertaken for different ends and therefore have quite different designs.

Oxford Record Linkage Study (ORLS)

The first study to be reported here (the Oxford Record Linkage Study) was undertaken specifically to look at the epidemiology of sudden infant death in an area of England. Previously, Jean Fedrick had carried out an investigation of all sudden infant deaths in Oxfordshire and West Berkshire in the period 1966 to 1970. This had produced a large number of results which were statistically significant, some of which had never before been investigated. In epidemiological studies if a new finding is produced it is normal to treat the discovery with discretion until a further study can confirm the original findings. The data presented here include the results from the subsequent study of sudden infant deaths in the same area, but covering the period 1971–75. A more detailed description is included in Appendix 1 (pages 224–5).

The Foundation Study

The second study to be reported here was carried out by Sylvia Limerick of the Foundation for the Study of Infant Deaths. It was not undertaken with a view to investigate the *causes* of sudden infant death but rather to assess the way the deaths were managed, the support given to parents, and the way these had changed over time. All parents who had contacted the Foundation were invited through its May 1978 newsletter, and since 1979 by personal correspondence, to complete a 'Procedural questionnaire' enquiring into their experiences following the baby's sudden death and practical problems which arose.

The survey includes information concerning 713 'cot' deaths: the management of the crisis immediately following the death, the coroner's investigation, cause of death and registration of death; the funeral arrangements and costs, the death grant and other administrative problems, the support given by primary health workers and others, the reactions of siblings and the community, and family changes associated with the loss. These will mainly be discussed in Part IV of this book. Any differences between management of the deaths occurring in the periods 1974–79 and 1980–81 will be described.

Epidemiological features of the deaths for which questionnaires were received are described in Appendix 2. There were no large differences in the pattern of deaths between the two time periods but, perhaps understandably, the sample surveyed represents a much higher proportion of articulate and literate parents than expected from other studies.

In other respects, such as age at death, seasonal variation, birthweight distribution, birth order and proportion of twins, the survey population was remarkably similar to other samples of sudden infant deaths.

Chapter 5

Variation of Incidence with Time, Place and Age of Infant

Incidence

The incidence of sudden infant death is usually expressed as the average number of such deaths that have occurred per 1,000 livebirths within a specific population. Thus, in a study of 7,000 livebirths, 20 of whom became sudden infant deaths, the incidence would be expressed as 2.9 per 1,000 livebirths. This could also have been written as 1 in 350 livebirths.

In view of the many difficulties described in case ascertainment, especially the fact that registered causes of death are unreliable, it is not wholly surprising that there have been relatively few population studies to ascertain the actual incidence of the condition. It is not always possible to tell from the published accounts whether the criteria are based on findings at post-mortem. Nevertheless, it is apparent that, within all the varying studies undertaken there is a fair amount of consistency (see Table 1), the incidence in North America being about 2.3 per 1,000, whereas that in Britain appears to be somewhat higher, ranging from 2.1 to 4.0. In Australasia, the reported incidences range from 1.6 to 4.1, with a mean approximating to that for North America.

In contrast with these rates, those for Sweden appear to be remarkably low, at about 0.6. It is difficult to compare data from Denmark, as the results are conflicting. One study in Copenhagen, followed all 8,425 children discharged from a large maternity hospital, and reported that 23 died suddenly and unexpectedly, giving a rate of 2.7 per 1,000. These figures cannot be extrapolated to the whole population though since the hospital was a reference centre for high-risk pregnancies. In contrast, a whole population study of deaths in Copenhagen identified an incidence of 0.9 per 1,000, but the criteria on which children were excluded were probably more rigorous than most.

TABLE 1

Incidence of sudden infant death in various populations.
(Studies with obvious large biases have been omitted.)

AREA	DATES	POPULATION DEFINED	SIDS IDENTIFICATION	INCIDENCE	BIAS	REFERENCE
NORTH AMERICA						
King Co. Seattle	1962–64	Residents of King Co, dying 7–364 days	Death Certificate perusal. Hosp. deaths excluded	2.9 (173)	?	Peterson, 1966
	1965–69	Deaths <2 yr. not resident in hospital	Detailed PM	2.3 (170)	—	Bergman et al, 1972
Douglas Co. Nebraska	1964–69	All sudden & unexplained deaths in the county	Review of death certificates signed by coroner's physician	2.5 (104)	?	Armitage & Roffman, 1972
Philadelphia City	1960	Deaths in city	Deaths reported to examiner & review of death certificates	2.5 (337)	—	Valdes-Dapena et al, 1968
Upstate New York	1974	All births in Upstate New York	Review of death certificates	1.4 (190)	PU	Standfast, Jereb & Janerich, 1979
Chicago	1966–69	All deaths in Chicago	Review of death certificates	3.4 (942)	PO	Greenberg, Nelson & Carnow, 1973
Charleston Co. S. Carolina	1973–4	Not clear	Report to Medical examiner	2.9 (16)	?	Bell, Sexton & Conradi, 1975

Table 1 cont.

AREA	DATES	POPULATION DEFINED	SIDS IDENTIFICATION	INCIDENCE	BIAS	REFERENCE
Olmsted Co. Minnesota	1946–65	Deaths of residents 2wk–2yr	Review of PM (Mayo clinic) & clinical notes	1.2 (37)	—	
Cuyahoga Co. Cleveland Ohio	1956–65	Deaths 10dy–2yr occurring in the county	Coroners PM	3.1 (1134)	—	Strimer, Adelson & Oseasohn, 1969
North Carolina	1972–74	Not stated	'Reported cases' – pm and/or clinical data from CMO	2.1 (534)	?	Blok, 1978
California	1960–67	Kaiser Foundation Pregnancy Health Plan: all births to members	not stated	2.3 (44)	—	Lewak, van den Berg Beckwith, 1979
San Diego, Calif.	1962–64	Residents of San Diego	Review of death certificates with certain diagnoses	2.7 (201)	?	Peterson, 1972
Sacramento Co, California	1964–70	All sudden deaths in Sacramento, 1–11mths	Review of PM reports all carried out by PM	1.8 (128)	—	Borhani, Rooney & Kraus, 1973
US Collaborative Study	1959–66	Prospective study of 59,379 pregnancies, in 12 city hospitals	Review of all PM & clinical data on all deaths by RN	2.3 (125)	—	Naeye, Ladis & Drage, 1976
Ontario, Canada	1965–66	Deaths 1–11mths	Death certificate review & discussion with attending physicians	3.0 (87)	PO	Steele, Kraus & Langworth, 1967

SID-C

BRITISH ISLES						
Edinburgh	NS	All sudden clinically unexpected deaths	Post-mortem	2.1 (108)	PO	Mason et al, 1980
Northern Ireland	1965–67	Residents in N. Ireland	PM data & clinical history	2.5 (162)	PU*	Froggatt, Lynas & MacKenzie, 1971
Hartlepool	1950–59 1960–69	Residents in the County Borough	Review of hospital & PM notes. Deaths 1–12 months only	3.6 (53) 3.0 (50)	— —	Milligan, 1974
Scunthorpe	1948–76	Residents	Non-hospital deaths 1wk–12mths. Coroner reported. Death certificate review	2.5 (142)	PO	Robertson & Parker, 1978
Grimsby & Cleethorpes	1953–76	Residents		4.0 (261)	PO	
Newcastle-Upon-Tyne	1974–76	Prospective study of all deaths 1wk–5yr in city	Review of Pathology & clinical information	3.8 (30)	—	J. Clarke et al, 1977
Oxfordshire & West Berkshire	1966–70	Deaths under 5 to residents of area	Review of death certificate information	2.8 (206)	PO	Fedrick, 1973
Oxfordshire & West Berkshire	1971–75	Deaths under 2 to residents of the area	Examination of PM & clinical history	2.6 (168)	—	Present study
EUROPE						
Sweden: Göthenburg	1972–3	Prospective follow-up of all births	Review of all deaths	0.5 (6)	—	Karlberg et al, 1977
Sweden: Stockholm	1968–72	Deaths 14–364 days	Review of PM and clinical history	0.6 (53)	?	Fohlin, 1974

Table 1 cont.

AREA	DATES	POPULATION DEFINED	SIDS IDENTIFICATION	INCIDENCE	BIAS	REFERENCE
Denmark: Copenhagen	1956–71	Residents of city	Home deaths – review of police report & PM	0.9 (139)	PU	Biering-Sørensen, Jørgensen & Hilden, 1978
Copenhagen	1959–61	Hospital births, followed-up	Not stated	2.7 (23)	—	Zachau-Christiansen & Ross, 1975
West Germany: Trier	1964	Births in Trier district	Deaths 1–11mths	5.2 (23)	?	Schneider, 1977
Stuttgart	1957–60	Births to US Army personnel	PM on all deaths & clinical history	1.9 (14)	PU	Canby & Jaffurs, 1963
Hamburg	1961–67	Not stated	Not stated	1.6 (294)	?	Eckert, 1976
Czechoslovakia: Prague	1960–69	Not stated	Not stated	0.8 (79)	?	Houstek et al, 1971
Middle Bohemia	1960–69	Not stated	Not stated	1.0 (170)	?	
THE ANTIPODES						
Tasmania	1970–76	Deaths in state under 12mths	Unclear	2.9 (155)	?	Grice & McGlashan, 1978
Western Australia	1973	Deaths in the state under 2 years	One pathologist doing all PMs	2.2 (44)	—	Hilton & Turner, 1976
Southern Australia	1965–70	Not stated	Deaths 2wk–2yrs. PM & clinical notes	1.6 (36)	—	Beal, 1972
South Australia	1970–79	Not stated	Not stated	2.1 (416)	?	Beal, 1983

New Zealand:						
Christchurch	Not stated	All births in maternity units to urban population	Not stated	4.1 (5)	—	Fergusson et al, 1978
Southland	1968–71	Not stated	PM review	2.9 (33)	PU	Asher, 1975
Auckland	1970–72	Deaths 1–11 months	Not stated	1.9 (86)	?	Tonkin, 1974
REST OF WORLD						
Israel: Haifa	1975	Jewish births in Haifa	Review of home deaths	0.7 (5)	PU	Winter et al, 1978
Ashkelon	1961–70	Jewish infants only – hospital deaths omitted	Review of PM & clinical notes	0.3 (10)	PU	Bloch, 1973
Japan	1974	Not stated	Not stated	1.2 (NS)	?	Naito, 1976

KEY:

—	very little bias
PU	probably underestimated
PO	probably overestimated
?	insufficient information to assess
CMO	County Medical Officer

* authors estimate 90% ascertainment

It is certainly apparent that the rate of sudden infant death in Sweden must be substantially lower than that found in the British Isles. During the years 1968–72 the incidence of post-neonatal deaths from all causes (i.e. all deaths aged 28–364 days) in Sweden, was only 3.3 per 1,000 which included about 0.6 per 1,000 sudden infant deaths. Within England and Wales over the same period the death rate was about 6.0 per 1,000 with perhaps 2.4 of these attributable to sudden infant death.

The other country in which several studies have confirmed a low frequency of sudden infant death is Israel, where several surveys among Jewish births have demonstrated very low rates. It would be interesting to know whether the rates vary within the various national origins of the Jews, and whether the rate amongst the Arab population of Israel is equally low.

Variation within Area

Many authors have, on looking at their data, suspected that cases of sudden infant death have clustered together in certain districts. There is even one report of 2 cases occurring within 5 days to different mothers living in the same house in Inner London. Nevertheless, even with a condition as rare as the sudden infant death syndrome, there are bound to be a certain number of coincidences of this sort arising by chance.

Within population studies in both the United Kingdom and Australia, it has been found that the incidence in the cities is greater than that found in the surrounding rural areas. This was demonstrated in Northern Ireland, Western Australia and in our own first study from Oxford and West Berkshire. In America, however, no such association was found in either North Carolina or Upstate New York.

Results from the ORLS Study

The earlier study from this area showed: (a) a gradient, with the incidence in the cities being higher than that in the towns, but the incidence in the towns (urban areas) being lower than that in the rural areas. (b) the incidence in Oxfordshire was consistently higher than that in Berkshire.

The results of the present study showed that overall, the rate in the cities was higher than that in the surrounding areas, but this time the urban rate was higher than that of the surrounding rural areas. Overall, the rate in Oxfordshire was again higher than that in West Berkshire. The result of combining the two ORLS studies is shown in Figure 1.

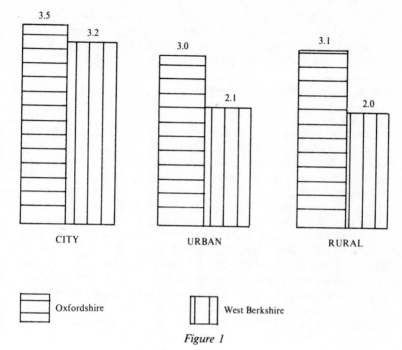

Figure 1

Incidence of sudden infant death by type of area and county; ORLS 1966–70.

It can be seen that although the rates are higher in the city, the risk of sudden infant death is higher in Oxfordshire, regardless of type of area. Explanations for this are not obvious. Both areas have, generally, a high standard of living with little overt poverty. An obvious explanation might be that the post-mortems were more thorough in Berkshire, but this is unlikely as the one experienced paediatric pathologist in the region is situated in Oxford.

Variation within a City
In Cardiff, Wales, areas of the city were divided into three categories, based on the type of housing. The incidence of sudden infant death was very low (0.25) in areas labelled 'good' where the property was almost totally owner-occupied and well-maintained. It rose to 1.38 in 'medium' areas and 3.51 where the housing was 'poor'.

Variation with Longitude
In the United States several studies of sudden infant deaths identified

from vital records have shown that the incidence increases with the longitude, the risk being higher on the Pacific than the Atlantic coast. Spiers has discussed possible reasons for such a finding, but failed to produce a convincing hypothesis. There must also be some doubt thrown on the evidence, since the population studies quoted in Table 1 fail to demonstrate an East–West increase.

Variation with Altitude

Another study from the United States attempted to assess whether infants living at high altitudes in Colorado were at increased risk of sudden infant death. Again, only death certificate diagnoses were used, and the authors were uncertain of the total numbers of infants resident at heights over 7,500 ft. Their results are uninterpretable, which is a pity since knowledge of whether these infants were at increased risk would be of great use in determining whether some longterm lack of oxygen contributed towards sudden infant death.

Subsequently, Alan Getts and Harlan Hill analysed information from Nebraska. They showed that, as the altitude increased so did the risk of sudden infant death – but there were several anomalies in their study. They found that the higher the area, the younger the mothers were, the more children they had and the shorter the birth intervals. As we shall show, all these factors are closely associated with sudden infant death. Nevertheless, it seems likely that the association they show could be a real one. It is interesting that the deaths at high altitude were more likely to have occurred at younger ages than those at lower altitudes. It can be seen from the figure below, that the increased incidence in sudden infant death only appears to exist at heights in excess of 725 metres (2400ft). It is important before acceptance of these results that they should be confirmed in another study.

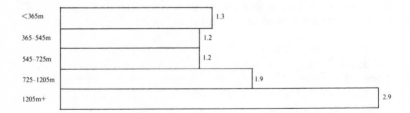

Figure 2

Variation in the incidence of sudden infant death by altitude (adapted from Getts and Hill).

Age at Death

Throughout the world, population studies have shown a typical pattern with age at death. In North America, Australasia and Britain, the pattern is similar to that shown for the combined ORLS studies in Figure 3 below. The majority of deaths occur between 4 and 20 weeks, with a peak incidence in the third month (i.e. age 8–12 weeks). The syndrome is not confined to the first year of life, though the risks get substantially lower thereafter. Sudden infant deaths can occur up to two years of age.

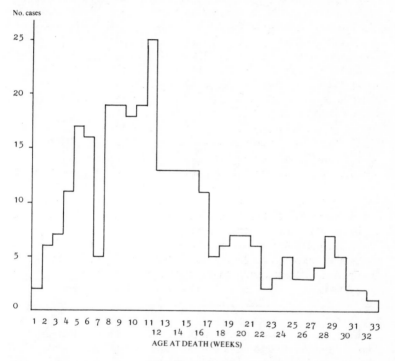

Figure 3

Distribution of 374 sudden infant deaths by age at death (in weeks); ORLS 1966–75.

There are interesting sex differences. As we shall show later, the risk of sudden infant death is increased in boys compared with girls. Boys and girls have a similar mean age at death. Yet the distributions are dissimilar, the deaths of boys having a relatively greater peak, than those of girls. In Table 2 we combine data from the two ORLS studies. For boys dying suddenly and unexpectedly 45% occurred at ages 8 to 15 weeks, whereas for girls only 36% of deaths occurred at this time.

Table 2

Age at death by sex: ORLS 1966–75.

AGE AT DEATH (completed week)	MALE No.	Cumulative %	FEMALE No.	Cumulative %
0–1	1	0.5	2	1.3
2–3	6	3.5	6	5.4
4–5	14	10.4	12	13.4
6–7	13	16.8	4	16.1
8–9	22	27.7	14	25.5
10–11	29	42.1	9	31.5
12–13	23	53.5	12	39.6
14–15	16	61.4	18	51.7
16–17	10	66.3	15	61.7
18–19	6	69.3	8	67.1
20–21	13	75.7	3	69.1
22–23	2	76.7	4	71.8
24–25	4	78.7	4	74.5
26–29	14	85.6	6	78.5
30–33	0	85.6	14	87.9
34–51	15	93.1	13	96.6
52–103	14	100.0	5	100.0
TOTAL	202	100.0%	149	100.0%

From the similarity of ages of death as shown in many areas of the world, it is possible to work out the daily risk that a particular child would run of suddenly dying. The risks shown in Table 3 are for areas in which there is an overall incidence of 2.5 sudden infant deaths per 1,000 livebirths.

There is some evidence from both our own study and that from Denmark, that children with short gestation are more likely to die at a later postnatal age. This suggests that if their age was measured from their expected date of delivery rather than their actual date of birth, their pattern of age at death might be similar to that shown in Figure 3. This is shown in Chapter 12 to be unlikely, however.

Table 3

Daily risk of a particular child dying suddenly and unexpectedly at each age in a population with incidence 2.5.

AGE OF CHILD	RISK OF DEATH/DAY
<4 wks	1 in 164,800
4–7 wks	1 in 82,400
8–11 wks	1 in 57,680
12–15 wks	1 in 74,425
16–19 wks	1 in 135,700
20–23 wks	1 in 209,750
24–39 wks	1 in 314,600
40 wks+	1 in 470,000

Time of Death

The exact hour at which infants die suddenly is frequently unknown. The typical picture has been thought of as an apparently well infant being put to bed in the evening and found dead the following morning. The common belief that a doctor can pinpoint the length of time a child has been dead with complete accuracy is a myth. From the information as it has been presented, it would appear that at least half of all sudden infant deaths occur between midnight and eight in the morning. In the subsequent day-time period from 8 a.m. to 4 p.m. some 36% of sudden infant deaths occur and only 14% appear to happen between the hours of 4 p.m. and midnight. Similar patterns are found on both sides of the Atlantic, and in the Antipodes.

Just how sound is the evidence that the majority of infants die while asleep during the night? All previous studies have merely presented information on when the child was found dead with an arbitrary time division in the morning which may obscure the distinction between those found dead on first being seen and those who had been seen alive in the morning but then died. Sylvia Limerick has, however, analysed information from 355 infants dying 1980–81 reported to the Foundation for the Study of Infant Deaths. If the information is presented in the traditional manner, as shown in Table 4a, there is an uneven distribution – over half the deaths being discovered dead in that quarter of the day from 6 a.m. to mid-day, implying that death occurred during the night.

If, however, one examines the data in the light of when the child was last seen alive, a totally different picture emerges. It would appear from Table 4b that the deaths are equally likely to have occurred during the day, as during the night. Information for deaths occurring in three time periods are shown in Table 5. All show that the infant was more likely to have died during the day than the night. To our knowledge, this is the first time any data have been analysed in this way. It is important that it should be verified in another series, but meanwhile it does call into question the tenets upon which much research into sudden infant death has been carried out – in the past no-one has ever questioned the popular belief that almost all the deaths occur during sleep at night.

Table 4

Time infant found dead (Foundation Study, 1980–81).

(a) traditional grouping

TIME FOUND DEAD	NO. SUDDEN INFANT DEATHS
Midnight–6 a.m.	21 (5.9%)
6.01–midday	183 (51.5%)
12.01–18.00	110 (31.0%)
18.01–24.00	41 (11.6%)
TOTAL	355 (100.0%)

(b) from when last seen alive

TIME LAST SEEN ALIVE	NO. SUDDEN INFANT DEATHS
Died at night between midnight and being first seen in morning	153 (43.1%)
Died after being first seen in morning and 9 p.m.	180 (50.7%)
Died during evening between 9 p.m. and midnight	22 (6.2%)
TOTAL	355 (100.0%)

Table 5

Time infant found dead in three sub-groups (Foundation Study).

TIME FOUND DEAD	PERIOD STUDIED		
	1974–77	1978–79	1980–1
Early morning: 6.01am–9am	28.7%	29.0%	33.8%
Daytime: 9.01am–9pm	55.3%	56.2%	54.1%
Evening/night: 9.01pm–6am	16.0%	14.8%	12.1%
NO. DEATHS (=100%)	94	217	355

Place of Death

Although the pattern of the child being found dead in his cot when the family awakes in the morning is the most often to occur, there are documented instances where the child has died suddenly in other circumstances. There are reports of the child suddenly expiring in the doctor's arms, in his mother's arms, in a car or almost any situation in which the infant is likely to be.

Another inaccuracy widely held is that all sudden infant deaths occur at home. Indeed some studies actually include in their definition that death must occur at home. In the ORLS study we found that only 65% of the children had died at their own home and a further 5% had died at some other address – either that of a friend or a neighbour or while in foster care. One child had died whilst at a Health Centre attending a Well-Baby Clinic! Some 22% of our children had died in hospital, but almost all had been taken to the hospital while *in extremis* and died very shortly afterwards.

There was a certain amount of discussion at one stage as to whether children who were actually already in hospital ever did die suddenly and unexpectedly. Originally it was thought that this never happened but there are now several instances where apparently well neonates had died while still with their mother in the Maternity Hospital. In addition, there have been well documented instances of older infants awaiting discharge from general hospital, apparently well, suddenly dying in the night. A statistical examination of the possibility that residence in hospital protects against sudden infant death was examined by Peterson and Beckwith in Seattle. They found two infants who had died suddenly whilst in hospital and worked out that less than 0.2 would have been expected in that childhood population over the time period they were studying. They concluded that hospital care did not protect against sudden infant death.

Variation over time

Since sudden infant deaths were first studied there have been various suggestions that the incidence is decreasing. Certainly, the overall rate of death in children aged 1 month to 1 year has fallen, though in a rather inconsistent manner in the years from 1950 to 1980, but there is no evidence for an overall fall in the incidence of *sudden infant deaths*.

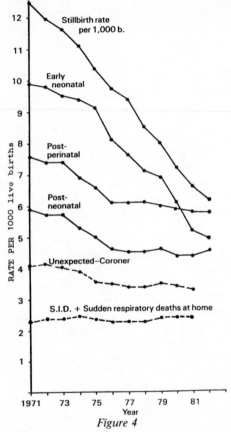

Figure 4

Mortality Rates per 1000 live births, England and Wales 1971–1982.

(Derived from OPCS tabulations with the permission of the Controller of Her Majesty's Stationery Office; Crown copyright reserved.)

Figure 4 compares the differences between the national statistics from 1971 to 1982. The incidence of both stillbirths and first week (early neonatal) deaths fell by almost a half over that period, yet the post-perinatal (1 week to 51 weeks) and post-neonatal (4 weeks to 51 weeks) death rates fell by less than a quarter. Identification of sudden infant deaths from death certificates is difficult, but taking all deaths said to be due to the sudden infant death syndrome together with sudden deaths at home certified by a coroner as due to respiratory causes (sudden respiratory deaths), an approximation to the true numbers can be made. The Figure shows no sign of a fall in incidence using these criteria.

There have been reports of static rates of sudden infant death over the time period 1956 to 1971 in Copenhagen and the whole of England and Wales. Within England, in the town of Hartlepool between 1950 and 1969 there was a slight, but insignificant fall in the rate; in nearby Scunthorpe there was a rise to a peak from 1948 to 1968 and then a fall over the next 8 years, whereas in the towns of Grimsby and Cleethorpes (also situated in the north-east of England) the rate was static.

Marie Valdes-Dapena reported in 1977 that the rates in 5 circumscribed populations had been falling. Examination of her evidence showed that in 2 of the populations the evidence had been communicated to her personally, and the information is missing on which a judgement as to the validity can be based (numbers involved, case ascertainment, etc.). There does appear to have been a genuine fall in Philadelphia between 1960 and 1974, but the study reported as showing a decrease in California was not claimed as doing so by its authors nor by our own statistical analysis of their data.

Peterson and Chinn also published secular information that had been reported to them personally, but their publication did not reveal methods of definition or completeness of ascertainment. It is impossible to assess such data.

Within Czechoslovakia, the incidence appears to have dropped slightly between 1960 and 1969 in Middle Bohemia, but this was balanced by a rise in Prague over the same period. More recently, in Tasmania, there has been evidence of a slight rise between 1970 and 1976.

Data from South Australia from 1970 to 1979 showed significant variation, but no consistent trend, in spite of the fact that the *overall* death rate fell. In Cleveland, Ohio, there were no marked differences between 1956 and 1965 and in King County, Washington, there had been no significant changes between 1969 and 1977.

It is remarkable that there has been no proven fall in incidence over a time period when the perinatal death rates and post-neonatal death rates due to other causes have fallen markedly. Changes in family composition have occurred, with fewer large families. This fact alone should have contributed towards a fall in rates.

Variation with season

In almost all large studies, a marked association has been found with season: infants being far more likely to die suddenly and unexpectedly in the winter than in the summer. Figures 5 (a) to (d) below show the variation in England (represented by our study in Oxfordshire and Berkshire) in Ontario, Canada, in California, USA and in Tasmania, Australia.

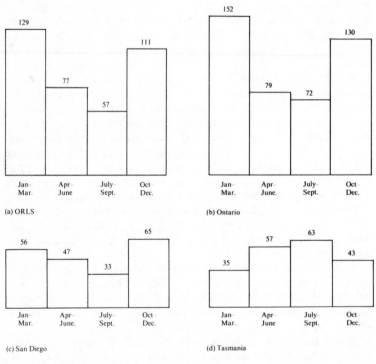

Figure 5

Numbers of sudden infant deaths occurring in each quarter of the year (a) ORLS 1966–75, (b) Ontario, 1960–61, (c) San Diego, California, 1962–64, (d) Tasmania, 1970–76.

In 1978, Farber and Chandra suggested that authors showing a seasonal variation in occurrence of these deaths had not taken account of the fact that more babies are born at certain times of the year than others. In Britain, the peak in births is in the Spring, but the variation is slight compared with the pattern found for sudden infant deaths. Analyses of the data from Colorado by Zoglo and his colleagues also concluded that taking the variation in birth rate with season into account made no difference to the general conclusion that there is a winter excess of deaths. This will be discussed in more detail on page 65.

Day of the week

There have been suggestions that sudden infant deaths are more likely to occur at weekends or on public holidays, the assumption being that parents are more reluctant, or find it more difficult, to obtain medical assistance at such times. Other possibilities concern a change in routine with parents sleeping later in the morning. In Sheffield, Emery showed that although there was no overall difference in the rate of sudden infant death by day of the week, there were differences in that the children were more likely to have died at home at the weekends, and more likely to have died en route to, or shortly after admission to hospital on a weekday. This may be the reason why the national data show an increased rate of sudden infant death at weekends – the definition used by the authors, Macfarlane and Gardner, required the death to have occurred outside hospital in cases where sudden infant death was not specifically written on the death certificate.

Other studies with numbers of sufficient size (over 100 deaths) have failed to demonstrate any consistent association between day of the week and risk of an infant dying suddenly and unexpectedly apart from one in Tasmania which showed marginally more deaths on a Monday.

Clustering of deaths on same day

Strange coincidences may occur. These may have happened by chance or they may provide a clue as to causation. Statistical methods should be able to distinguish one from the other. To do this, large population studies are necessary. For example, in Minneapolis, a study over an 18-month period had identified 84 sudden infant deaths, 2 of which occurred during the same night, a very hot summer night with a temperature of 93° F. Such a finding is suggestive but cannot be interpreted. Information from other studies is necessary.

Among other studies, days with 2 or 3 deaths have occurred fairly frequently, but it is important to calculate whether the numbers of such days are greater than one would have anticipated by chance alone. The relevant data are shown in Table 6 below. It can be seen that in all but one study, there were more days with clusters of deaths than would have been expected by chance. None of these, however, were days with exceptionally high temperatures.

Table 6

Number of days on which two or more deaths occurred compared with the number expected by chance – ORLS and cases in the literature.

AREA OF STUDY	NO. DAYS 2+ DEATHS	
	Observed	Expected
Seattle, Washington	15	12.3
San Diego, California	22	15.9
Ontario, Canada – Study a	8	3.7
b	4	4.7
c	8	5.2
ORLS		
1966–70	15	11.4
1971–75	12	8.0
ALL	84*	61.2

* $P < 0.01$

The Weather

In view of the marked seasonal variation in the incidence of sudden infant death, it is hardly surprising that various authors have suggested that some aspect of the weather might be involved. In Cardiff, it was shown that the months with the lowest night temperatures were those with the highest rate of sudden infant death. Within our study in Oxfordshire and Berkshire we found a similar pattern. Figure 6 shows that as the daily temperature rises, the death rate falls. Similar correlations have been shown in Southern Tasmania.

Not only the temperature, but also the hours of sunshine are negatively correlated with the incidence of sudden infant death in that

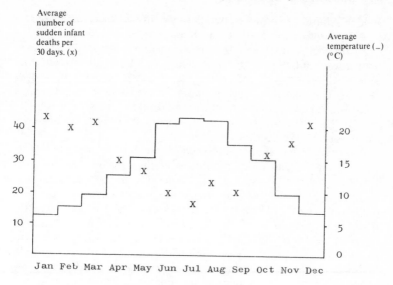

Figure 6

Seasonal variation in the incidence of sudden infant death by maximum daily temperature; ORLS 1966–75.

the months with the least number of hours of sunshine are those with the highest rates of sudden infant death. Conversely, there are positive associations between the monthly incidence of sudden infant deaths and (a) the average wind speed; (b) the number of days with snow and (c) the relative humidity. There is no such correlation with the mean barometric pressure.

Leaving aside the monthly association, several authors have examined the pattern of weather on or shortly before the day of death, and compared it to the weather on surrounding days. In Chicago, Greenberg and his colleagues found no association with the air pollutant, sulphur dioxide. In the first ORLS study we found that the days on which the death occurred were more likely to have had no sunshine, and to have been preceded by a day with no sunshine, but this has not been found in the second ORLS study. In neither of the ORLS studies was there an association between days and deaths and barometric pressure, temperature, wind speed, amount of rain, or presence of snow.

In contrast, with these largely negative findings, a study within Ontario produced two weather patterns which in their series preceded

sudden infant deaths more often than would be expected. These two factors, known as Factors A and B are defined as follows:

Factor A: A drop of 10° F between two successive days to a temperature of below 10° F, associated with little or no precipitation. This combination occurred on the date of death or one of the 3 days prior to the death for slightly more of the sudden infant deaths occurring at ages 5 months or more than would have been expected by chance. The effect was not found in Chicago or our own ORLS series where such low temperatures rarely occur.

Factor B: A maximum wind speed for one hour or more of at least 20 mph on the day of death or one of the previous five days. In Ontario, this effect was strongest in the period April to November, and for infants dying at ages 5 months or more. Again, this association was not found in either Chicago or the ORLS area. The definition of factor B was later changed slightly by the Canadians to: 'winds of 25 mph or more on the day of death', after a later survey of sudden infant deaths in Ontario had found no association with either Factor A or Factor B. In Tasmania, McGlashan and Grice showed that the deaths were most likely on days where the minimum temperature was between 4° and 12° C, and that deaths were less likely to happen when there were large changes in temperature.

In conclusion, although the seasonal variation with sudden infant death is strong, there is no verified evidence that the weather in the days immediately preceding the death is concerned with the death.

Clustering in time and space

For many infectious diseases it is possible to follow the way an epidemic moves through a community by plotting the geographic clustering within time periods. For example, in a typical measles epidemic the first cases will tend to be clustered together, subsequently cases will develop in contiguous areas, and gradually the disease will spread.

There are a variety of statistical methods which can be used to determine whether there is any evidence for such a phenomenon to be occurring. The three studies that have been published concerning sudden infant deaths in Northern Ireland, Cardiff and the ORLS area have produced negative results. Curiously, however, there are two reports that suggest a clustering in the date and place of birth. These will be discussed later.

Chapter 6

Characteristics of the Parents

So far we have mapped out the bare facts about the frequency with which sudden infant deaths occur in the population, and the way in which the death rate varies with the age of the child and the season of the year. In this section we will be describing ways in which the risk of sudden infant death appears to vary with various characteristics of the household.

Social Class

In Britain, since the beginning of the century, attempts have been made to categorise families according to the occupation of the head of the household. A scale has been devised which can be used to divide families into five main categories: social class I, which consists of the higher professionals, the doctors and dentists, chartered accountants, ministers of religion and academics; social class II are the semi-professionals – the business managers and executives, school teachers and nurses, farmers, company directors and journalists; social class III contains the largest proportion of the population and is used for skilled occupations: it includes all the craftsmen, the police and firemen, lorry drivers, shop assistants, secretaries and mechanics: the semi-skilled professions comprise social class IV, and include farm workers, caretakers, machine operators, postmen, sorters and checkers. Social class V is reserved for the relatively small proportion of workers who are in unskilled occupations, such as labourers, cleaners and refuse collectors. Persons in the Armed Forces are usually considered separately, whether officers or persons in the ranks. Students and unmarried mothers are included in a residual group.

The classification is rarely used outside Britain, but within Britain it is of major importance in the study of many diseases and disorders.

Frequently, there is a linear trend in incidence with social class: for mortality in general, and especially perinatal mortality, there is a strong trend, with the incidence in social class I being only about half of that in social class V. Conversely, in conditions such as cancer of the prostate the trend is reversed, the incidence to men in social class I being the highest.

An even more marked trend with social class has been found in the British Isles for sudden infant death. The data from the ORLS studies are illustrated below using the concept of relative risk. Relative risk is a useful method of illustrating the magnitude of any association. The overall risk to all children in the study is taken as 1, and then the risks to sub-groups are measured in relation to this. In Figure 7, it can be seen that the risk to children of mothers in social classes I and II was only 70% of the average risk, whereas that to children of fathers of social class V was almost twice that found overall. It is of interest that the trend between social classes I, II and III is far less pronounced than for perinatal mortality. The remarkable factor in sudden infant deaths is the significant increase in risk in social classes IV and V. Similar information was apparent from Edinburgh.

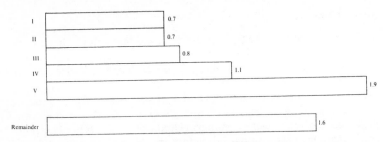

Figure 7

Relative risk of sudden infant death, ORLS 1966–75 by social class.

Of note, too, is the high risk to the infants who were not classified. These include children whose fathers are in the armed forces, and those who were born to an unmarried mother. Both groups appear to have a high risk.

Studies of trends in social class are a beginning rather than a conclusion. Having shown an association the immediate question arises as to what it actually means. It has been shown that many parameters vary with social class – from diet, parental smoking, likelihood of the mother to breast feed, attitude of the mother to child-rearing, her income, her leisure activities, education and type of

housing. The mother of social classes IV and V is also far more likely to have started having children in her teens, more likely to have several children and to have short intervals between pregnancies.

Within the United States, Naeye and his colleagues have looked at variation in the incidence of sudden infant death by a socio-economic index which was derived from parental education, income and occupation, a high score indicating high levels of these factors. They found that 56% of sudden infant deaths came from households with low scores compared with 39% of the rest of the population. They showed that the association between low score and sudden infant death was not explained by the lack of education of the parents or by whether the household was over-crowded (i.e. more than 1 person per room).

In California, the longitudinal study of pregnancies to women registered in the Kaiser Health Plan, showed that the incidence of sudden infant death was higher in families of blue-collar as opposed to white-collar workers, but they too found no relationship with maternal education. In Upper New York State, though, a high incidence of sudden infant death was found when the mother had had less than 12 years education, and this was shown to be independent of the maternal age effect. No other factors, however, were taken into account. In Cleveland, Ohio, it has been shown that the incidence in small areas (census tracts) with relatively low mean income was twice that found for census tracts with a higher mean income. Such indirect evidence raises similar questions to those prompted by the British trends in social class.

Outside the United Kingdom and the United States, the only other report to examine such social factors has been that from Denmark. Their criteria for categorising the father's occupation distinguished between those paid a weekly wage and those paid a monthly salary. They found that significantly more fathers of sudden infant deaths were wage rather than salary earners. They looked at details of the household economy, defined as money available rather than money spent. They found that significantly more families who had sudden infant deaths had below average income.

Unemployment

Men in social classes IV and V are far more likely to have periods of unemployment than are men of the higher social classes. It is therefore not surprising that authors in Cardiff, Canada and Northern Ireland, have found that the fathers of infants dying suddenly and unexpectedly were more likely to be unemployed than were fathers of

surviving infants. Whether paternal unemployment itself confers an increased risk awaits further study.

Marital status

In all large studies where the topic has been addressed, the risk of sudden infant death is raised in infants born to unmarried mothers. The increase has been reported as over two-fold in places as far apart as California, Upper New York State, Northern Ireland, Canada and Copenhagen. In the longitudinal British Births 1970 study, the relative risk of sudden death among infants whose mothers were unmarried at delivery was 2.2. In the ORLS studies, the risk to infants born illegitimate was 2.3 compared with a risk to legitimate births of 0.9.

Unfortunately there is not yet sufficient published information to indicate whether the currently fashionable state of remaining unmarried but living in a stable union with the father of the child is associated with an increased risk to that child, when compared with the risk to the child of parents of similar age and social class who are married. The one available study (from Copenhagen) suggests that infants born out of wedlock, but living with both parents are still at increased risk, though not as great as that to the infant living in a single parent situation.

Mother's age

A universal association with sudden infant deaths is found when the incidence is plotted according to the age of the mother. In the ORLS study we also showed a marked association, as can be seen from Figure 8, with children born to mothers under 20 being over twice as likely to die suddenly and unexpectedly compared with the children of mothers aged 25 or more.

Similar findings of markedly increased incidence in young mothers have been published for Chile, Copenhagen, many parts of the British

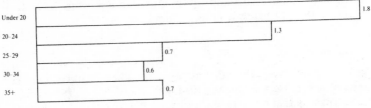

Figure 8

Relative risk of sudden infant death, ORLS 1966–75 by mother's age.

Isles and the United States. In King County, Washington, Peterson and his colleagues have shown that this pattern has remained constant over time.

Birth Order

The younger the mother, in general, the more likely the child to be the first born in the family. In view of the association between young motherhood and sudden infant death it would be logical to expect that overall the first-born child would be more at risk than the later-born infant. In actuality, however, the reverse is found, the more children the mother has already borne, the greater the risk of sudden infant death (see Figure 9).

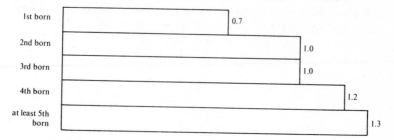

1st born	0.7
2nd born	1.0
3rd born	1.0
4th born	1.2
at least 5th born	1.3

Figure 9

Relative risk of sudden infant death by the order of birth of the child; ORLS, 1966–1975.

Studies in Northern Ireland, Canada, Britain and California have produced similar results. This immediately prompts the question of how the distinctive birth order pattern might be associated with the mother's age.

Within the ORLS study we have been able to calculate the relative risk of sudden infant death within each birth order group for each maternal age group separately. The results are shown in Figure 10 below. It can be clearly seen that for each birth order the risk of sudden infant death is higher the younger the mother. Conversely, whatever the age of the mother, the more children that she already has, the higher the risk of sudden infant death. A similar pattern has been shown for King County, Washington.

Analysis of data from Upper New York State showed that there was a relationship between the age at which the mother had had her *first* ever child and the risk of sudden death to her current infant. This was

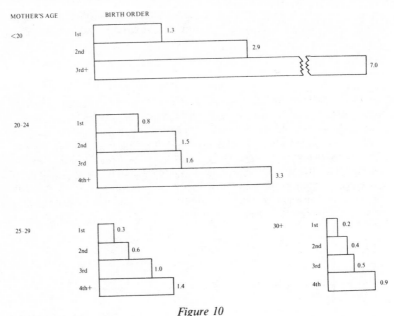

Figure 10

Relative risk of sudden infant death, ORLS 1966–75, by mother's age and birth order.

not surprising in view of the finding of a high incidence of sudden infant death with maternal youth and high birth order. Indeed once these latter factors have been taken into account, Jacquie Roberts has shown that there is no additional association with age of the mother at her first delivery.

Inter-relationship of mother's age, birth order and social class

As we have shown, the associations in risk of sudden infant death, vary consistently and independently of one another. In addition, the association with illegitimacy is equally strong, as is that with social classes IV and V. All of these factors are associated with many of the other facets of the parents and the child. In order, therefore, to ensure that in examining other relationships we are not just looking at a different way of measuring social class, we have therefore compared the parents of the ORLS sudden infant deaths with a group of parents of similar maternal age, birth order, social class and marital status, giving birth in the same hospital in the same year. The details are

described in Appendix 1. The comparison group will be referred to as the controls.

Height of the Mother

Naeye compared the mean height of mothers of sudden infant deaths with two control populations. He found no significant differences although the index mothers were, in general, one centimetre shorter. Comparison of cases and controls in the second ORLS study is shown in Figure 11. (Unfortunately, the information had not been collected in the earlier period.) The risk of sudden infant death appears to be greatest at the two extremes – the very short women (under 5ft 1in) and the tall women (over 5ft 6½in). Before speculation as to the possible meaning of this can take place, it is essential to see whether the finding can be confirmed in another study.

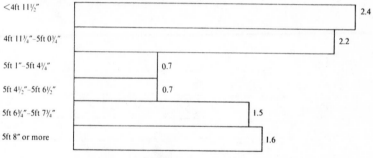

Figure 11

Relative risk of sudden infant death by maternal height; ORLS 1971–75 (comparison with controls matched for age, parity, social class and marital status).

Race

Within several, but not all, studies in the United States there are strong differences between incidence in white and non-white infants. In the longitudinal Collaborative Study, the incidence of sudden infant death was 1.9 among white, and 3.0 among non-white infants. In Nebraska, the differences were 1.9 compared with 5.9, in North Carolina the figures were 1.2 and 3.8 and in Upper New York they were 1.2 and 3.9. It is important to attempt to determine whether such differences are inherited genetically or are a function of the environment. The American non-white population is more likely to

live in areas with relatively poor housing and lower incomes. An analysis in Cleveland, Ohio, subdivided the area into 6 groups according to the characteristics of average income within the census tracts. Although, overall, the differences between incidences was large (2.4 white compared with 5.8 non-white) within each of the 6 income strata there were no racial differences. In other words the differences between white and non-white risks appeared to be a function of socio-economic or environment circumstances.

Within Britain, it is not felt to be ethically justified to record the colour of a person's skin. It is permissible, however, to record the place of birth of an individual and, since most of the coloured population are recent immigrants, it is possible to identify persons originating from various parts of the world. In the ORLS studies, the

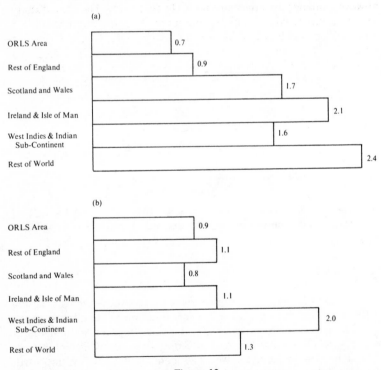

Figure 12

Relative risk of sudden infant death by place of birth of the mother: comparison with controls matched for maternal age, parity, social class and marital status (a) ORLS 1966–70; (b) ORLS 1971–75.

place of birth of the mother of the child who died suddenly and unexpectedly was compared with the control group. As can be seen from Figure 12a, for the first study the lowest risk was found among women actually born in the study area, which is situated roughly in the centre of England. The risk was slightly higher if the mother had been born elsewhere in England, and rose substantially thereafter. The fascinating point is that the women who were probably coloured (those from the West Indies and the Indian subcontinent) were no more at increased risk than those from other parts of the British Isles, or indeed those from the rest of the world.

The second study confirmed that women who had been born outside the ORLS area were more likely to have an infant who died suddenly and unexpectedly than those who were born in the area and still resident there at the time of the baby's birth. The differences were, however, smaller than those found in the first study. The second study found an increased risk among infants of West Indian mothers, but numbers are small. Combination of the two ORLS studies gives a relative risk for infants of West Indian mothers of 1.7 which is not statistically significant being based on only 12 index mothers and 20 controls. There is no convincing evidence here that non-white infants are at higher risk than other immigrants from outside the British Isles.

In conclusion, the ORLS data are consistent with the hypothesis that women who are resident in the area in which they themselves were born are slightly less at risk of having an infant dying suddenly and unexpectedly. There is also a suggestion that British infants of women born outside the British Isles are at greater risk than those whose mothers were born within Britain.

Blood Groups

The various blood groups vary in prevalence with geographical location and race. The two most commonly identified blood groups are those of the ABO and Rhesus systems. These groups are normally identified in pregnancy so that compatible blood can be given should a transfusion be necessary.

Various diseases have been found to be more prevalent with particular blood groups, for example – the incidence of peptic ulcer is 35% higher among persons of blood group O, whereas cancer of the stomach has its highest prevalence among persons of blood group A.

The mother's blood group is mainly considered of importance in relation to the possibility of incompatibility between mother and foetus. This is well known in respect of the Rhesus system whereby a Rhesus negative mother can become sensitised to the blood of her first

Rhesus positive conceptus, and therefore will produce antibodies to any subsequent Rhesus positive conceptus.

Conflicting information exists regarding any possible association between ABO blood groups of mothers of sudden infant deaths. British data from Sheffield suggested that fewer mothers of sudden infant deaths were of blood group A than expected. In the two ORLS studies as well as in those from Cardiff, Southampton, Birmingham and Newcastle there were no differences between cases and controls.

Only one study has produced any evidence for the maternal Rhesus group to differ from controls. All others have shown no association. No information on paternal blood groups is available.

Previous pregnancy loss

The question of whether pregnancies prior to that resulting in the sudden infant death were abnormal in any way has been examined by several authors. None found any statistically significant differences in the number of previous miscarriages or abortions, stillbirths or child deaths other than sudden infant deaths. This was confirmed using the ORLS data. As we shall show later, however, there is evidence that there is an increased risk of sudden infant death when there has already been a similar death among the immediate family.

Chapter 7

Characteristics of the Pregnancy

We have already shown that there is considerable evidence to suggest that babies born to mothers who are relatively young, unmarried, of low social class and with several children are at increased risk. It is the purpose of this section to assess whether there is any evidence that details concerning the pregnancy itself differ from those which would be expected, given the social and environmental background.

Interval since marriage

Given the association with maternal youth, it is hardly surprising that many of the mothers had only been married for a short time before conception. In the second ORLS study we were able to compare the relationship between the date of marriage and the date of the last menstrual period (LMP) between the mothers of sudden infant deaths and the control mothers who were of the same age, parity and social class at delivery. Although 28% of sudden infant death mothers had been married within 12 months of the LMP, compared with 17% of control mothers, the difference was not statistically significant.

Inter-pregnancy interval

The interval from one delivery to the first day of the last menstrual period before the subsequent conception is known as the inter-pregnancy interval. There is some evidence that the risk of neonatal death is increased among infants conceived within 6 months of a previous delivery, and we examined our data from Oxfordshire and Berkshire to assess whether a similar phenomenon was found among sudden infant deaths.

Obviously young mothers with several previous pregnancies are

likely to have short intervals between pregnancies. Comparison with controls of the same age and the same number of previous births should enable us to ascertain whether there is an additional association with short inter-pregnancy interval. As shown in Figure 13 below, the risk of death is over twice as high as the average if the inter-pregnancy interval is less than 3 months, and also high if it lies between 3 and 5 months. Thereafter there was no trend in risk. Similar associations have been found in Canada, California and Upper New York State.

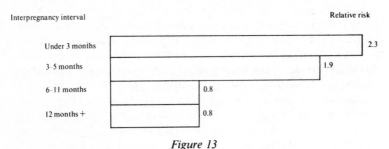

Interpregnancy interval   Relative risk

Under 3 months   2.3

3–5 months   1.9

6–11 months   0.8

12 months +   0.8

Figure 13

Relative risk of sudden infant death according to 'interpregnancy interval': ORLS 1966–1970.

Fertility

Only one of the ORLS index mothers had been noted as having been previously infertile compared with five controls. There is no suggestion in the literature that infertility was more of a problem for index rather than control parents.

Planned pregnancies

The above information suggests that it might be the mother who is unlikely to plan her pregnancies who is at greater risk of having a sudden infant death. This was considered by Lewak and colleagues in their prospective study of women enrolling in the Kaiser Health Plan. Women who subsequently had a sudden death were, however, no more likely to have described their pregnancy as unplanned than the rest of the population.

One study has tried to determine whether the mothers of sudden infant deaths were more likely to have requested termination of the pregnancy than the rest of the population. The authors found no evidence to support such a suggestion. The British Births 1970 cohort

study did show, however, that women who subsequently had a sudden death were less likely to have ever taken the oral contraceptive pill. The available data therefore supports the suggestion that these children were as much wanted and planned for as their surviving peers.

Antenatal Care

Various authors have attempted to determine whether there is any evidence of mothers being more likely to book late or to make fewer visits for antenatal care than might be expected. In Upper New York State, Ontario, Cardiff and in London, mothers of sudden infant deaths were more likely to book late. In Copenhagen and California they were found to have had fewer antenatal visits, but interpretation of such figures is extraordinarily difficult. Young mothers, unmarried mothers and mothers who have already had several successful pregnancies are less likely to book early compared with the mature mother expecting her first baby or one who has lost previous infants. It would seem possible, therefore, that findings of infrequent antenatal visits, or late booking, are merely a consequence of the background of the mother rather than being meaningful in themselves.

Naeye and his colleagues have attempted to analyse their longitudinal population data to take account of such background variables as socio-economic status and gestation – but unfortunately not maternal age or number of pregnancies. They found that the mothers of sudden infant deaths were more likely to have fewer antenatal visits, but the fact that the authors had not taken other factors into account again makes the interpretation difficult. In the ORLS study, only one mother of a sudden infant death had had *no* antenatal care compared with 8 matched controls.

Date of last menstrual period

One of the factors that helps the midwife and physician in their management of pregnancy is accurate knowledge of the date of the first day of the last mentrual period prior to conception. A large study from California showed that the risk of sudden infant death was raised if the mother had not been able to report this date.

There is evidence that women who are, in general, unable to be specific about their dates are more likely to come from socially disadvantaged circumstances and to be teenagers. In our ORLS studies we took account of such biases by choosing controls matched for maternal age, number of pregnancies, marital status and social class. If the mother was able to report the date of her last menstrual

period when reporting her pregnancy, the relative risk of the child dying suddenly was only 0.9, but that to the child of a mother who did not know her dates was twice as high at 1.9.

Month of Last Menstrual Period

In view of the marked seasonal association with the incidence of death, it is not unexpected that there should be an association with the month of conception. In the ORLS data, however, as shown in Table 7, there were only slight differences with conceptions in the summer (July to September) having the lowest risk. The differences were only just statistically significant.

Table 7

Distribution of month of LMP of mothers of sudden infant deaths, 1966–75, compared with the population in the ORLS area.

MONTH OF LMP	Sudden Infant Death	Total population	Relative risk
January–March	76 (26.9%)	22.8%	1.18
April–June	74 (26.1%)	25.9%	1.01
July–September	53 (18.7%)	26.4%	0.71
October–December	80 (28.3%)	24.9%	1.13
ALL KNOWN MONTHS	283 (100.0%)	100.0%	1.00

$P < 0.05$

Smoking in pregnancy

Whenever data have been available for analysis it has been shown that infants of women who smoked during their pregnancy were at increased risk of sudden death in infancy. The two major longitudinal studies in America showed this, as did the 1970 British Births Survey and the Cardiff Birth Survey. The results of the latter are shown in Figure 14 below, from which it is apparent that the risk to infants of smokers is at least twice that to non-smokers. This study found that smoking in pregnancy was the factor with the highest predictive value.

Three other major retrospective studies have been carried out on this topic, where parents of sudden infant deaths were questioned

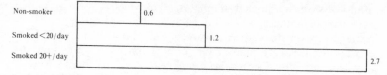

Figure 14

Relative risk of sudden infant death in Cardiff according to whether the mother smoked during pregnancy (from Murphy, Newcombe & Sibert).

concerning the events of pregnancy and similar questions were asked of a control group. The Canadian study found that 68% of the mothers of sudden infant deaths had smoked during the pregnancy, compared with 39% of control mothers. In San Diego, there were 39% of index mothers smoking during pregnancy compared with 21% of controls. In Seattle, a similar study was carried out by Bergman and Wiesner as a result of their impression at meetings with parents of sudden infant deaths, that the amount of smoking seemed unusually heavy. They showed that the consumption of tea, coffee and cola was identical in the two groups, as was paternal smoking. They found a very strong relationship with maternal smoking though, and were able to show that the more cigarettes the pregnant mother had smoked, the greater was the risk of sudden infant death (Figure 15).

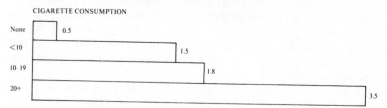

Figure 15

Relative risk of sudden infant death by numbers of cigarettes smoked by the mother: calculated from case/control study published by Bergman and Wiesner; mothers under 25 years of age only.

Information on maternal smoking was only collected in some of the case notes of the second ORLS study. Nevertheless, a similar association was shown, even though numbers were small.

Drug addiction

There have now been 6 published studies of sudden infant death in

infants of women addicted to opiates, all of which reported very high incidences. Combining all the information, Finnegan showed that the incidence to opiate addicted women was about 20 per 1,000. All studies published to date have been from America where the prevalence of addiction has been higher than in the British Isles.

Of course, on average, addicts are more likely to be at high risk of having a sudden infant death anyway: they are more likely to smoke cigarettes, to live in poor social circumstances and to have extramarital pregnancies. A study by Chavez and colleagues in Detroit compared the outcome of 688 infants born to drug addicts with 388 infants of non-addicts who were from similar socio-economic backgrounds. Seventeen of the addicts' babies were sudden infant deaths compared with two of the controls. They concluded that opiate addiction in the mother probably raises the risks of sudden infant death by a factor of 5.

Non-obstetric disorders occurring during pregnancy

The major study from Sheffield, comparing the histories of 94 pregnancies resulting in unexpected infant death with 135 normal infants who did not die, found that 6 of the mothers of sudden infant deaths had had influenza during the pregnancy compared with only 1 control. In the United States, the Collaborative Study had also collected information on infectious diseases during pregnancy. Naeye, Ladis and Drage also reported that when the mother had had influenza during pregnancy, the infant was more likely to die suddenly and unexpectedly.

During the analysis of the early ORLS data, information on major events that had occurred during the pregnancies of the index mothers was compared with similar information on the matched control pregnancies. It was shown that not only were the mothers more likely to have had viral infections (mumps, rubella and influenza) but they also appeared to be more likely to have been involved in other events requiring hospital admission (appendicectomy, severe fall).

For the second ORLS series all clinical obstetric case notes were scanned to identify any reports of infections or other disorders that may have happened during the pregnancy of both mothers of infants who died suddenly and unexpectedly and of control mothers. We found no indication that operations were more likely to have occurred in the sudden infant death pregnancies, but there was a strong association with infection. In all, 23 of the 153 pregnancies which were to result in a sudden infant death had been associated with an

infection, compared with 36 of 454 control pregnancies. The result is statistically significant.

Breakdown of the data according to type of infection shows that both infections of the urinary tract and those of the respiratory tract were strongly related, as shown in Figure 16.

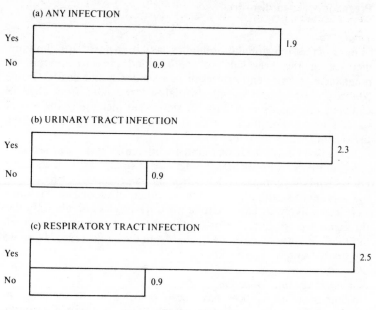

(a) ANY INFECTION

Yes — 1.9
No — 0.9

(b) URINARY TRACT INFECTION

Yes — 2.3
No — 0.9

(c) RESPIRATORY TRACT INFECTION

Yes — 2.5
No — 0.9

Figure 16

Relative risk of sudden infant death by whether the mother was recorded as having had (a) any infection (b) urinary tract infection or (c) respiratory infection, during pregnancy: ORLS 1971–75.

In contrast with the information on infections, there was no evidence that there were more falls or other accidents among mothers who had sudden infant deaths. In addition they were not more likely to have been in contact with rubella, to have had varicose veins, skin disorders or a history of psychiatric disorder. Mothers who had sudden infant deaths were, however, more likely to be noted as having an allergic disorder, the risk of sudden infant death appeared to be raised by a factor of 2.4 if this history was present. Caution should be used in the interpretation of this finding though, since no other authors have yet shown this.

Information concerning maternal congenital defects was recorded for only one index mother (she had a bicornuate uterus) but ten

control mothers (one cleft lip, one cleft palate, one umbilical hernia, one oesophageal atresia, one kyphoscoliosis, one accessory nipple and four with defects of the urogenital system).

Pregnancy-related disorders

Toxaemia

In none of the large population studies has it been possible to show any increase in the prevalence of *high* blood pressure among the pregnancies subsequently to result in a sudden infant death. On the contrary, Naeye has recently reanalysed the data from the US Collaborative Study and shown a significant increase in the risk of sudden infant death if the maternal blood pressure had *fallen* during the third trimester to under 61mm.

In the first ORLS study we found no differences in the proportion of index mothers to have clinically diagnosed toxaemia. In the second ORLS study we compared the highest blood pressures recorded prior to the onset of labour and found that mothers of sudden infant deaths were more likely to have systolic pressures that were relatively low throughout pregnancy. Unfortunately, information concerning a fall in blood pressure was not abstracted from the clinical records, so we are unable to test Naeye's finding.

Haemorrhage and Anaemia

No significant differences have been reported in the incidence of bleeding in the two major longitudinal studies in America, or in the British studies. The ORLS studies also failed to demonstrate an association.

Maternal anaemia was reported to be associated with sudden infant death by Naeye, but other series have not found this. Reanalysis of Naeye's data, however, showed an increase in risk if the mother had had either low (under 9gm/dl) or high (12+gm/dl) haemoglobin levels. This was only significant at the 0.05 level and without confirmatory evidence should probably be ignored. There was no evidence from the ORLS studies of an unexpectedly low haemoglobin level in mothers of sudden infant deaths.

Other pregnancy disorders

The Danish study looked at the mothers whose pregnancy health was described as poor, and found equal proportions among mothers of sudden infant deaths as compared with the rest of the population.

The only significant pregnancy-related finding to be reported so far

has been proteinuria. This was found in a significant proportion of mothers of sudden infant deaths in the American Collaborative Study, and there was also a difference in the Sheffield data. Proteinuria is found in severe toxaemia, and associated with urinary infections, but need not be predictive of either.

In the ORLS study, too, there were more mothers of sudden infant deaths who had had proteinuria during pregnancy (21%) than matched controls (11%). The excess among the index mothers did not appear to have been due to urinary infection.

In the ORLS studies, there was no evidence of an association with vomiting in pregnancy, of vaginal discharge or infection, or of abnormal glucose metabolism. Only one of the mothers was diabetic (her infant died suddenly aged 57 weeks).

Among factors significantly associated with pregnancies resulting in sudden infant deaths, was a history of hydramnios. This occurred in 9 index cases and 8 controls. Other factors significantly associated involved the mention of pain (other than the backache often associated with pregnancy). Some 11% of index mothers had complained of pain, frequently involving hospital admission, compared with 5.5% of matched controls. It is not immediately obvious whether such a finding is meaningful. No other study has looked at such a comparatively vague symptom.

Although we have shown an association with both short and tall women, there was no increase in the numbers of index mothers who were described as obese, or in those who had been noted as having poor weight gain or a period of weight loss. For the period 1971–75 in the ORLS study an index of obesity, taking account of height, was calculated for women at term. This statistic is derived by dividing the woman's weight by the square of her height. There were no differences between cases and their matched controls.

Procedures during pregnancy

In the American Collaborative Study, Naeye showed that women who had a sudden infant death were no more likely to have had an abdominal X-ray during pregnancy than the rest of the population. A similar lack of association was found in the ORLS study for X-rays, ultrasound scan and amniocentesis during pregnancy.

Pharmaceutical drugs in pregnancy

Few studies have examined the possibility that medicinal drug ingestion during pregnancy might be associated with a later sudden infant death. Analysis of the American Collaborative Study showed that overall the mothers of sudden infant deaths had taken fewer

medicinal drugs than the mothers of controls matched on socio-economic group and race. There was a suggestion, though, that infants of mothers who were taking either iron dextran, hydrochlorothiazine or phenobarbitone were at increased risk.

The retrospective enquiry in Sheffield also found no significant differences between cases and controls in the overall use of drugs. More mothers of sudden infant deaths than controls, however, were reported to have taken both sedatives and antibiotics, but numbers were too small for any reliance to be placed on these results without confirmatory evidence.

Wherever an infant's condition has been shown to be associated with illness during pregnancy one of the possible explanations is that medication taken by the mother for the disorder may have affected the fetus. Information on medication is very difficult to obtain, and that obtained from the ORLS study is far from ideal. The study listed all the drugs that were recorded as being taken in the clinical obstetric notes. Interestingly, the only drug group which showed significant difference between cases and controls involved the barbiturates. In view of Naeye's similar finding it is likely that this association is not one that is spurious. In all, 20 of 153 index mothers took barbiturate preparations during pregnancy compared with 26 out of 454 controls ($P<0.01$).

Chapter 8

Labour and Delivery

Place of birth

In the first ORLS study an unexpected association was found with the type of hospital in which the infant had been delivered. It was shown that infants born in hospitals with a large number of deliveries per year were more likely to have died suddenly and unexpectedly than infants who were born in small family General Practitioner units. The second ORLS study showed a similar association. Infants delivered in hospitals with more than 1000 births a year were more likely to die (relative risk 1.1), than those delivered in smaller hospitals (relative risk 0.7).

Interpretation of such findings is not easy. Mothers referred to large hospitals for delivery include those having their first baby and those who are relatively elderly. These categories of infants are those at least risk of subsequent sudden death. Other factors that prompt delivery in a large hospital include complications of pregnancy, yet we have been unable to show an increased incidence of the major complications. Factors such as urinary tract infections and influenza in pregnancy are not likely to change the policy for booking.

There was some evidence for clustering of births at certain hospitals. In the 1970 British Births cohort, Chamberlain and Simpson showed that among 35 sudden infant deaths, there were 4 pairs who had been born in the same hospital. This is out of a sample of some 16,000 births throughout the United Kingdom during one week in April, 1970. Although no statistical tests were used, the authors felt that the 4 birth pairs were far more than would have been expected.

In the first ORLS study, there were 7 pairs of sudden infant deaths born at the same hospital within 10 days of one another who subsequently died within two weeks of each other. This was estimated at being twice the number that would have been expected. In the second ORLS study, however, no such findings were apparent. Altogether there were 14 pairs of infants who subsequently died

suddenly and who had been delivered in the same hospital within 7 days of each other. Statistical calculation estimated that, just by chance, one would have expected 13.8 pairs to have been delivered in the same hospital within this period of time.

Onset of Labour

In the first ORLS study, there was an association between sudden infant deaths and induction of labour. This has not been found in any other studies, including the second ORLS study.

Length of Labour

The collaborative study in the U.S.A., and the Danish study in Copenhagen were unable to find any differences in the type of labour between infants who subsequently died suddenly and unexpectedly and those who did not. Other studies have found that the infants who had died suddenly and unexpectedly were more likely to have had a short second stage of labour. This has been reported from Cardiff, Southampton and Sheffield. There are difficulties in analysing the lengths of the second stage of labour, since there are normally shorter labours when the mother has had previous infants. The woman having her first delivery, is likely to have a much longer second stage of labour than the woman who has delivered before. Since sudden infant deaths are less likely to be first births, there will automatically be an association between sudden infant deaths and a short second stage of labour. Whether this accounts for the entirety of the findings from Sheffield, Cardiff and Southampton awaits discussion. The analysis of the information from the second ORLS study (the information was not collected for the first ORLS study), showed no significant differences between the length of either the first or second stages of labour in the infants who subsequently died suddenly compared with those controls matched for birth order, mother's age and social class.

Duration of Membrane Rupture

Information has also been analysed concerning the length of time the membranes had ruptured prior to delivery of the infant. A feature of prolonged membrane rupture is that the fetus is at increased risk of developing an infection before or during the process of delivery. The second ORLS study, as in all other studies where the factor has been examined, showed no association between subsequent sudden infant death and prolonged membrane rupture.

Drugs in Labour

During labour, information is frequently written into the clinical notes concerning whether the mother was 'distressed' or not. In the second ORLS study, approximately the same proportion of mothers of sudden infant deaths as control mothers were reported as being distressed (43.5% compared with 37.3%). In relation to whether the mother showed signs of distress or not is the medication that she was given. The study shows that similar proportions of mothers of sudden infant deaths as matched controls were given narcotic type drugs, antipsychotic type drugs, hypnotics, sedatives or barbiturates. There was no evidence in these data for an association between short-term ingestion of opiates such as heroin and subsequent sudden infant death.

Type of Delivery

No other studies have found an excess of deliveries by forceps, breech, or caesarean section among groups of sudden infant deaths. Neither of the ORLS studies showed any differences in mode of delivery.

Time of Delivery

There was no indication that infants who were delivered during the night or at times when the obstetric units might be short of staff were at an increased risk of later sudden infant death. The proportions delivered during normal working hours were identical in the deliveries of sudden infant deaths and their matched controls (42.3% compared with 42.6%). There were, however, major differences in the season of birth.

Season of Delivery

Since the majority of studies of sudden infant death demonstrate a marked increase of deaths occurring in the winter months, and the majority of deaths occur between the second and fifth months of life, it is not surprising that more sudden infant deaths are born in the summer or late autumn. This has been found in Denmark, Los Angeles, Seattle and various centres within the United Kingdom. Similarly, in both South Australia and Victoria more children who become sudden infant deaths are born between January and April (their summer and autumn). The relative risk of sudden infant deaths as described by Carpenter and Gardner from information on death certificates is shown in Figure 17. It can be seen that the lowest risk of

sudden infant death is found in infants born in March and April and the highest risks are found for those born between September and November.

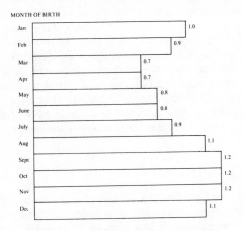

Figure 17

Relative risk of sudden respiratory death by month of birth (calculated from Carpenter and Gardner, 1982).

The information from Los Angeles, that from the registered statistics of England and Wales and the two ORLS studies showed that children born in the summer were more likely to die at an older age than those born at other times. It is pertinent to question whether the variation in season of birth is responsible for the variation in season of death or vice versa. This is a complex statistical problem which warrants further attention.

Chapter 9

Characteristics of the Infant in the Early Neonatal Period

Sex differences

As with studies of the *incidence* of sudden infant death, it is important that studies of other aspects should involve a defined population of deaths, rather than those that a particular pathologist happens to see.

In all studies based on a population, and where an effort has been made to include all cases of sudden infant death, it has been clearly found that there are more boys than girls. Of course, on average there are always more male infants born than females – but the sex ratio (i.e. the number of males divided by the number of females) is never as high as 1.10. With sudden infant death, the major population studies have always shown a greater proportion of males than this, the sex ratio occasionally being as high as 2.0. There is a suggestion that the sex ratio in the Scandinavian countries is higher than elsewhere. For Britain, the sex ratio is more or less constant at 1.4 giving the relative risks of 1.13 for boys and 0.86 for girls.

Interestingly, in populations such as Upper New York State, where the rate among black infants is three times that among white infants, the risk to non-white boys relative to non-white girls shows no difference when calculated from data published by Standfast and her colleagues. A similar finding was reported by Naeye using data from the American Collaborative Study.

Gestation

The length of time from the first day of the last menstrual period prior to conception until the date of delivery is known as the length of gestation. The majority of infants are delivered '*at term*', which is defined as 37 to 41 weeks, when the risk of perinatal death is at its lowest. Those infants delivered later than this i.e. 42 weeks+, are

defined as '*post-term*'; they tend to have a higher perinatal mortality rate and a higher incidence of abnormal neonatal symptoms.

'*Pre-term*' infants are those delivered before 37 weeks gestation, they have a high risk of many disorders because of their immaturity. In particular they are more likely to have respiratory difficulties, more prone to infection and to jaundice.

Accurate assessment of gestation is difficult if the mother is unsure of her dates. There are methods by which the paediatrician can examine the child and make an estimate, but the potential error is still measurable. Restricting the analysis to studies of infants for which the mother has recorded her dates accurately, a striking pattern emerges, as can be seen from the ORLS data in Figure 18. This shows the relative risk of subsequent sudden infant death, according to the length of gestation after having taken account of factors such as maternal age, birth order, social class and marital status. It can be seen that the shorter the period of gestation the more likely the infant to become a sudden infant death. Similar findings of an increased risk in pre-term infants have been reported from Canada, the United States as well as elsewhere in England.

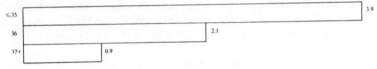

Figure 18

Relative risk of sudden infant death according to length of gestation: ORLS 1966-1975.

In analysing information on the deaths in California, Kraus showed that pre-term infants dying suddenly and unexpectedly were likely to have died slightly later than those born at term. The first ORLS study reported similar results, with only one of the 7 very pre-term (<35 weeks) sudden infant deaths dying within 12 weeks of delivery. In the second ORLS study a similar result was apparent – of the 15 deaths to infants born pre-term, 11 died after the 12th week of life. This is described further on pages 100–101.

Birthweight

Far more authors have reported on the birthweights of sudden infant deaths than on their gestations. This is not surprising since birthweight is far more likely than gestation to be recorded accurately.

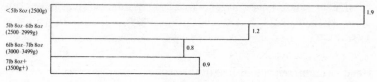

Figure 19

Relative risk of sudden infant death by birthweight, ORLS 1966–75.

Increased incidence of sudden infant death in low birthweight infants has been recorded in all parts of the world where the topic has been studied. The results from the ORLS area are presented below. They are typical of those in the literature – the risk of sudden infant death being greater among the smaller infants.

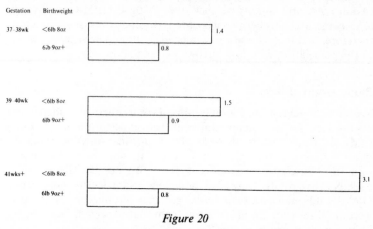

Figure 20

Relative risk of subsequent sudden infant death in infants born at or after term, according to birthweight within gestation group: ORLS 1966–1970.

Low birthweight will have occurred if the infant has been born pre-term, but it is also found in the condition of growth retardation. In those studies where the genesis of low birthweight has been examined, it has been shown that infants who subsequently die suddenly are frequently mildly growth retarded at birth. There are thus two separate associations: (a) infants born at early gestation, and (b) infants showing lower birthweight than would be expected from other factors. For example, from the first ORLS study, we were able to look at the proportion of infants weighing under 6lb 8oz (2950g) who had been born at term or later. The relative risk of sudden infant death is shown in Figure 20. It can be seen that, regardless of gestation,

the smaller children were at increased risk. Similar findings have been reported from the U.S. Collaborative Study and from Upper New York State.

Head circumference and length

In contrast with birthweight, the birth head circumference and length of the infants who subsequently died were, in two studies, exactly the same as found in survivors. In Copenhagen, however, the birth lengths of the infants who died were slightly lower than that of those who survived. No account was taken of gestation however.

Information on neonatal head circumferences was collected in the second ORLS study. There were significantly more very small head circumferences (under 33cm) among the sudden infant deaths. Only two of these nine infants weighed over 2500g at birth, two were pre-term twins, and another two were pre-term singletons. It seems likely, therefore, that the association with head circumference was secondary to the association with low birthweight and short gestation.

Blood group of baby

We have shown that the blood groups of the mothers of sudden infant deaths were not consistently different from expectation in the ORLS study. In three studies, there has been information concerning the blood groups of the infants who died. In only one was there a significant difference – an excess of infants of group B in the American Collaborative Study. Only 17 of the sudden infant deaths in the second ORLS study had had their blood group ascertained at birth; there were no differences in distribution from that expected. None of the infants were of blood group B.

Twins

In the two ORLS studies there were 14 twins who were sudden infant deaths, twice as many as would be expected by chance. Similarly increased risks have been reported from other parts of Britain, from Denmark and from the United States. A large population study in California was able to provide data on both twins and triplets. As can be seen from Figure 21 below, according to their estimates the risk to triplets is more than twice that of twins, and the risk to twins is more than twice that of singletons.

In South Australia, Beal reported 21 of 446 sudden infant deaths to have been twins: in three of these the co-twin had been stillborn. The

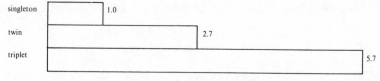

Figure 21

Relative risk of sudden infant death in singletons, twins and triplets: calculated from data published for the State of California (from Kraus and Borhani, 1972).

21 included both members of a pair, both having died the same night. Of the remainder, attention was paid to the birthweights of the pair. Among the seven where the birthweight difference was 300g or more, the lighter twin had died, whereas among the six pairs with birthweight differences of less than 300g, the heavier twin was as likely to have died as the lighter twin.

In Upper New York State, Susan Standfast and her colleagues showed that there were no differences in risk of sudden infant death in the lighter as opposed to the heavier twin, but the second-born twin was more likely to have died than the first-born twin. Similar findings were reported for Wisconsin by Alan Getts. Among 14 twins dying suddenly and unexpectedly, 11 were second born.

Information on the 14 twins in the two ORLS studies is shown in Table 8. In all, there were 9 sudden infant deaths that had been first-born and 5 that were second-born. There were 6 instances where the weight of the co-twin differed by 300g or more from that of the twin that died. In all of these, the smaller twin died. In all other pairs, the smaller of the twins was at no greater risk than the larger. Thus, the evidence presented here supports the findings of Susan Beal that there is an increased risk for the smaller twin if the differences are 300g or more in birthweight. It does not support the finding of an increased risk to the second-born twin.

In California, the data on twins were analysed after stratifying for birthweight. The results in Figure 22 indicate that there is an interaction: for twins of low birthweight the risk of sudden infant death is greater than that of a low birthweight singleton, but twins of 2500g or more were at similar risk to singletons of this birthweight. Similar results were reported by Susan Beal in South Australia.

The problem of risk to a surviving co-twin is important to both parents and health professionals. There are well documented instances of both members of a twin pair dying on the same night, but this is relatively rare. In the large California study summarised above, only one

Table 8

Twins occurring in the two ORLS studies.

	SUDDEN INFANT DEATH					CO-TWIN		
Case No.	Sex	Order	Birth Weight	Age at Death	Month of Death	Sex	Order	Birth Weight
401	M	I	2620	10 wk	10	M	II	2950
402	M	I	2500	12 wk	11	F	II	2410
403	M	I	1450	9 wk	12	F	II	1700
404	M	I	2130	8 wk	1	M	II	2550
405*	F	I	NS	16 wk	12	F	II	NS
406	M	I	3540	10 wk	3	M	II	3856
407	M	II	1865	15 wk	8	F	I	2381
408	F	II	2720	2 yr	7	M	I	2580
109	F	I	2330	1 yr	9	M	II	3085
24	F	I	1930	27 wk	12	F	II	1955
121*	F	I	1890	21 wk	5	F	II	2190
12	M	II	1600	11 wk	10	M	I	1580
113*	M	II	NS	9 wk	2	M	I	NS
136	F	II	2060	8 wk	5	F	I	2210

* twins were not diagnosed before delivery

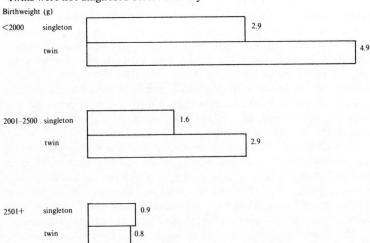

Relative risk of sudden infant death syndrome in singletons and twins by birthweight (calculated from Kraus, 1983).

pair died together on the same night. Recently, the British national press reported a pair of female twins sleeping in separate rooms, both being well on being put to bed, and both being found dead in the morning.

A study in North California attempted to address the problem by analysing the incidence of deaths registered as having occurred at home. As we have indicated earlier, this is likely to underestimate the true rate of sudden infant deaths. Nevertheless, the author Philip Spiers, was able to show that of the twins dying suddenly, 8% had their co-twin die suddenly at home. Almost all of the deaths of pairs had occurred within 30 days of one another, and there were no differences in risks to the co-twins of like-sexed pairs compared with male–female twin pairs.

In a questionnaire study of parents of infants dying suddenly and unexpectedly in North America, 63 had been a twin. The co-twin of three of these had died subsequently (5%). The numbers were small but there was no evidence to suggest that identical (monozygotic) twins were more at risk than non-identical (dizygotic) twins (1/24 monozygotic, 2/37 dizygotic).

It would appear, therefore, that the risk to a co-twin is high in the month after his co-twin's death, but that it falls thereafter. In the first ORLS study, the co-twins of 3 of the 8 twins who died were admitted to hospital immediately after the death, and this does appear to be a reasonable method of management.

Neonatal disorders

It would be useful if the infant were to present some abnormal sign or symptom that could be easily spotted during the neonatal period and that would alert everyone to the child being at high risk of sudden infant death. Unfortunately, although at various times it has seemed that such a breakthrough was about to be made, there is still little evidence for such a predictor.

One of the confounding factors is that, in so many of our major neonatal centres, a large number of measurements are being made and different conditions noted. The research worker anxious to find the 'cause' of sudden infant death may look at every factor he can lay his hands on – forgetting that the more factors that are examined, the more likely is a spurious finding to be made. The only way to assess the validity of any association is then to see whether it is repeated in another study.

Of the prospectively collected data sets, many associations have been found but little concordance reached. In the British Birth cohort

study, the major finding was that the sudden infant death babies were more likely to have been referred for 'Special Care', and more likely to have had jaundice. In the Kaiser Health Plan cohort, there were no differences in signs of asphyxia or need for resuscitation. But elsewhere in America, Standfast and her colleagues compared the Apgar scores at birth of 52 black infants, who subsequently died suddenly and unexpectedly, with 52 control infants. There were no significant differences in 1 minute Apgars, but the index infants had slightly but significantly lower 5 minute Apgar scores. The larger U.S. Collaborative Study, in contrast, found an increase in low 1-minute Apgar scores (a measure of asphyxia at delivery) and increased use of resuscitation in these infants. They were also, in this study, more likely to be given oxygen and antibiotics, to develop the respiratory distress syndrome, to have an abnormal Moro reflex, to have muscles described as generally hypotonic, and to have symmetrical but abnormal reflexes.

In the case-control study from Sheffield there was no association with Apgar score, but the sudden infant deaths were more likely to be nursed in an incubator, to be retained in the hospital for at least 10 days, and to suffer from a variety of symptoms – none of which stood out in particular.

Other studies which have purported to show major associations have been based on relatively tiny numbers of cases. For example, in a comparison of 15 cases of sudden infant death with 30 control infants, Lippincot reports lower 1 minute Apgar scores, increased respiratory abnormality, especially associated with atelectasis, and elevated serum bilirubin.

Rebecca Anderson and Judy Rosenblith studied 9 cases of sudden infant death, the definition of which was based on clinical rather than post-mortem information. They referred back to the results of an extensive neonatal examination, and found that the cases had had relatively low scores on the tactile adaptive scale. This measures the response of the infant to cotton and cellophane placed over the nose. The same authors later added another 3 presumed cases of sudden infant death, reanalysed their data and found a large variety of other abnormalities including jaundice, oxygen therapy and multiple minor findings.

Information from the neonatal case notes was obtained for index cases and their matched controls in both ORLS studies. Initially, the only difference related to an increase in reported jaundice among the infants who later died. In spite of the fact that the index infants included more of short gestation and/or low birthweight, there were few differences in the distribution of symptoms when compared with

the controls. No differences were statistically significant. In particular, there were *no* differences in the prevalence of apnoeic attacks.

From a slightly more objective point of view, there were no differences in Apgar scores between sudden infant deaths and controls. There was no evidence that the sudden infant deaths were more likely to be clinically jaundiced, nor did they have higher serum levels of bilirubin.

Only slightly more sudden infant deaths than controls had been admitted to a special care baby unit 42 (27%) cases; 92 (20%) of controls. The differences were not statistically significant.

Congenital Malformations

By definition, the term 'sudden infant death' is generally excluded if the infant has a major malformation which would have contributed towards death. This is in spite of the fact that there is much anecdotal evidence that infants with spina bifida, for example, are likely to die suddenly and unexpectedly with no major pathological lesions being found at the time. Nevertheless, even though by definition the sudden infant death cannot have a potentially lethal malformation, various studies have shown that these infants are more likely to have minor malformations than might have been expected.

Detailed examination of 17 infants dying suddenly and unexpectedly in New York, revealed that 29% had single palmar creases (a minor defect, frequently associated with more major abnormalities). In Copenhagen, there were over three times as many infants with congenital malformations among the group that died suddenly and unexpectedly compared with a control group. The malformations had all been noted during the life of the child and were not found solely at post-mortem.

In the first ORLS study there was also an increased incidence of malformations among the children who died suddenly and unexpectedly. We found that 12 (7%) of the 170 sudden infant deaths had malformations compared with 15 (3%) of the 510 controls – a two-fold difference. It was interesting that two of these infants had had repaired atresia of the gastric system (one oesophageal and one ileal). Relevant to this is the study of 158 cases of oesophageal atresia that were followed up in Sheffield, the authors noted that sudden infant death was unusually common in cases that had apparently been treated adequately.

In the second ORLS study, there were 16 (10.5%) of 153 sudden infant deaths that had been noted as having a malformation compared with 25 (5.5%) of 453 matched controls. This difference is just

statistically significant. Several striking differences were noted: 5 of the sudden infant deaths had some mention of abnormalities of the face, compared with 3 controls: 7 of the sudden infant deaths had malformations that would probably have required surgical correction (one abnormal thighs, one hypospadias, three cleft palate, one inguinal hernia, one oesophageal atresia) compared with only one control (large umbilical hernia). Four of the sudden infant deaths had single transverse palmar creases compared with only three controls.

Drugs given to Babies

The second ORLS study involved perusal of the clinical neonatal notes of the sudden infant deaths and their matched controls. There were no significant differences between the two groups apart from an association with vitamins and other nutrients. Ten such preparations were given to the 133 infants who later died compared with 7 of 400 control infants. All the infants who received these preparations were of low birthweight, however, and it seems likely that the finding of an excess of vitamins given merely reflects the association between low birthweight and sudden infant death.

The Placenta

One important indicator of certain aspects of fetal well-being in utero can be assessed from the placenta. Lewak and his colleagues have compared the weight and description of placentae of sudden infant deaths with a control population. They found no differences in placental weights, abnormal cord insertion or presence of infarcts in the 44 cases in their study. Naeye, also in the United States, found no differences in the placental weight of 48 sudden infant deaths although he did show histological differences which have not yet been fully explained.

Comparison in the ORLS study of index cases and controls showed that there were no differences in placental weight. Various terms were used to describe the placenta – from 'healthy' to 'infarcted'. The only difference noted was an excess of 'gritty' placentae among sudden infant deaths. The finding was significant only at the 5% level and involved 29 of 115 sudden infant deaths (25%) as opposed to 52 of 341 matched controls (15%). This finding would need to be repeated in another study before being taken seriously.

Chapter 10

Characteristics of the Older Infant

Housing

In view of the other social factors shown to be associated epidemiologically with sudden infant death it would not be surprising if these children were found more often in areas of poor housing. In both Copenhagen and Cardiff, this has been confirmed, but no study has looked to see whether the homes are of poorer quality than would be expected from the other social variables.

As already indicated, Naeye found no association with overcrowding in his longitudinal American data after controlling for maternal age, birth order and socio-economic index. In Britain, data from Newcastle showed that the sudden infant death rate was higher among those who lived in state-subsidised council houses as opposed to privately owned homes, but again this study did not control for the socio-economic and other factors we have shown to be important.

In the second ORLS study the clinical case notes were read to pick out any mention of adverse housing or social conditions. These were often recorded either in the general practitioner's referral letter or in the report by the midwife responsible for ensuring that the home is suitable for early discharge of mother or baby. There were 7 sudden infant deaths and 9 controls where adverse housing conditions were mentioned. The difference was not statistically significant.

There is a curious study analysing information from Hamburg, West Germany and Philadelphia, Pennsylvania which indicates that the risk to infants living in the basement or ground floor is higher than that to infants living at higher levels. Dr. Eckert relates these findings to electromagnetic fields. He incidently also purports to show that the regional variation of sudden infant death in the two areas is a function of uncommon magnetic fields and stray electric currents. No other study has been carried out to assess the validity of these findings – but it is important to point out that in countries with AC current such as

Britain, any electromagnetic fields induced are of minimal strength.

One other housing factor which may be relevant concerns the setting of the thermostat of the central heating system. Here national habits vary, as does the prevalence of such systems in the community. In Britain, for example, in 1975 only half the young families had homes with central heating – and there is no information as yet on whether such an acquisition has an effect on the risk of sudden infant death. In Canada, the question is apparently not whether the house has central heating, but rather what is the thermostat setting? The homes of sudden infant deaths were more likely to have a setting of 70° F or more, but the study was too small for this finding to be statistically significant. It would be interesting to have more information on this topic, especially in view of the hypothesis that hyperthermia may actually be responsible for some cases of sudden infant death.

A further instance of the way in which the environment of the infants who were to die suddenly differed from those of the general population was shown in the study in Canada. The authors demonstrated that the control infants were in general far more likely to spend time out of doors. For the five days prior to death, the sudden infant death babies were far more likely than control infants to have been kept indoors. This, of course, begs the question that these children might have been kept indoors because the mothers felt that they were slightly unwell. Nevertheless, another finding concerns the likelihood of having a window open in the child's bedroom. Again, in the Canadian study, it was found that the control infants were more likely to sleep in a room with a window open at least 4 inches (10cm). Unfortunately, no other study has collected or published information on these topics.

Social Conditions

Investigators can always find some adverse social aspect of a household if they look hard enough. Families of sudden infant deaths can be scrutinised in this way, and results compared with control families. Such discussions are always biased by the fact that the interviewer knows which family suffered the sudden infant death. The information collected is mostly subjective rather than objective.

During the second ORLS study we abstracted from the obstetric case notes all social comments that were recorded. Such comments were made usually during the pregnancy, and never after the death had occurred. Twenty-two of the sudden infant deaths (14%) had such comments compared with 25 controls (6%), a statistically significant

difference. As mentioned earlier, the housing conditions were not responsible for the associations, nor are there clear categories of social problem involved.

Clinic Attendance

We showed earlier that pregnancies which resulted in infants who were subsequently to die did seem to have been associated with later attendances for antenatal care and fewer antenatal visits than a control population. We pointed out, however, that the data so far available was difficult to interpret.

Although several authors have collected information on attendance of the mothers of sudden infant death children at Well-Baby Clinics, prior to the death, it is not easy to interpret the results here either. Later in this chapter, we shall be showing that the sudden infant deaths are more likely to have had various illnesses during their short lives, and therefore the possibility of their attending Well-Baby Clinics would be reduced. Bearing this in mind, it was found in Copenhagen that sudden infant death babies were less likely to have kept appointments with the Health Visitor. In one Sheffield study, where sudden explained as well as unexplained deaths were included, as many as 55% of mothers failed to keep their appointment for post-natal follow-up compared with 14% of control women. Unfortunately, this analysis did not appear to take account of the number of children who had already died or were ill at the time of their post-natal follow-up appointment. Similarly, in a study in Lambeth, London, there were 26 out of 50 mothers of sudden infant deaths who defaulted from their post-natal follow-up compared with 10 of 48 controls. Again, no account appears to have been taken of the number of mothers who had already lost their infants.

As with analysis of antenatal care, therefore, interpretation of whether a mother keeps appointments for Well-Baby Clincs or post-natal check-ups, can be difficult. In addition, the available data do not appear to have taken account of those social factors that we know are important in the genesis of sudden infant death. The results are impossible to interpret. The suggestion that mothers of sudden infant deaths are less likely to take full advantage of the primary health care available is thus not proven.

Breast Feeding

For many years it was common to hear statements such as 'I have never come across a case of cot death in a totally breast fed baby'.

Based on such widely repeated wisdom, the emphasis of much early research on the topic relied on the cows' milk allergy hypothesis, and women are still being told to breast feed and prevent a sudden infant death.

Just how much evidence is there for any of these statements? The first studies on the subject were carried out either at times or in places where breast feeding was comparatively rare. For example, in the study in Northern Ireland, it is true that only 27 (16.7%) of the 162 mothers of sudden infant deaths had attempted to breast feed their babies at all, but this must be compared with the figures for the matched controls (29/164 = 17.7%) an almost identical proportion. Similar findings of a lack of negative association between breast feeding in the first week and later sudden infant death, have been found in the U.S. Collaborative Study, the Canadian Study, one from San Diego and both ORLS studies. Others, such as those in Sheffield, Cardiff, Southampton and Copenhagen have found that fewer mothers of sudden infant deaths were breast feeding than would have been expected.

The Danish authors discuss their findings in some detail and point out that although the rate of breast feeding had, in general, been declining over the 15 years of the study, the rate of sudden infant death had been static. They suggest that their results could be explained if the prevalence of breast feeding was linked with social variables which were themselves associated with sudden infant death.

Within Britain, there is substantial evidence that the social factors which are associated with lack of breast feeding are those which are largely associated with sudden infant death. In Figure 23 we show the proportion of women who breast fed in 1970 according to (a) social class, and (b) their smoking habit. By comparing the patterns with those shown for the risk of sudden infant death on pages 44 and 57, it can be seen that the Danish predictions are fulfilled: the mothers socially at risk of sudden infant death are those who would be unlikely to breast feed. It is therefore not surprising that the major studies that have controlled for social factors in their analysis found no association with bottle feeding.

There were 277 ORLS sudden infant deaths for which information on feeding practice in the first week was available. Almost identical proportions of their mothers had been breast feeding (31.8%) as had the mothers of the matched controls (32.2%). Thus there was no evidence that sudden infant death was more likely in infants who had never been breast fed.

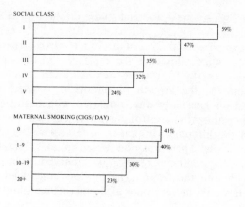

Figure 23

Proportions of women in Britain in 1970 who breast fed in the first week of life according to social class and maternal smoking (from the 1970 British Birth Cohort, Butler, Golding and Howlett, 1984).

Postnatal Growth

Again, the topic of postnatal growth is full of difficulties. In general, the growth is measured from two points: measurements made at birth, and those made at death. In some studies there has been information available on the children during their lives, but this always appears to have been a biased set of children. For example, from the U.S. Collaborative Study, Naeye and his colleagues reported on the growth from birth to 4 weeks of 28 of the 125 sudden infant deaths in the study. He reported that although on average their birthweight was at the 40th percentile, by the time they reached the age of 4 weeks, their mean weight was on the 20th percentile as were their lengths and head circumferences. The major defects of the study lie in the fact that the percentile values he is using are standards published for the whole population and do not necessarily relate to the population of infants from which the deaths were obtained. There must also be considerable unease in any study where information for analysis exists in only 20% of the sudden infant deaths.

In the study in Northern Ireland, the authors stated that 'most cases seemed well nourished at post-mortem', and plotting their growth on a standard growth curve 'suggested that sudden infant deaths have

thrived normally'. In one of the first studies in the United Kingdom, it was reported that 60% of the sudden infant deaths had a below average weight gain compared with 27% of random controls. Again, there was no attempt to make allowance for the fact that the sudden infant deaths differed socially from the control children.

In Copenhagen, the growth of infants who were later to die suddenly and unexpectedly was compared with that of controls of similar birthweight. After controlling for type of feed, they found that there were slight differences in that the infants who later died, gained weight more slowly. There was no attempt to take social factors into account, however, and no suggestion of a marked decrease in weight gain shortly before the death. The authors concluded that infant growth charts would be very poor at predicting an infant who was to die suddenly.

A further study has been carried out by Naeye. He elicited the cooperation of 45 families who had had a sudden infant death and compared the growth of the infants with that of their siblings. He showed that two thirds of the sudden infant deaths had a decrease in weight percentile after birth compared with 35% of their sibling controls. These data are the most convincing that exist concerning the possibility of reduced growth in sudden infant death children but again a word of caution must be raised – there was no attempt to ascertain how representative these families were of all sudden infant deaths. It could be, for example, that the parents who decided to cooperate in the study were those who already felt that the child differed in some way from his siblings.

An interesting study was carried out in Seattle. The head circumferences, lengths and weight gains for a group of sudden infant deaths were compared with similar information from two separate control groups. The first control population was obtained from a group of healthy children measured in a clinic in a socially well off area and the second group consisted of children from deprived homes. The sudden infant deaths showed mean values that were worse than either control group but the difference in weights between the sudden infant deaths and children from so-called deprived homes was not statistically significant. No account had been taken though of the fact that the children who were sudden infant deaths had a lower birthweight to start with.

A further study was then carried out by Peterson. In his original study in Seattle, he had compared sudden infant death children with controls who were either from well off areas or from deprived circumstances, but in his latest study he compared the growth curve of the children who were to die suddenly and unexpectedly with a group

of children whose mothers had smoked during pregnancy. He found that the two growth patterns were virtually identical, and concluded that the reduced growth rate in infants who died suddenly was associated with the fact that their mothers had smoked during pregnancy.

Passive Smoking

We have already shown that there is a strong association between maternal smoking in pregnancy and sudden infant death. Of course, mothers who smoke during pregnancy are very likely to continue to do so when the child is born. It is therefore quite feasible that it is not the smoking during pregnancy, but the smoking subsequent to delivery that is the vital association with sudden infant death. Because women who smoke during pregnancy are almost always the same as those who smoked after pregnancy, it is difficult to distinguish between the two effects. Bergman and Wiesner examined this possibility in Seattle, comparing the smoking history of 100 parents whose infants had recently died suddenly and unexpectedly with 100 control parents with children born at the same time, of the same sex and race. In the event, they only had replies from 56 cases and 86 controls, the large number of parents not replying were all people who had moved from their last address and not left a forwarding address! (As we shall discuss later, this in itself seems a highly disturbing fact, implying that the parents who have sudden infant deaths feel unable to stay in the same area). Of the replies that were received, 61% of the sudden infant death mothers had smoked during pregnancy compared with 42% of control mothers; for smoking after delivery the figures were 59% and 37%. There was no association at all with paternal smoking. It is impossible from these data to state which factor is the most important but pending further information it would seem advisable to assume that neither smoking during pregnancy nor after pregnancy is a safe habit, given a vulnerable infant.

Postnatal Temperament

In retrospect, it is very difficult to give an unbiased view of the temperament of an infant who has recently died. Any study therefore that relies on questioning persons closely involved with the infant, especially the parents, is liable to the criticism that the information obtained would rely heavily on parental reactions to the sudden death.

A study has been carried out in America whereby 46 parents of sudden infant deaths were given questionnaires to fill in concerning

the temperament not only of the infant who died, but also of one other surviving child. Comparison of the replies concerning the infant who died with those of the siblings who were alive and well resulted in several statistically significant differences. The infant who died was reported as having had less reaction to environmental stimuli, to have been less active physically, to have been more breathless and exhausted during feeding and more likely to have had abnormal cries.

To our knowledge, only one other group of authors has attempted to ascertain the development of the infant who died. From health visitor records, the Copenhagen team showed that among infants weighing 2500g or more, the children who subsequently died were slightly less likely to have started to smile by two months of age. They were also less likely to have started to 'babble' than their controls. It is possible though that this could merely have reflected a difference in gestation. No information is given on this possibility.

Further investigations of postneonatal temperament are necessary. They should rely on prospectively gathered information, the recording of temperament being made prior to any death. Obviously, this requires a number of observations on a large number of infants, very few of whom will die, but many health visitors keep such records and the project should be possible.

Postnatal Illness

As with a study of post-neonatal temperament, an assessment of the symptoms and illnesses of the child during its life is likely to be biased by retrospective recall. The parents who have lost their child suddenly and unexpectedly are likely to have racked their brains for abnormalities that might have existed which perhaps they felt they ought to have taken more note of. Alternatively, some parents feel so guilty that they hide the fact that symptoms were present.

For a child that has survived, such intense questioning is unlikely to occur. Consequently, any study which relies on asking such questions of the parents of a sudden infant death and comparing the answers with those of the parents of a healthy child is likely to be misleading. Probably the first authors to document illness in the child prior to death were Carpenter and Shaddick. In analysing information from London and Cambridge they reported that 80% of the deaths had had symptoms prior to the death compared with 39% of controls. The differences concerned respiratory rather than other symptoms. In Sheffield, Carpenter et al reported on 97 explained and unexplained sudden deaths and compared the results with 97 controls. The deaths had apparently had 260 different symptoms in the three weeks prior to

death compared with 48 symptoms in 97 controls. The symptoms concerned, included snuffles (40 cases; 17 controls), cough (32; 7), irritability (32; 2), vomiting (29; 3), diarrhoea (20; 3), fever (9; 1), and change of cry (15; 0).

Further data were published by Stanton et al involving 145 explained and unexplained sudden infant deaths from various centres in Britain. This time there were no significant differences in the prevalence of snuffles, but there were again more deaths with a history of cough (31 cases; 8 controls), irritability (37; 8), vomiting (14; 2), diarrhoea (9; 2), fever (13; 2) and change of cry (14; 0).

These details are difficult to interpret in assessing the association between symptoms and the truly unexpected sudden infant death as we have defined it in this book. Nevertheless, such investigations can be helpful in deriving hypotheses, providing these can then be tested in an objective fashion. One of the ways in which more concrete data can be obtained is in looking at events, such as hospital admissions, or visits to the family physician during the child's life.

In Northern Ireland, there were more admissions to hospital of the children who subsequently died, than of the control children. A similar finding of increased risk of hospital admission to infants who had later died was found by Carpenter and his colleagues in Sheffield. In the first ORLS study we found a similar pattern. As many as 17 (10%) of the 170 children in our study had been admitted to hospital and been discharged prior to their death, compared with only 16 (3%) of the 510 control children who had been admitted during the time during which their matched case had been alive. The biggest difference in the causes of hospital admission, lay in the admissions for respiratory disorders, especially bronchiolitis. Three of the children had died suddenly within a week of discharge from the hospital.

Bedding and Sleeping Positions

In one of the first epidemiological studies, that of infant deaths occurring suddenly at home in Cambridge and London, enquiry of the coroner's officers concerning the softness of clothes and mattresses, was compared with health visitor's assessment of those of control children. Any such study where one group of people is responsible for making assessment of cases and another group assessed controls is obviously prone to bias. It is therefore with a large 'pinch of salt' that one reads the results of a comparison between the two sets of information. In fact it was found that the sudden infant deaths were more likely to have had pillows, and more likely that the pillows were softer than the random control population. The infants who died were

also apparently more likely to have had a soft mattress. No attempt was made to take account of social circumstances in this study. Very little in the way of other evidence is available on the associations of types of bedding with sudden infant death. It is relevant, however, that although soft pillows are now rarely used, and mattresses have become harder, there has been no reduction in the rate of sudden infant death.

The same study examined the *normal* sleeping position of the deaths and of control infants. They found no differences between these two groups, although the 'deaths' were more likely than expected to be *found* lying face down. It was thought that this was probably a position which the infant got into before its terminal state. In Northern Ireland, Froggatt and his colleagues found that the majority of deaths occurred with the baby in his/her normal sleeping position. Of those where there was a difference, the baby was found face down (nine), face up (eight) and face to side (five). Thus, there is little evidence that putting the child to bed on his stomach, on his back, or on his side, influences his likelihood to die suddenly.

Chapter 11

Medical History of the Siblings and the Mothers

The Siblings

As with enquiries of the symptoms or temperament of the child who died, so with the characteristics of siblings. The possible bias introduced in comparing answers of parents of sudden infant deaths with those of controls concerns not so much the ability of either to tell the truth, but their ability to recall in the same amount of detail abnormalities that have occurred. We are, therefore, presenting here previously unpublished data from our own study concerning the deaths and hospital admissions to the siblings of both the sudden infant deaths in the first ORLS series and the siblings of control infants. It must be remembered that the controls were picked so that they had the same maternal age, maternal marital status, social class and birth order as the cases of sudden infant death. To avoid possible bias we ascertained the names and dates of birth of those siblings who were born within the area and for whom we had records on the file. We independently traced these children through the Oxford Record Linkage records to ascertain all instances of neonatal abnormality, hospital admission and/or death.

Mortality

From a population study in Northern Ireland, there were 8 siblings of sudden infant deaths who had themselves died suddenly and unexpectedly. If all of these were genuine cases of sudden infant death, the risk to siblings would be 2.2%.

Questionnaire response from 1,194 parents of sudden infant deaths in North America revealed that 18 of 839 (2.1%) subsequent births also died suddenly and unexpectedly; this is about ten times the expected rate in the normal population.

In South Australia also, 2% (6/302) of the siblings had died suddenly and expectedly. In 652 second degree relatives the incidence

was 1.4% and in third degree relatives it was 1.3% – but no details are given as to accuracy of diagnosis. This point is relevant when we consider a study carried out by Jacquie Roberts on British families who had abused one of their children. There was a high rate of post-neonatal death, attributed by the parents and many health workers to the sudden infant death syndrome. Review of post-mortem reports, however, showed that most of these deaths were not cases of sudden infant death syndrome at all.

Of the 164 siblings of the first ORLS cases there were three children who died suddenly and unexpectedly. All 3 were born to the same mother. In comparison, of the 308 siblings of controls three were sudden infant deaths. Apart from this finding, there were no differences in the risk of other types of death between the siblings of the sudden infant deaths and the siblings of the controls.

The family for which there was a repeated history of sudden infant death was interesting in many respects. This was a large family, the four eldest children being alive and well. The mother had remarried after the birth of the last of these children and the subsequent children to be born all died suddenly and unexpectedly. The first two were apparently well until both went into hospital with dysentery: the younger of the two died within 6 days of discharge (at 9 weeks of age) and the elder died some 16 days later at 73 weeks of age. The next sibling was born some 14 months later and also died suddenly at 9 weeks. No abnormalities were found at post-mortem. A subsequent infant was born during the period of the second ORLS survey. He was given a great deal of care by the paediatric services, and by his very anxious mother. Nevertheless, he also died suddenly at the age of 9 weeks. One of the possibly significant factors about this family was that both the mother and the father were very heavy cigarette smokers – the mother smoking as many as 50 cigarettes a day. The other factor possibly of note was that this child was known to be allergic to cows' milk.

Combining the numbers of siblings who were sudden infant deaths in the ORLS study with those identified by Froggatt and his colleagues in Northern Ireland suggests that the incidence of sudden infant death is increased by a factor of 10. If, however, the risk is related to controls of the same social and maternal background, the relative risk of sudden infant death among siblings is possibly raised by only a factor of about three.

Curiously, the American study indicated that further cases of sudden infant death were more likely to occur if the mother had originated from a family with half-siblings, step-siblings or adopted siblings. In Australia, mothers with more than one sudden infant

death were more likely to have had previous miscarriages or problems in the index pregnancy. Such findings require other observations to confirm the associations before much weight can be placed upon them.

From the genetic point of view, the most interesting finding from the American study was that the first cousins of sudden infant deaths had a rate of sudden infant death almost identical to the population as a whole.

We have already shown that twins of infants who die suddenly and unexpectedly are at increased risk, but that most of this risk is restricted to the four weeks of time from the death of the co-twin. There is an elevated risk thereafter, compared to the general population, but this does not appear to be more than for any siblings. There is no evidence that monozygotic (identical) twins are at increased risk.

Congenital Malformations in Siblings
From the files of the ORLS we identified siblings with congenital malformations from information available at birth as well as that obtained from details of hospital admission and, where relevant, post-mortem findings. In the following analyses we will be omitting those siblings who were to die a sudden infant death. Altogether 8 (5%) of the 164 siblings of sudden infant deaths had congenital malformations of some magnitude compared with a similar proportion (5%) of the siblings of controls.

Other factors which might have had a prenatal origin were, however, found in the siblings of sudden infant deaths more than might have been expected. Two of the children (both siblings of one sudden infant death) were suffering severe hypothyroidism resulting in mental retardation; there was one other sibling with mental retardation, and one case of cerebral palsy among the 164 siblings of sudden infant deaths. These were all identified from hospital admission records. In contrast, there were no such cases among the 308 siblings of controls. A possible association with hypothyroidism is tempting, but further evidence is required from larger studies.

Neonatal Illness
The various signs and symptoms that were noted in the neonatal period of the siblings of the sudden infant deaths are compared with the siblings of controls in Table 9 below. It can be seen that there was little in the way of consistent difference apart from one factor: an association with prematurity. Ten of the 164 siblings of the sudden infant deaths received special care for low birthweight compared with

only 5 of the 305 control siblings. Of perhaps more interest is the analysis of subsequent hospital admission of siblings.

Table 9

Neonatal signs and symptoms among siblings of sudden infant deaths and controls (ORLS 1966–70).

Neonatal signs and symptoms	SIBLINGS OF	
	Sudden infant deaths	Controls
"prematurity"	10	5*
asphyxia at birth	16	31
apnoeic attacks	1	1
hypotonia	2	1
cyanotic attacks	1	1
systolic murmur	1	1
convulsion	1	0
respiratory distress	1	2
jaundice	2	9
Rhesus incompatibility	0	2
stillbirth	2	2
neonatal death	2	9
ALL SIBLINGS CONSIDERED	164	305

* $P < 0.05$

Later Hospital Admissions

Altogether, 29 of the 164 siblings of sudden infant deaths (17.7%) had been admitted to hospital during their early life. This compares with 30 of the 305 siblings of controls (9.8%). Altogether, 53 hospital admissions had been recorded for the 164 siblings of sudden infant deaths (a mean of 0.32 per child) compared with 55 hospital admissions to the 305 siblings of controls (a mean of 0.18 per child). A comparison of the major causes of the admissions is shown in Table 10 below. It can be seen that the greatest difference was in admissions for gastro-enteritis.

Pertinent to the possibility of a hypothetical relationship with child abuse is the fact that the siblings of the sudden infant deaths were at no greater risk of admission with injuries of any kind. Relevant to the possibility of an association between sudden infant death and febrile

convulsions is the fact that only two of 164 siblings (1.2%) of sudden infant deaths were admitted with convulsions, compared with 2 of 305 control siblings (0.7%). These points will be discussed in more details in Part III of this book.

Table 10

Later hospital admissions to siblings of sudden infant deaths compared with the siblings of control infants: selected reasons. ORLS 1966-70.

REASON FOR ADMISSION	SIBLINGS OF SUDDEN INFANT DEATHS	SIBLINGS OF CONTROLS
Gastroenteritis	8 (7)	2 (2)*
Respiratory disorders	9 (6)	13 (9)
Otitis media	5 (1)	1 (1)
Septicaemia	1 (1)	1 (1)
Injuries	4 (4)	13 (13)
Convulsions/fits	2 (2)	3 (2)
Abscess	2 (2)	3 (3)
Hernias	4 (4)	3 (3)
Feeding problem	2 (2)	1 (1)
Malformations and developmental disorders	11 (7)	7 (5)
Total children considered	164	305

In parentheses are the number of children involved.

* P<0.05

Maternal Medical History

The hospital admission records of one hundred and sixty-eight mothers of sudden infant deaths were compared with that of 510 mothers of control infants in the first ORLS study. Records of all non-obstetric hospital admissions during the period under consideration were obtained and coded to conditions (a) arising before pregnancy, (b) during the pregnancy, (c) after delivery, but before the death occurred, and (d) after the death (Table 11). Altogether there were more admissions to mothers of sudden infant deaths than to mothers of controls. The difference, however, was mainly in admissions after

the death had occurred, as can be seen from Table 11. After the sudden deaths, 16 mothers of cases had 21 admissions, more than would have been expected from the admission rate to mothers of controls.

Table 11

Comparison of hospital admissions to mothers of sudden infant deaths with matched controls. (Excluding all admissions for obstetric/gynaecological reasons.) ORLS 1966-70.

No. of Hospital Admissions	Mother of sudden infant deaths (n=168)	Mother of control infants (n=510)	Statistical significance
Prior to pregnancy	9 (8)	20 (18)	N.S.
During the pregnancy	4 (3)	3 (3)	N.S.
From delivery to death	2 (2)	4 (4)	N.S.
After death	21 (16)	32 (24)	$P<0.05$
ALL	36 (24)	59 (45)	N.S.

No. of women involved are shown in brackets.

Four of the admissions after death were associated with taking overdoses and a further three with depression. A further woman had schizophrenia and one woman was a long-standing alcoholic, indeed she had had an admission during the pregnancy itself for alcoholism. Another woman was admitted in an hysterical state. Altogether, therefore, there were 8 women with admissions for mental depression or psychosis after the death had occurred. This must be compared with only three such women among the controls.

To assess whether the mothers of sudden infant deaths are overall mentally more unstable than controls, admissions prior to the death should be analysed. Only 3 of the mothers of sudden infant deaths had such admissions prior to the death compared with 6 of the controls. It does therefore appear that the excess of post-mortality mental disorders among mothers who had had a sudden infant death was in response to the death rather than being a characteristic of the mothers involved.

Subsequent Fertility

There has been only one published study on subsequent fertility of mothers who have had a sudden infant death, and it appears to indicate that they had extreme difficulty in conceiving again and that among those who had conceived there were a large proportion of spontaneous abortions.

The data from the ORLS files was used to assess the fertility of the group of women who had a sudden infant death compared with control women of the same social background, age and number of pregnancies. The results are shown in Table 12 below. Altogether there were far more subsequent pregnancies to the women who had had a sudden infant death than there were to the controls. There was no excess of spontaneous abortions among women who had had sudden infant deaths (though it must be pointed out that only spontaneous abortions resulting in hospital admissions have been identified). Neither group were very likely to request and obtain termination of pregnancy and a large number of successful deliveries occurred within our study period. We have no information on the number of women who were involuntarily infertile but the evidence from this study is that the women with a sudden infant death are normally fertile, and appear to have little difficulty in giving birth to another child.

Table 12

Subsequent pregnancies to mothers of sudden infant deaths and matched controls. ORLS 1966–71.

SUBSEQUENT PREGNANCIES	To: mothers of sudden infant deaths	To: mothers of controls
Spontaneous abortion (miscarriage)	7	7
Termination	4	7
Birth	97	143
Total number pregnancies	108	157
No. of mothers	168	510

P<0.001

Chapter 12

Summary of the Epidemiological Findings

Throughout this section of the book we have presented data from the two ORLS studies together with that reported from other investigators. Examination of the evidence has shown many findings that are consistent, not only within certain areas, but across the world. These are summarised in Table 13.

From this it is apparent that in all caucasian populations studied, there is a typical age distribution, more boys are affected than girls, death is more likely to occur in winter, the risk increases in social classes IV and V, to infants of young mothers, to infants with a large number of other siblings, if there was a short interval between this birth and the previous one, if the child is illegitimate, a multiple birth, delivered pre-term or of low birthweight. Sudden infant death is more common in infants with congenital defects and in infants whose mother was not aware of the date of her last menstrual period.

Table 13

Listing of epidemiological findings in the two ORLS studies and in the world literature.

	1st ORLS Study	2nd ORLS Study	Other Studies
Sex	Excess of males	Similar to 1st	Similar in caucasian
Age at death	Peak 8–17 wks	Similar to 1st	Similar
Season of death	Winter excess	Similar to 1st	Similar
Day of death	No association	Similar to 1st	?
Type of area	City excess	Similar to 1st	?
	Oxfordshire> Berkshire	Similar to 1st	—

Social class	increase in IV and V	Similar to 1st	Similar
Maternal age	increase with young mothers	Similar to 1st	Similar
Birth order	increase with high birth order	Similar to 1st	Similar
Short interpregnancy interval	increase	—	Similar
Illegitimacy	increase	Similar to 1st	Similar
Maternal origin	increase in immigrants	Similar but less strong	—
Maternal blood group	no association	Similar to 1st	?
Previous pregnancy loss	no association	Similar to 1st	Similar
Month of delivery	excess in Autumn	Similar to 1st	Similar
Place of delivery	excess in large hospitals	Similar to 1st	—
Multiple births	excess	Similar to 1st	Similar
Gestation	excess in pre-term	Similar to 1st	Similar
Birthweight	excess in low birthweight	Similar to 1st	Similar
Obstetric complications	no association	Similar to 1st	Similar
Non-obstetric	excess "insults"	Excess infections	Similar
Induction of labour	excess	no association	Similar to 2nd
Length of labour	no association	Similar to 1st	?
Neonatal jaundice	excess	no association	no association
Congenital defects	excess	Similar to 1st	Similar
Breast feeding	no association	Similar to 1st	?
Unknown date of LMP	excess	Similar to 1st	Similar
Maternal smoking	—	excess	Similar
Maternal barbiturates in pregnancy	—	excess	Similar

— = study/studies not done   ? = lack of consistent reports
Similar = results similar in direction to those found in the first ORLS study

Maternal cigarette smoking in pregnancy and maternal opiate addiction both carry increased risks to the infant. There is evidence that infants of mothers who had had an infection or taken barbiturates were at increased risk.

On the negative side, there is no consistent evidence to support the generalisation that breast feeding protects against all sudden infant death. Nor is there any strong evidence that particular neonatal abnormalities such as apnoeic attacks indicate that the infant is at increased risk of sudden infant death. Finally, we question whether these deaths

are more likely to occur during the night rather than the day.

The epidemiological information that has been discussed to date has made the assumption that sudden infant death is a definable entity, with the possibility that a distinct cause will be found for it. In actual fact of course, the label 'sudden infant death' is derived by a process of elimination rather than of positive identification. It is quite possible that the label hides a number of distinct entities.

If this were so, the relevant question is whether an epidemiologist might be able to distinguish between different types, even though most pathologists seldom do so. A simple example of a way in which the epidemiologist could assist is given below.

Suppose post-mortems were not carried out in a population, but the clinicians were able to categorise which members of the population had died from heart disease. An epidemiologist might plot the ages at death of all with heart disease, and derive a graph such as Figure 24 below. There are two distinct distributions – one occurring among young children and the other among the elderly. The epidemiologist would then suggest that there might be two distinct disorders, and of course he would be right. The young children would mostly have died of congenital heart disease and the older deaths would mainly be due to degenerative heart disease.

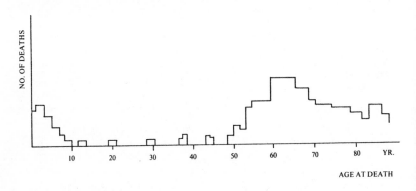

Figure 24

Hypothetical distribution of deaths from heart disease by age at death.

Analysis and interpretation of the information on sudden infant death is not as simple. Nevertheless, there is a certain amount of evidence to suggest that an effort is warranted.

The age at death distribution is not obviously bimodal. Neverthe-

less, the smooth distribution noted could easily be derived from two separate distributions. Suppose, for example, that one type of sudden infant death affected only infants in the first 4 months of life with a peak incidence at 8 weeks (Figure 25A), and that a second form of sudden infant death rarely occurred before 6 weeks of age and had its peak incidence at 15 weeks (Figure 25B). Combination of the two would give the picture shown in Figure 26, the typical sudden infant death distribution.

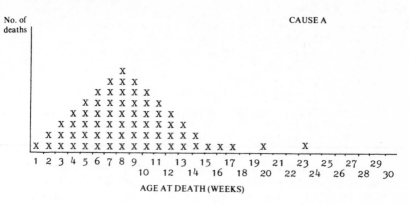

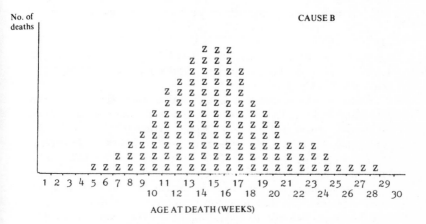

Figure 25

Hypothetical distribution of two distinct types of sudden infant death by age at death.

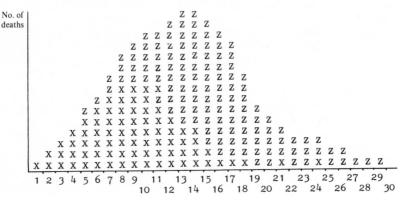

Figure 26

Combination of the two distributions shown in Figure 25.

Is there any evidence for such a combination of two distributions? If they were to occur one would anticipate that division of sudden infant deaths by age at death would distinguish between them. Thus if one considered the deaths occurring under 8 weeks in the example above, 84% of the deaths would have been due to cause A. If one had taken all deaths aged 12 weeks or more, 87% would have been due to cause B.

The first intimation that there were epidemiological differences between early deaths and later deaths was published by Fedrick after analysing the first ORLS study. It was found that the deaths that occurred from 12 weeks onwards differed from the earlier deaths in that they were predominantly winter deaths, more likely to be of low social class and high birth order.

The strongest confirmation of such a difference was produced by Carpenter and Gardner when they analysed national data. Their results are illustrated in Figure 27, which is copied from their original publication. It shows that the seasonal variation in sudden respiratory death rates is lower for the deaths at early ages and rises to a peak at between 3 and 6 months, falling slightly thereafter.

Similar findings were reported by Susan Beal in Australia. She found that deaths under 8 weeks showed no seasonal differences, but that the deaths between 16 and 24 weeks were predominantly winter deaths.

Although most population studies show little evidence of a bimodal distribution in age at death, information from deaths for which data were collected during the Foundation Study show two marked peaks at 8 weeks and 13 weeks (see page 227). It could be that these indicate

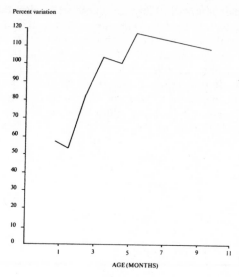

Figure 27

Seasonal variation in SRD rates, 1965–76*, England and Wales. (Reproduced from Carpenter and Gardner, 1982.)

*The rates are averaged over the years 1965–76 and the variation is measured by the difference between the December–January rate and the June–July rate expressed as a percentage of the average rate for the age groups.

two different modes of death in this markedly different sample, 50% of whom were from social classes I and II.

A comparison was made of the epidemiological findings in the two ORLS studies for sudden infant deaths occurring before 12 weeks of age and those occurring later. Numbers are small and associations would need to be confirmed elsewhere. The factor that appears to be consistent in regard to the deaths at under 12 weeks is:

more maternal smoking

Factors that are particularly associated with later deaths are:

winter excess
low gestation
low birthweight
illegitimacy
'lower' social class
other children in the family

The fact that infants of short gestation are likely to die later has often been noted. It has been suggested that correction to age after *expected* date of delivery rather than the age calculated from *actual* date of birth (the postnatal age), might result in the infants of short gestation displaying a similar distribution to the infants delivered at term. We have done this for all sudden infant deaths of gestation under 38 weeks. The results are shown in Figure 28. It can be seen that correcting for gestation fails to produce a distribution that is more like that found for all the other deaths.

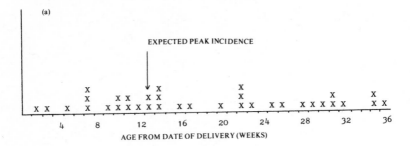

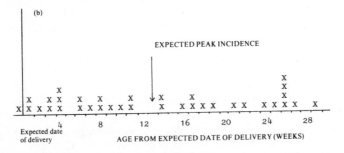

Figure 28

Age at death of all sudden infant deaths of gestation under 38 weeks calculated from (a) date of delivery, (b) expected date of delivery; ORLS 1966–1975.

A similar exercise was carried out for all deaths who had been delivered post-term, correcting for the duration of gestation. It can be seen from Figure 29 that the pattern of deaths conforms to the expected distribution if the age is taken from the actual date of delivery, but is far less clear if the age is calculated from the expected date of delivery. It seems reasonable, therefore, to suggest that gestational age should not be taken into account when dividing the infants according to the age of death. It is therefore true that the

children of short gestation are more likely to be in the group of later deaths.

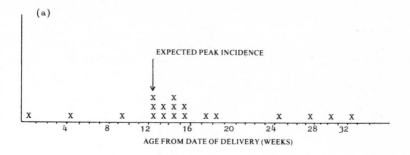

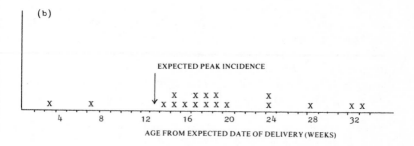

Figure 29

Age at death of all sudden infant deaths of gestation 42 weeks or more, calculated from (a) date of delivery and (b) expected date of delivery: ORLS 1966–75.

The distribution of age at death of the low birthweight infants is shown in Figure 30. Seventeen of the infants had been of short gestation and all but two of them died at 12 weeks or later. Fifteen, however, were delivered at term and were severely growth-retarded: over half of these had died before the age of 12 weeks. It is likely, therefore, that growth retardation is one of the factors more associated with the early deaths.

The combination of this information with that of other sudden infant deaths might elucidate further ways in which the groups differ from one another. Large numbers will be needed to show any significant differences.

Although we have shown some evidence for a division at 12 weeks into two groups there are more cogent reasons for the deaths to be split

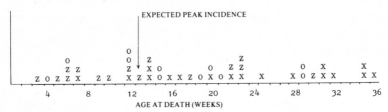

x = immature (gestation 38 weeks)
z = growth retardation (gestation 38 weeks+)
0 = gestation not known

Figure 30

Age at death of infants of birthweight 2500g or less: ORLS 1966-75.

into several groups – but the overlapping of groups will become more and more difficult to assess. Nevertheless, we are sure that this is the way in which future epidemiological studies should be directed.

This analysis of risk factors statistically associated with sudden infant death when considered as a single entity has illustrated the degree of risk associated with the factors for which data is available.

It is important to appreciate 2 points. First, the distinction between risk and proportion; for example, although infants of unmarried mothers are at increased risk they form in England only one fifth (20%) of all sudden infant deaths. Second, if sudden infant deaths comprise a collection of different conditions with a common final pathway, some factors which are not statistically significantly associated with the whole group may be highly relevant to a small number of deaths. For example the method of feeding may be very important to the few babies who are allergic to cows' milk but not relevant to the majority who are not.

In the next four chapters, we shall be discussing the epidemiological findings in the context of the various hypotheses that have been produced to try to explain the causes of sudden infant death, and indicating which of these seem feasible.

Part III

Possible Causes of Sudden Infant Death

Chapter 13

Methods of Generating and Testing Hypotheses

The fact that sudden infant death is often called 'sudden infant death *syndrome*' does not mean that there is a proven single cause of the deaths. Indeed, as we have already pointed out, the label sudden infant death is arrived at by a process of elimination, not of positive identification. It is often suggested that most of the deaths are unlikely to have been caused by a single factor but rather that it may be a combination of disorders that results in the death, such as a mild infection in a child with an inherited weakness on a cold night in mid-winter.

In the next three chapters we shall try to outline some of the recent areas of research and suggested causes of the deaths. Hypotheses have proliferated to an enormous extent in the last twenty years, and it has been impossible to cover all of them. We have tried, however, to outline those theories that are, at the present time, most discussed in the medical literature or which seem to have some basis for consideration. Part of the function of this section will be to attempt to see whether any of the hypotheses fit in with the epidemiological evidence available.

Research into the aetiology of sudden infant death has divided into four main categories: (a) the creation of a hypothesis from the available evidence; (b) the testing of hypotheses by assessing the levels of biochemical markers at post-mortem; (c) the investigation of so-called 'near-miss' cot deaths; (d) the detailed study of infant siblings of sudden infant deaths.

Creation of Hypotheses

As we have already indicated, ideas as to the cause of sudden infant death have been legion. Most have been ignored – and this may have occurred for several reasons: first, the sheer quantity of hypotheses

tends to militate against serious consideration of any particular one; second, the argument may have been poorly presented, focussing on only one aspect of the known facts concerning sudden infant death; third, it may be such that it is impossible to test in any way.

In this volume we cannot hope to consider all the suggestions that have been advanced – we can merely present the arguments for and against some of the hypotheses. In all arguments, however, it is important to remember that the condition we are dealing with may be due to a variety of causes, and the contribution of each cause may differ in different parts of the world. Thus, as we shall discuss, botulinism may account for a discernible proportion of deaths in California where the micro-organism is more common – but not be in other areas where the botulin microbe is rarely identified.

Testing Hypotheses at Post-Mortem

The above argument is wholly relevant to the interpretation of a scientist's results. Suppose a hypothesis suggests that sudden infant death is due to a particular condition which can be detected by measuring the level of a certain chemical at post-mortem. Two scientists might carry out a study on sudden infant deaths in different parts of the world. They might obtain totally different results, with one rejecting and one accepting the hypothesis. Both may be right for their particular area. This, of course, makes it very difficult to compare results and assess the validity of a hypothesis. Nevertheless we shall attempt to examine the evidence to assess whether there are grounds for considering each hypothesis as revealing a major cause of sudden infant death.

Other ways in which post-mortem measures may be misleading lie in lack of adequate control measures, and biochemical changes that occur after death. Clear examples of the latter will be shown in Chapter 14. There is little chance of obtaining adequate controls – since these should be representative of the population and without a history of serious illness. The only candidates are either children who are still alive, or infants who died from accidental injury. Ideally, the control specimens should be obtained from infants of the same ages, and at the same season, as the sudden infant deaths. This rarely occurs, and hence results are difficult to evaluate.

The 'Near-Miss'

In trying to carry out research on possible causes of sudden infant death, scientists, by the very nature of things, are unable to study many of the infants before they die. This is obviously because there is no

clear way of predicting which infants are going to die. There are, however, a large number of studies of the so-called 'near-miss' sudden infant death syndrome. This term is used to describe infants that have been found collapsed with no respirations, pale, limp and lifeless, but have, nevertheless, been resuscitated or started to breathe again spontaneously on their own. It has often been assumed that these children are representative of sudden unexpected infant deaths. Yet the relationship between 'near-miss' and actual sudden infant deaths is by no means clear. What is certain is that these 'near-miss' infants do include children who have a large number of different problems including hypoglycaemia, abnormalities in the regulation of breathing, abnormalities of heart beat, ear infections, convulsions, and other disorders. Once the children with identifiable diagnoses have been excluded, there remain a number of infants for whom no definite explanation of their sudden collapse was subsequently found.

It is assumed that this group of infants are similar to sudden infant deaths, and investigation of such children has been considered to provide valuable clues in the search for the causes of sudden infant death itself. Certainly, it is true that the infants who have suffered a near-miss episode are slightly more at risk of subsequently dying suddenly and unexpectedly.

For example, in Boston, Massachusetts, Dorothy Kelly and her colleagues arranged for home cardio-respiratory monitoring for 84 near-miss children. These children had had extensive evaluation in hospital and their parents had been trained in how to use the monitors. Four of the children who were in the study subsequently died at home in spite of the monitors.

Such studies as these suggest that infants who do have a so-called near-miss are at increased risk of subsequent death. There is no conclusive proof that these children are representative of sudden infant deaths in general though. Indeed, at a recent conference, Donald Peterson went so far as to say 'so-called SIDS near-misses, have been employed as SIDS surrogates despite any quantitative evidence of their value as predictors. *Near-myth* might be a better description of these events than "near-miss".' Consequently, it is with discretion that we shall report some of the information that has been derived from studies of 'near-misses'.

Studies on Siblings

Many studies have now been carried out on the subsequent siblings of sudden infant deaths. The assumption here is that these infants are at such high risk of dying that by studying them one might gain clues as

to the ways in which the infants who died might have differed from the rest of the population.

Such studies therefore assume that there is a genetic component to sudden infant death – yet, as we have shown in Part II, there is no evidence for this. True, there is an increased risk of sudden infant death in this group, but this only affects 1 in 50 siblings. Investigations based on detailed studies of siblings are unlikely to prove enlightening.

Conclusions

Having shown the difficulties in evaluating the hypotheses, we have to admit that much evidence is so prone to error and misinterpretation that it is rarely possible to make a firm conclusion. Nevertheless, as we shall show, some of the theories appear more plausible than others.

Chapter 14

Excesses and Deficiencies

Hypernatraemia (high sodium in the blood)

In very small babies the kidneys, which are responsible for excreting such substances as sodium and urea from the body and thus maintaining a carefully balanced level in the baby's blood and body, are very much more immature than in the adult. Much of their ability to get rid of these substances is related to the amount of fluid which is also being excreted. If the baby's intake of fluids is severely reduced then the kidneys are only able to excrete a reduced amount of sodium and urea.

As early as 1911 it was realised that anyone with gastroenteritis, which was especially common in young infants at that time, lost large amounts of body fluid via the gut. This resulted in insufficient fluid going through the kidneys, and thus the retention of both urea and sodium within the body. A paper published in 1955 identified high sodium levels in the blood (hypernatraemia) as a cause of death and brain damage in infants.

It was not realised until about 1972 that this problem might be exacerbated by the high concentration of sodium in artificial feeds. The amount of sodium in cows' milk is approximately four times that of breast milk and in the early 1970's many of the artificial feeds consisted of dried powdered cows' milk. Instructions to mothers at that time on how these feeds should be made up were not precise, and many mothers made up over-strong feeds with the idea that this would be of greater benefit in helping their infants put on weight.

In 1974, a study from Sheffield was published concerning 25 infants who had died suddenly, although deaths which were explained at post-mortem were also included. The authors showed that the levels of sodium and urea in the blood indicated severe electrolyte imbalance in 12 of these children.

Following this an inquiry was instigated into the preparation of artificial feeds for children in Sheffield. Of 301 mothers questions, 172 (57%) were found to prepare over-concentrated feeds. Consequently a report from the Department of Health and Social Security was published emphasising the importance of breast feeding and recommending that when artificial milks were used that these should be low in sodium. Early mixed feeding was also discouraged as many cereals also contained a high level of sodium.

Some evidence that sudden infant death was associated with sodium consumption was found when data from Scunthorpe were published. In this town there had been changes in the incidence of sudden infant death from 1948 to 1976. This was thought to be related to the artificial softening of the town water supply since methods of artificial softening tend to increase the concentration of sodium in the water. In the ten years 1948–57, there was no softening and the incidence of sudden infant deaths was 1.8 per 1000 births. From 1958–68 softening took place, with high levels of sodium in the drinking water; the rate of sudden infant death was then 3.25 per 1000. In the subsequent eight years the process was modified and the concentration of sodium dropped slightly. The rate of sudden infant death was 2.2 per 1000.

Comparison of the incidence of sudden infant death in two cities in the United States with softened water (Miami and Minneapolis) was then made with four cities that did not have artificially softened water (Cleveland, Memphis, Philadelphia and Seattle). Phillip Spiers showed that, contrary to the hypothesis, the cities with *higher* sodium content had *lower* rates of sudden infant death.

A retrospective study from Sheffield showed a significant decrease in deaths associated with hypernatraemia between 1969 and 1978. The authors put this down to the decreased incidence of gastroenteritis, the change to artificial feeds low in sodium, an increase in the incidence of breast feeding and a local campaign to increase awareness of the dangers of making over-concentrated feeds. In spite of the initial finding of a high proportion of sudden infant deaths with hypernatraemia in the early part of the study, other authors have not been able to confirm the finding.

Two further British post-mortem studies, one in Edinburgh and one in Northamptonshire, failed to find raised levels of sodium in 108 and 54 sudden infant deaths respectively, although they did demonstrate high levels of urea in a large proportion of cases. The deaths with high urea were predominantly bottle fed, and were associated with younger mothers. In the light of this, it is important to note that, as we have shown in Chapter 10, even in studies carried out at the same time as the Sheffield one, there is no clear-cut association between artificial feeds

and sudden infant death. The high levels of urea indicate the type of feed, not the cause of death.

A study from Canada examined the concentrations of various elements including sodium in 127 children who had died. Fifty nine had died from medical and surgical diseases, 21 from acute trauma and 47 had died suddenly and unexpectedly. There was no difference in any of the mean values of the substances looked at between the three groups.

In summary, there is some evidence that, in the early 1970's in Britain, infants were being fed artificial feeds with high sodium levels. Dead infants who had been fed in this way were found to have high levels of urea in their blood, but there is no conclusive evidence that the high ureas led to the death nor that hypernatraemia had ever been a major cause of sudden infant deaths.

Deficiency of Trace Elements

It is now known that, although only very small amounts of certain trace elements are necessary, without such elements the human body would cease to function. Eleven elements are absolutely essential: molybdenum, chromium, manganese, cobalt, iron, copper, zinc, silicon, fluorine, selenium and iodine. Other elements may be discovered to be essential as more information becomes available. The young infant will have gained most of his trace elements from his mother while in the uterus. Nevertheless, he may become deficient if receiving an inadequate supply during his first months of life. Other ways in which he may become deficient would result from a possible inability to digest particular elements or to metabolise them in the normal fashion. The study of trace element deficiencies is in its infancy. Nevertheless, several theories have been put forward in regard to sudden infant deaths.

In 1972, Joan Caddell suggested that sudden infant death might be due to a deficiency of magnesium. She suggested that such a deficiency might occur during the rapid growth of a young infant fed a diet poor in the element, and suggested that premature and low birthweight infants with rapid growth rates would be the most vulnerable. This, of course, would fit in with the known association between sudden infant death and low birthweight. In addition, she suggested that women who had breast fed a large number of infants beforehand, have reduced stores of magnesium in their breast milk.

Following up this hypothesis, several studies were carried out. A study by Godwin and Brown divided the 21 counties of California into three groups according to whether they had high, medium or low

incidence of sudden infant death. The magnesium and calcium concentrations of the water supplies were compared for each of these groups. The median magnesium concentration was certainly lower in counties with high rates of sudden infant death, although there was no difference between counties with low and medium rates of sudden infant death. A similar picture was shown for the calcium concentration in the drinking water. The authors felt that the information was particularly difficult to interpret. Other studies have looked at the actual concentration of magnesium in various organs of infants who had died suddenly and unexpectedly. In only one was there a significant difference between infants with sudden infant death and those dying from other causes: Erickson & colleagues actually found *more* magnesium in infants dying suddenly with no discernible cause of death, when compared with infants dying suddenly but due to a disease process.

Other authors have looked at concentrations in the tissues of sudden infant deaths of substances such as zinc, copper, calcium, manganese, iron and potassium. The only significant differences were found in one study by Chipperfield and Chipperfield. They compared the levels of seven trace elements in heart muscle of seven sudden infant deaths with over one hundred control deaths, but it is important to note that the controls were all adult. The differences they found were in the levels of potassium and calcium. The sudden infant deaths had significantly lower levels of potassium and higher levels of calcium in their heart muscles. It is difficult to know how to interpret these findings.

Selenium deficiency has also caused a great deal of interest. This deficiency is common in parts of China where the fatal heart condition Keshan disease is prevalent among children. In 1970, Money in the United States, reported that deficiency of selenium and Vitamin E was responsible for sudden infant death in piglets. He suggested that a similar deficiency in human infants could also lead to sudden infant death and prompted a great deal of research.

In New Zealand, the selenium status of the population is relatively low, but the incidence of sudden infant death does not seem to be particularly high. In Auckland, the selenium level is higher than the rest of the country, however, and the incidence of sudden infant death is lower. Within the Southland area of the country however, the variation in selenium levels did not mirror the variation in the incidence of sudden infant death.

A number of authors have now looked at the levels of selenium in the blood of infants who died suddenly and unexpectedly and found no difference when compared with the levels in controls. Thus the

balance of the evidence indicates that selenium deficiency is not a major cause of sudden infant death.

Vitamin Deficiency

Only one study appears to have looked at whether infants who die suddenly and unexpectedly had received vitamin supplementation during their lives. This was carried out in San Diego, California, by Gerhard Schrauzer and his colleagues. They found that the infants who had died a sudden infant death were slightly less likely to have had vitamin supplementation, but there were many reasons why this study was unsatisfactory, not least of which was that less than a third of the study and the control parents actually responded to the question-naires. More important, there is no indication that the age at which the infant had died had been taken into account. Obviously, sudden infant deaths occurring in the first month or so of life are probably less likely to be receiving vitamin supplementation than children who are older.

Nevertheless, there have been several theories involving specific vitamin deficiencies in the aetiology of sudden infant deaths.

Vitamin E Deficiency

Vitamin E is closely linked to selenium, and most of those studies which have looked for a deficiency of selenium have also looked for deficiencies of vitamin E in cases and controls. Only one study has shown lower serum levels in sudden infant deaths. This was carried out in England and compared the vitamin E levels in the serum of 14 sudden infant deaths, with 7 control babies who died from other causes.

Vitamin C Deficiency

The possibility that vitamin C may protect from sudden infant death was expounded by Archie Kalokerinos in Australia. He studied the infant mortality in Australian aborigines and suggested that the very high infant mortality was often due to gross vitamin C deficiency. He postulated that some of these deaths which were sudden and unexpected may well have been associated with vitamin C deficiency. In other correspondence he has suggested that among infants not grossly deficient, a slight infection may result in a rapid fall in serum levels of this vitamin, and children who suffer from repeated minor illnesses may be at exceptional risk. He also suggests that immunisation results in an increased utilisation of the vitamin, and that sudden infant deaths are more likely to occur after immunisation.

In support of this hypothesis, is the fact that infants born to mothers

who have smoked during pregnancy appear to be at increased risk of sudden infant death, and it has been shown in the literature that women who smoke have a lower blood level of vitamin C. It seems feasible to conclude that the fetus will have received less vitamin C before his birth if his mother smoked. Another factor which supports the possibility that infants who die suddenly and unexpectedly were more likely to have been born deficient in vitamin C lies in the seasonal variation. The lowest levels of serum vitamin C are found in the winter, and the highest in the summer, roughly mirroring the seasonal risks to infants born at those times. Within Britain, too, national food surveys have shown that women of social classes IV and V consume less vitamin C. Infants in this group are at higher risk of sudden infant death. Thus, there is circumstantial evidence to suggest that there may be a link between sudden infant death and prolonged vitamin C deficiency.

On the other hand, there has been no direct evidence that serum vitamin C levels of infants who died suddenly were any different from infants who survived. The Australian College of Pediatrics examined the evidence that large doses of vitamin C might prevent sudden infant death, but Phelan reported that they found no supporting evidence. On the other hand, they reported that such doses may predispose to the formation of kidney stones.

Vitamin D Deficiency
Reasons why deficiency of vitamin D was thought important in the possible mechanism of sudden infant death were largely epidemiological. The hypothesis was first raised by findings from Canada that sudden infant deaths were less likely to have spent time outdoors than control infants, implying that they would have received less direct sunlight, and hence that their vitamin D concentration would be lower. This hypothesis was supported to a certain extent by the first study from the Oxford Record Linkage Area, where we showed that infants were more likely to have died on a day when the sun did not shine. The second study from the ORLS area failed to confirm this. No other study appears to have looked at sunlight in relation to sudden infant death. Other factors supporting the hypothesis include an increased rate of microscopic rickets in a series of sudden infant deaths from northern Europe and the fact that vitamin D deficiency is related to fetal growth retardation (abnormalities of fetal growth have certainly been noted in sudden infant deaths). Clinical rickets associated with vitamin D deficiency has a peak incidence at age 3 months, identical to that found for sudden infant deaths. The incidence of both rickets and sudden infant death are higher in

premature babies. Within Britain, Asian immigrants are known to have a high incidence of rickets, and their rate of sudden infant deaths is also thought to be high, although, as we have shown, this has yet to be proven.

One study has measured part of the vitamin D content in the blood of 31 sudden infant deaths, 7 acute death controls and 17 hospital death controls. The authors found no differences between the groups but pointed out that the particular fraction of the vitamin D that they were measuring was not the one that was most biologically active. The possibility that vitamin D is related to sudden infant death must therefore remain open.

Biotin Deficiency

Marginal dietary deficiency of biotin does cause sudden unexpected death in young chickens exposed to mild stress. The mode of death is hypoglycaemia, and it was suggested that this might be a model for sudden infant death in humans.

In man, biotin is derived both directly from the diet and from chemical reactions brought about by bacteria in the gut. In human infants some weeks are required for the bacteria in the gut to develop sufficiently to produce biotin. In the first weeks, therefore, the infant probably relies upon the biotin in the diet as its main source. It is known that the vitamin is lost during the processing of certain infant formulations, so some infants may be receiving a diet which is marginally deficient. Johnson and his colleagues in Australia therefore examined the tissues from sudden infant death victims and compared the levels of biotin with those from deaths from other causes. They found that the children dying suddenly and unexpectedly had lower levels in their livers when compared with the livers of other children. Such a finding does support the hypothesis, but other evidence suggests that there is no excess of hypoglycaemia in infants who die suddenly and unexpectedly. Since the hypoglycaemia was thought to be the way in which biotin would cause death, the conclusions are far from clear.

Thiamine Deficiency

Like so many of the hypotheses which have been suggested for sudden infant death that of thiamine deficiency is plausible. The hypothesis arose after consideration of children with Leigh's disease, which is an inherited disorder of thiamine metabolism. These children occasionally develop sleep apnoea, thought by many to be associated with sudden infant death. Certainly, among apparently well infants with proven thiamine deficiency, sudden death has occurred. The mortality

from identifiable infantile thiamine deficiency has a peak age between 2 and 4 months, identical to that found for the sudden infant death syndrome. Overt thiamine deficiency is often precipitated by minor febrile episodes.

Apparently maternal thiamine deficiency is common in western communities ingesting diets with high levels of carbohydrates containing various thiamine antagonists. An interesting story comes from Australia early in this century. The Australian administration had outlawed the fermentation of a certain type of beverage which was an important source of thiamine to the community. Subsequently the population consumed large amounts of sugar and food such as white flour and tinned meats which contain little or no thiamine. The result was sudden death at the age of about 3 months of breast fed infants apparently in good health. There was a pronounced seasonal variation in the death rates and some 40% of infants were affected. The problem was resolved rapidly by the compulsory treatment of both mothers and babies with a drink rich in the vitamin.

Beri-beri is also due to thiamine deficiency. The peak mortality from beri-beri in the developing world is also found between the ages of two and five months.

If the mother is carrying twins, it has been reported that she is more likely to develop beri-beri. This would imply that a twin is more likely to be born deficient of thiamine. Twin infants are, of course, more susceptible to sudden infant death. Thiamine deficiency has also been reported to be more common in lower socio-economic groups. The other important factor in the development of the hypothesis is that where deaths have occurred suddenly in overt thiamine deficient individuals, there have been no clear findings at post-mortem.

An initial study by Peterson and his colleagues tested this hypothesis by measuring the enzyme TPP which is considered a test for thiamine status, high levels indicating a deficiency of thiamine. In comparing the post-mortem blood levels of 20 infants dying of sudden infant death syndrome with 17 controls they found no significant differences. Davis and his colleagues, however, measured the actual amounts of thiamine in blood and to their surprise showed that there was a large *excess* of thiamine in infants dying suddenly and unexpectedly. Indeed, they found that of 233 infants tested, 220 had levels of thiamine which were above the normal range. Discussion is continuing as to whether the hypothesis should be changed to read 'an excess of thiamine is associated with sudden infant death', or whether the finding of excess thiamine in the blood indicates an abnormality in the child's ability to metabolise the substance. It is interesting that when animals are given injections of thiamine, death occurs because of

failure of the animal to breathe. It would appear that the hypothesis of overall dietary thiamine deficiency in sudden infant death is no longer tenable, and we await further developments concerning thiamine metabolism with interest.

Hypoglycaemia

As already mentioned, a possible mechanism by which sudden infant death may be precipitated is as a result of low levels of blood sugar. Sumbilla and his team have now compared biochemical measures of glucogenic enzymes from 74 sudden infant deaths with 36 infant deaths of known causes. They found no differences between the two.

Thyroid Hormones

A hypothesis that low levels of the thyroid hormones thyroxine and tri-iodothyronine would be found in sudden infant deaths was derived from the suggestion that these children were suffering from chronic hypoxia (or starvation of oxygen). The suggestion was based on the observation that the rate of utilisation of oxygen in humans is related to the levels of these hormones. Moshang and colleagues had verified this by showing significantly lower values in children with cyanotic heart disease, a disorder which certainly results in chronic hypoxia.

Various investigators have now measured the levels of these two hormones in the plasma of sudden infant deaths, deaths from other causes and live controls. All have found that, far from reduced levels, the sudden infant deaths had elevated levels of one of the hormones (tri-iodothyronine) but not of the other. A discussion of all available evidence by Root has indicated that high levels of the hormone are not predictive of sudden infant death, but that most of the findings are probably the result of changes occurring after death.

Over-heating

The idea that a very high temperature in a child might play a part in sudden infant death, were first put forward by Robert Dallas in 1974. He pointed out that the mother's reaction to cold weather or to illness in the child was usually to put plenty of clothing on the child and have a larger amount of bedding. He thought that fever combined with excessive insulation might be a dangerous combination. Supporting this theory is the fact that babies of more than a month of age are better at producing and conserving heat than at losing it.

The hypothesis came to mind once more in 1979 when Christopher

Bacon and his colleagues published the case histories of five children. They were aged between 3 and 8 months and had a history of slight illness, were well wrapped up by the mother and had often been left near a fire. They were found in a shocked state, had repeated convulsions and all but one died soon after admission to hospital. The one survivor was left spastic, blind and grossly retarded in development.

This study was followed up in 1980 in Newcastle, when the hypothesis was investigated that over-heating could be associated with sudden infant death. In 8 of 34 sudden infant deaths there were post-mortem findings of the kind usually associated with heat stroke. In five of these cases, there was overwhelming clinical evidence of over-heating. Supporting evidence that over-heating may be associated with sudden infant death has also been obtained from post-mortem studies, with a frequent finding that the temperature of the dead infant even after he has been dead for some time, is abnormally high. This was found in 10 out of 24 sudden infant deaths in Sheffield, and 32 out of 60 cases in London.

There is a strong tradition, both in England and the United States, as well as other countries with similar climates, of over-clothing and over-wrapping babies. Undoubtedly, young infants are vulnerable to cold, but the reverse also tends to be true. Not only is there a general inclination to dress babies up in many layers of clothes, but these may often not be removed when the child moves from a cold into a warm environment. With infection, even small babies can generate high temperatures.

How exactly over-heating may cause death is not clear, although experimental evidence of over-heating in young animals shows that death can occur early without any convulsions and before recognisable pathological changes have had time to develop. In humans, there is evidence that heat stroke can develop suddenly and unexpectedly. Another mechanism for possible sudden deaths, could be that children die during a febrile convulsion.

The link between over-heating and febrile convulsions as a possible cause of sudden infant death was examined by Robert Sunderland and John Emery. They compared the rates of hospital admission for a first febrile convulsion over a five year period with the numbers of cot deaths appearing in each month. They found no relationship. There was no evidence that winter months, when the sudden infant deaths were most likely to occur, were associated with an increase of hospital admissions for convulsions. In later correspondence, Caroline Berry suggested that the best way to determine whether sudden infant deaths were associated with febrile convulsions was to look at the family

history. If a sibling has febrile convulsions then the risk to the index child of febrile convulsions is around 20%. There were some negative data from the first ORLS study concerning hospital admission to siblings of sudden infant deaths. As shown in Table 10 (page 91), only two of 164 siblings of sudden infant deaths were admitted to hospital with febrile convulsions.

Febrile convulsions are common among children aged between 6 months and 6 years with a peak incidence at 3 years of age. Epidemiological studies of febrile convulsions, though, have shown that there are no associations with maternal youth, social class, number of children in household or any of the other sociological factors we have shown to be associated with sudden infant death. It is quite conceivable that the child could die during such a convulsion, while unattended. Nevertheless, it seems unlikely that this accounts for many sudden infant deaths since febrile convulsions are rarely found at ages below 6 months.

A possible relationship between over-heating and sudden infant death was taken in a different direction by Denborough and his colleagues in Australia. They had observed that the father of a sudden infant death had a condition which predisposes to malignant hyperpyrexia. Malignant hyperpyrexia is a sharp rise of temperature which occurs in certain individuals who have a particular disorder of their muscles when they are under anaesthetic. It is relatively rare. Experiments with pigs who also can have this disease, have shown that sudden death can occur as the result of stress in individuals with the disorder.

The authors tested the hypothesis that some sudden infant deaths were associated with this disorder by obtaining muscle samples from 15 parents of sudden infant deaths. They found that 5 of these parents had this disorder of the muscles. Clearly, it is important that these results should be taken further and other studies be undertaken. In some areas tests are now available to parents who would like to have them.

Chapter 15

Sleeping, Breathing and Heart Rate

Internal Mechanical Obstruction to Breathing

Up to 30% of new born babies are obligatory nose breathers. This means that they breathe through their noses and that if their noses are occluded, they do not automatically open their mouths to breathe. Knowledge of this, together with the fact that the nasal passages of young babies are extremely small, caused Dr. Shaw in America, to propose that nasal obstruction may be responsible for some sudden infant deaths. He illustrated his theory with observations regarding infants who had been born with choanal atresia (a very rare condition in which infants are born without any nasal passages at all). These infants do not naturally and automatically breathe through their mouths and, unless stimulated to do so, will die.

A mechanism by which the nostrils may be obstructed was demonstrated by Professor Kenneth Cross, in London, who pointed out that, in a series of post-mortems on sudden infant deaths there had been signs of respiratory infection in two-thirds. In consequence, he suggested that a common sequence of events might be a mild nasal infection in an obligated nose breather; if this occurred in winter months in a cool environment, when the demand for oxygen is naturally increased, the nasal obstruction would cause decreased ventilation during a time of increased oxygen need. This might finally lead to the death of an infant.

Other theories of means by which mechanical obstruction might affect breathing have been put forward. In particular, Dr. Shirley Tonkin, working in New Zealand, proposed in 1975 that since the normal infant's tongue was relatively large, it might be that there was relaxation of the jaw muscles during a period of infection, which might result in a mechanical blockage.

None of these theories have yet received great credibility. There is a lack of post-mortem evidence, including X-ray evidence, possibly

because such functional disorders are unlikely to be apparent at post-mortem.

Another possible mechanism for causing obstruction of the airways was suggested by Kravitz and Scherz. After writing to 1,400 paediatricians concerning their experience of sudden infant death, they found that 88% of deaths had occurred in the baby's cot (crib). Very few of the deaths had occurred when the infant was in a sitting or upright position. The authors therefore suggested that lying prone might cause the weight of the jaw, the tongue and the soft palate to press downwards and block the airway. They suggested that infants should be put to bed in a slanting position by raising the head of the infant's bed, but acknowledged that the cots would have to be redesigned to prevent the infants from sliding down.

External Mechanical Obstruction to Breathing

Sudden infant deaths have always been tainted with the suggestion that the parents were in some way responsible for the death, whether deliberately or accidentally. As already suggested in the introduction, the belief in 'over-laying' as a cause of these deaths faded at the beginning of this century, although in some instances it was substituted by a belief that soft-pillows or mattresses had caused the deaths. The situation is confused, since at post-mortem there is little to distinguish the sudden infant death from an infant which had actually been asphyxiated in such a way. In 1968, a report from America suggested 'a large percentage of crib deaths are actually infanticides presenting as part of a post-partum depression, unknown to or undiagnosed by the family and/or family physician'. Reviewing this paper other American investigators examined the rates of known homicide in the United States. The period of study covered the years 1950–74 during which time there was a 4 fold increase in the infant homicide rate. Although the rate of sudden infant death was some hundred times greater than the rate of infanticide, there were no similar time changes to lend support to the hypothesis that the sudden infant deaths were in a large proportion of cases, infanticides.

Before the recognition of sudden infant deaths as a discreet entity and, alas, in some cases afterwards, many parents who suffered the misfortune of having their child die suddenly were accused of having killed their infant either deliberately or accidentally. In recent years there has been increasing emphasis on avoiding this error and paediatricians rarely consider child abuse as part of the initial diagnosis when sudden infant death occurs. Nevertheless, case reports

tend to hit the headlines. There have been two recent reports of 'missed cot deaths' where the mother was very clearly producing symptoms of collapse by deliberately asphyxiating the child. One has to be very careful in drawing parallels with sudden infant deaths, nevertheless there are isolated occasions when mothers confess to being responsible for the sudden death of their child. Although statements concerning child abuse tend to be emotional rather than scientific, and are rarely submitted to epidemiological analysis, Professor John Emery has recently reported that he thought that three of the deaths for which he had information in Sheffield were due to so-called 'gentle battering'.

There are on the face of it two potential fallacies in linking severe social circumstances and sudden infant death. First, that if cases exist satisfying two criteria, there must be an association between them. Second, that if there is an association it must be causal. To demonstrate an association one needs to take, for example, a number of cases of sudden infant deaths and compare their background with that of infants from a comparable population, who have not died suddenly and unexpectedly. If having done this there is evidence that the proportion of sudden infant deaths with a history of child abuse or neglect is substantially and significantly greater than the proportion of controls with child abuse, one can state that there is an association. This has not been found, although initial reports were suggestive.

In the Oxford region, Jacquie Roberts and her co-workers had investigated the families of children who had been abused by their parents. They found that there were three times as many infant deaths in these families than would have been expected from their social backgrounds. Although many of these deaths had been reported by the mother as 'cot deaths', review of the post-mortem reports showed that most of the deaths were 'explained'. There was, in fact, no significant excess of sudden infant deaths in these families.

Facts that support the hypothesis that sudden infant deaths may be associated with child abuse lie in the similarity of epidemiological patterns. Both are more likely to occur if the mother is very young, unmarried, of social classes IV or V, if the infant was of low birthweight, whether due to immaturity or growth retardation, or had congenital malformations.

In addition to these factors, a study in Oxford by Margaret Lynch and Jacquie Roberts had shown that certain strong predictors of child abuse could be identified from obstetric case notes. The factors they found included: (a) age of mother when her first child was born, (b) whether there was any evidence during pregnancy of psychiatric or emotional disturbance, (c) whether the family had been referred to a medical social work department, (d) whether the baby had been

admitted to the special care baby unit, and (e) whether the hospital staff had recorded concern over the parents' ability to cope with the child. In order to test the possibility that some cases of sudden infant death might be predicted in the same way, Jacquie Roberts carried out a further study in Oxford in collaboration with the Oxford Record Linkage Study. She was given the maternal obstetric notes of 45 infants who died suddenly and unexpectedly and compared each with three controls matched for maternal age, parity, social class, year and hospital of delivery.

The comparison of cases and controls was carried out blind, in that Mrs. Roberts was not told the identity of those mothers whose children had died. In this way, she was able to assess the information in the clinical notes without being biased by knowledge as to the outcome. After she had collected and coded all the information she was informed as to which infants had actually died and which had survived. She found that there were no differences between mothers of sudden infant deaths and mothers of controls in four of the five factors. Only in respect of the mothers needing advice and support with feeding was there a slight difference.

The conclusion of this survey was that behavioural characteristics of mothers of sudden infant deaths did not, on the whole, resemble that of mothers who subsequently abused their child.

Abnormal Surfactant in the Lung

Over the last few weeks of pregnancy, as the fetus is developing inside the womb, a substance known as surfactant is beginning to be produced in the lining of the baby's lungs. The major function of the surfactant appears to be to decrease the surface tension in the alveoli of the lungs. After the baby is born, when these alveoli are expanded with the first breath, the molecular structure of the surfactant helps prevent them from collapsing again.

Surfactant has been of interest for many years since babies born very prematurely have very low levels of this substance and their lungs tend to collapse easily, giving rise to what is known as the 'respiratory distress syndrome'. Many of these pre-term babies need to be artificially ventilated until natural surfactant is produced.

It was somewhat by accident that Dr. Colin Morley and his colleagues discovered that, at necropsy, the surfactant contents of the lungs of sudden infant deaths was far less than had been expected. They had compared the surfactant from the lungs of 16 sudden infant deaths with 16 infants who had died of congenital abnormalities or neurological problems and 35 babies dying from the respiratory

distress syndrome. They found that although the babies with congenital abnormalities or neurological disorders seemed to have normal levels of surfactant in their lungs, the sudden infant deaths had low levels, of the same order as that found in the premature infant dying of respiratory distress syndrome. Furthermore, the results suggested that there was an abnormal type of surfactant rather than just reduced production. If these findings are repeated by other research workers, and shown not to be an artifact, the possibilities for future research are exciting. It would be important to ascertain whether, if there is indeed an abnormality in surfactant in the sudden infant death, it has been present from birth, whether it has developed during the child's life or has been created while the baby is actually dying.

Recurrent Apnoeic Episodes

On the basis of the assumption that most sudden infant deaths occur during a period of sleep, attention has been paid to the results of research into the mechanisms of sleep. With different types of sleep, there are marked alterations in several fundamental physiological functions, including heart rate, blood pressure and respiratory patterns.

Alfred Steinschneider pointed out that periods of arrested breathing (apnoeic attacks) tended to occur more often in babies within certain patterns of light sleep. He therefore suggested that further research in this area might be important in uncovering the aetiology of sudden infant death. He reported the results of studying 5 infants from 3 different families. Three of these infants had had cyanotic attacks at the age of one month. These attacks, in which the babies turn blue from lack of oxygen, appear to have no definite cause. Two other children who were siblings of these initial patients were also studied. During his research, he discovered that all the children showed periods of arrested breathing lasting longer than 2 seconds, and that they occurred most commonly during those periods of sleep when there are rapid eye movements behind the lid – the so-called rapid-eye movement sleep pattern (or REM sleep). He found that the periods of apnoea increased as the children got older. All the infants studied had prolonged episodes of arrested breathing and cyanotic attacks during sleep, some of which required the child to be vigorously resuscitated. The prolonged periods of apnoea occurred more frequently when the child had an infection in the upper respiratory tract. Two of the infants died suddenly and unexpectedly.

The difficulty with studies of this kind lies in the fact that there are

no control values for comparison. Later studies have indicated that periods of apnoea are extremely common in normal infants. One important study compared the frequency of apnoeic attacks in three groups of children. The first comprised 9 infants who had been so-called near-miss cot deaths. The second were 9 children who were siblings of sudden infant deaths and the third group were 9 normal control children. The measures were of the number of periods of apnoea lasting longer than 6 seconds measured over a period of 12 hours. In all, the first group had 144 such periods, the second group had 68 such episodes, and the third group, the normal controls, actually had most – 161 periods of apnoea.

A study from Boston in 1977 compared 12 normal infants with 11 infants who had had 2 previous periods of severe apnoea during sleep. The infants who had already had prolonged apnoeic attacks showed reduced ventilation of the lungs during quiet sleep. They responded poorly when an increased amount of carbon dioxide was introduced into the air they were breathing (the normal child would under the circumstances increase the amount of air it was taking into its lungs).

In Connecticut, scientists looked at the frequency of apnoeic attacks in 23 normal infants during the first weeks of their lives. Whilst they were carrying out the study, one of the infants died aged 3 months, and another began to have episodes of prolonged apnoea at the age of 5 months. When they looked back at the observations carried out during the early weeks of life, they found that the two babies who had the later problems had had the *lowest* rate of apnoeic attacks during this period.

Since the original suggestions of Steinschneider, Richard Naeye, a paediatric pathologist suggested that periods of arrested breathing over a long period of time, would lead to a decreased amount of oxygen in the blood and that this chronic lack of oxygen would lead to other changes which might be recognised at post-mortem. He therefore looked at the post-mortem results of a number of sudden infant deaths and reported that in 60% of cases, there was an abnormal increase in the amount of musculature in the small arteries of the lung. This, he suggested, was due to chronic under-ventilation of the lungs causing prolonged constriction of the small arteries. He suggested that constriction of the small arteries would increase the resistance of the blood flowing along them, which in turn would mean that the right ventricle of the heart would need to exert greater pressure in order to produce the necessary blood flow through these constricted vessels. At post-mortem it was noted that in cases where there was increased musculature there was also an increase in the size of the right ventricle of the heart. He then looked for other evidence of chronic decrease in

the oxygen supply and found seven so-called 'tissue markers', which he suggested were the result of under-ventilation, possibly due to recurrent apnoeic episodes. These were brown fat around the adrenal glands; red blood cells being produced in the liver; abnormalities of the carotid body which is responsible for monitoring the oxygen content of the blood; scar tissue in the nerve centres in the brain which control breathing and cardiac action; excess of specialised nerve tissue in the adrenal; increased musculature around the walls of the small arteries in the lungs, and increased musculature of the right side of the heart.

Of these tissue markers, only two have been confirmed by other pathologists (brown fat around the adrenals and red cell production in the liver). In view of the fact that there is no concrete evidence that sudden infant deaths are more likely to have had prolonged apnoeic attacks during their life, the findings of Naeye, without confirmatory evidence from elsewhere, must remain dubious.

The strongest evidence against the hypothesis that sudden infant death is strongly associated with prolonged apnoeic attacks comes from three studies in Britain. Stanton and Oakley showed that of 467 unexpected deaths (including those with evidence of infection) occurring in several areas between 1976 and 1979, there had been none with previous admissions to hospital for apnoea and none designated as near-miss cot death. In our own ORLS study, as we have shown in Chapter 9, the infants who subsequently died were not more likely to have had apnoeic attacks in the first week of life, than their controls.

The third study was by David Southall and his colleagues who studied breathing movements on over 9,000 infants during the first weeks of life. Twenty-nine subsequently became sudden infant deaths, but none had shown prolonged apnoea or other breathing abnormalities.

Other Abnormalities of Sleep
In the previous section we discussed ways in which repeated apnoeic attacks might result in oxygen depletion in the infant. There are other ways, however, in which oxygen depletion might occur. Dr. Paul Johnson, working in Oxford, has shown that during deep sleep (i.e. sleep not associated with rapid eye movement), respiratory drive and rhythm is very dependent on sensory input. In contrast, during rapid eye movement sleep the drive appears to be essentially unaffected by such factors and he suggests that hypoxia arising during this phase may be less likely to be responded to appropriately by the infant.

The question of whether infants who die suddenly and unexpectedly have a different response to levels of carbon dioxide has been

evaluated in two studies of 'near miss' infants. One of these studies showed a decrease in the response of the infant to low levels of carbon dioxide in the air that he was breathing and the other showed increased responses! No such studies have been done on populations of infants some of whom later became sudden infant deaths. Whether, indeed, some irregularity of breathing is responsible for some sudden infant deaths has therefore to remain speculative for the moment.

The possibility of a failed control mechanism over ventilation has also been tested indirectly by Philip Schiffman and his colleagues in New Jersey. They compared the ventilatory response of 12 parents of sudden infant deaths with 12 control parents. They found that there was a lower ventilatory response to carbon dioxide among the parents of sudden infant deaths. Again, this study would need to be repeated on larger numbers of parents before one could draw any useful conclusions.

Abnormalities of Heart Beat

In Ireland in the early 1960's a group of families was studied. Children in these families suffered from recurrent fainting attacks. After electrical recordings were taken of their heart, it was found that the fainting attacks were associated with a fast and inefficient heart beat, a condition known as ventricular fibrillation. Occasionally, one of these children died suddenly and unexpectedly due to the fact that the rhythm of the heart had not reverted back to normal. The abnormality appeared to be inherited and was in some cases associated with deafness. These findings led the investigators to wonder whether a similar mechanism was associated with sudden infant death. A study was then carried out to look at the genetic and epidemiological aspects of sudden infant death in Northern Ireland. In the course of this study, the hearts from sudden infant deaths and from children who had died from other causes were specially examined. It was found that in all deaths, part of the electrical conducting system of the heart appeared to have become altered soon after birth. It was therefore suggested that during this period of alteration, the heart might have been more susceptible to certain abnormal rhythms. Subsequent studies have shown that there are actual changes during this time, but there is still argument about whether such changes do result in heart beats so abnormal as to cause death. For example, in early life there are strange rhythms and extra beats of the heart, but most of these disappear without any apparent harm to the babies.

In the families described above, where the children had abnormal ventricular patterns and fainting attacks, a particular part of the

electrical cycle of the heart known as the QT interval was abnormally prolonged. It is possible that some sudden infant deaths have had prolonged QT intervals. One study has found more prolonged QT intervals in parents of sudden infant deaths as well as their siblings, compared with controls. Three other studies have failed to confirm any relationship whatsoever.

The most convincing results have been obtained from Southall's two population investigations. This research monitored the heart rate and rhythm and the breathing patterns of a large number of infants in early life. In the first investigation out of 5,247 infants studied there were fourteen sudden infant deaths, three of whom had had high QT indices but none had had irregular heart beats. The subsequent study monitored 9,251 infants, 29 of whom were sudden infant deaths. None of the deaths showed abnormal QT intervals and only one had abnormal heart rhythms.

Two further theories connected with the heart have been put forward as possible explanations for sudden infant deaths; they are concerned with the stimulation of the heart by the vagus nerve. This nerve slows the heart down and may in some cases cause it to stop. The first theory concerns the so-called 'diving reflex', the most common example of which occurs in vertebrates when their bodies are suddenly immersed in cold water. This results in an automatic cessation of breathing and slowing of the heart rate. In humans, this can be triggered merely by a cold stimulus to the face. Such an event could, in theory, occur if an infant's face got wet and he was left outside in a cold wind, but there is no evidence for such weather conditions to be more likely to have occurred at the time of sudden infant deaths.

The second reflex is the so-called 'oculo-cardiac' response. Pressure on the eyeballs will cause vagal nerve stimulation and slowing of the heart beat. It has been suggested that the weight of the baby's head pressing downwards on the mattress may bring about this response, but again there is no clear-cut evidence to support such a suggestion.

Chapter 16

Infections and the Immune System

Immunological mechanisms

The immune system is of vital importance in combating infection. If an infant were to be immunologically deficient, then he might succumb rapidly to an infection. The newborn infant's immune defences will have resulted from the transfer of immunoglobins across the placenta. In the first weeks after the delivery the breast fed infant will be obtaining further immunity via the breast milk, but all infants will begin to develop their own immunological systems. Several authors have suggested that the child may be immunologically incompetent during the period of transition from the maternal to the infant system. This period spans 2 to 3 months of age – the time when sudden infant death is most prevalent.

Additional factors that support a role for a reduced immunological mechanism in the aetiology of sudden infant death include the fact that pre-term infants have a relatively high incidence of sudden infant death and they are known to have lower levels of acquired antibodies and an immature immune system. Further, the more the mother has smoked the greater risk of sudden infant death, and infants of mothers who have smoked during pregnancy have been shown to be deficient in certain immunoglobins. Finally, it has been suggested that young mothers who have had several infants in quick succession may be suffering from protein deprivation. It has certainly been shown in rats that infants born to mothers deprived of protein are immunodeficient.

There are two methods by which an abnormal immune mechanism might work. In the first there would be little protection against bacteria or viruses and the infant would die rapidly of fulminating infection. The second possibility is of an allergic reaction. Thus if an infant is introduced to a substance to which it is allergic, it is quite feasible that the reaction could be so severe that the baby's heart would stop in shock. Such a rapid death would leave little evidence at post-

mortem. The substance that could set off such a reaction could be a virus, a constituent of the food or something in the atmosphere.

What evidence then is there that these infants might have succumbed to such a reaction? There are three ways in which such a hypothesis may be tested; (a) sudden infant deaths should be found more often in families with a history of allergic disorders such as asthma, eczema and hay fever; (b) levels of immunological components of sudden infant deaths might differ from controls; (c) allergens might be present more often in the home environment of sudden infant deaths.

Among animals, Henschel and Coates have reported a high sudden death rate among artificially fed young rabbits. They found two ages at which the deaths occurred – the first was between 7 and 10 days and the second between 15 and 20 days. They showed that the deaths appeared to be due to an allergic reaction to the diet.

The idea that infants might become allergic to cows' milk and die suddenly was a most popular hypothesis in the 1960's. The basis of the theory was that the baby would be sensitised if, after drinking cows' milk, the sleeping infant regurgitated some and inhaled a small amount into the lungs. The cows' milk protein would become absorbed and set off an immediate anaphylactic reaction. There are well-documented cases of sudden infant death among children who are allergic to cows' milk, but the fact that totally breast fed infants are not protected from sudden infant death suggests that there are other more important causes of sudden infant death.

A study by Coe published in 1963 in which he looked at the serum antibodies to cows' milk protein in 28 sudden infant deaths and 67 control infants showed no difference in antibody levels between the two groups.

House dust mites are found universally. They were first recognised as important allergens in the aetiology of asthma in the early 1960's and a suggestion was put forward that there might be a correlation between sudden infant death and the presence of house dust mites. In 1972, Mulvey in Australia reported a significant increase in house dust mites in the homes of sudden infant deaths. Following this lead, investigators began to look for IgE antibodies to house dust mites and other factors in the blood of sudden infant deaths.

Although no differences in the various total immunoglobulins IgE, IgA, IgG or IgM levels were found in the blood of sudden infant deaths, Turner and his colleagues in Australia found elevated IgE antibodies specific to the house dust mite and two other common allergens, including cows' milk. The sudden infant deaths were more likely to have antibodies to 2 or 3 of these allergens (8/44), compared

with other deaths (0/14) or control survivors (0/57). An American study attempted to replicate these findings, but they found no instance of IgE antibodies to house dust mite and only three of 61 sudden infant deaths had antibodies to cows' milk compared with four out of 24 explained deaths.

In Seattle, Clausen and his team had collected blood from 8,400 newborn infants. Of these, 23 later became sudden infant deaths. The authors returned to examine the blood that had been collected at birth and found no differences in the immunoglobulins IgM and IgA in these deaths compared with the survivors. They also took blood from 65 sudden infant deaths and compared the levels of specific antibodies to 14 viruses but found no differences.

Dr. Clare Raven and her colleagues in Detroit examined the lungs of 22 sudden infant deaths and compared the results with a group of infants who had died from trauma. They did find evidence of bound IgG in the lungs of the sudden infant deaths but none in the other deaths. The findings indicate a local immune reaction in the lungs, and it was suggested that this might be a reaction to a virus.

We have already shown that, from the ORLS study, the mothers of sudden infant deaths were more likely to have a history of atopic disorders than the control mothers. This was not found in Newcastle-upon-Tyne when Dr. Warnasuriya and his team enquired about the history of atopic disorders such as asthma and eczema in a group of 36 parents of sudden infant deaths and 36 parents of controls. No differences were found in these or in the results of skin tests. Atopy was common in both groups. Nevertheless one is not quite sure from the published description whether bias might not have been introduced by the choice of controls. These were picked by the index parents after the aims of the study had been explained to them. They might well have assumed that those friends of theirs who had allergies would be more willing to cooperate.

A different approach was used in Australia when Tait and his co-workers typed the HLA antigens present in the parents of 33 sudden infant deaths. Different HLA compositions have previously been shown to be associated with diseases that are related to the immunological system, such as ankylosing spondylitis and diabetes. In this study they found an association with certain parental antigens in the A group. This has yet to be confirmed in a further study.

Mavis Gunther in 1975 suggested that sudden infant death may result from an anaphylactic reaction with central effects, that the antibodies may be of the IgE or IgG class, and that the antigen may sometimes be from an 'infecting' agent, sometimes from food. The evidence for such an event is still equivocal, but the possibility that viruses or other micro-organisms may be involved is fairly strong.

Infections

The young infant may become infected in a variety of ways and with a number of different organisms. He may have acquired an infection early in pregnancy, during the process of delivery as he descends through his mother's birth canal, from the food he is given, the bottle or nipple at which he sucks or from the atmosphere he breathes. In this chapter we shall be considering the evidence for and against such possibilities.

Botulinism

There is a bacterium, Clostridium botulinum, which produces a toxin so virulent that one milligram contains enough to kill 20,000 people. In Britain, fortunately, only 21 deaths from botulinism have been reported in this century – and no fewer than 8 of these resulted from a single unfortunate episode in 1922, when a party of fishermen in Scotland ate sandwiches filled with contaminated duck paste.

Interest in botulinism was generated in America in 1976 when it was shown that botulinism affected infants in California far more often than it had previously been supposed. Between 1976 and 1978, 40 hospital admissions for infant botulinism were reported in California, and since then the other states in North America have identified cases. This form of infant botulinism affects infants aged between 3 and 36 weeks of age. The incidence pattern is remarkably similar to that found for sudden infant death, with a peak in the risk at two months of age. The source of the organism is not always discovered but in America, honey has often been implicated.

Because of the associations with an age at which sudden infant death was common, all 280 dead infants occurring in California in 1978 were examined to assess whether the Clostridium was present. The organism was in fact identified in 10 of these deaths, all of whom were sudden infant deaths. Stool specimens were also examined from 160 normal, healthy infants, and in only one was the Clostridium isolated. These findings suggested that the bacteria might be a possible cause of sudden infant death. To support this, it has been shown that post-mortem findings on children for whom botulinism had been diagnosed in life are as equivocal as those found in sudden infant death. Nevertheless, there have been no reported cases of sudden infant death in Britain which could be ascribed to botulinism. Indeed, only one infant has so far been identified as having had this disorder in Britain. He survived.

The epidemiological associations of surviving infants admitted to hospital with botulinism in America were extremely interesting. There was no differences between the sexes, but the risk was far higher if the

infant was breast fed than if he was being artificially fed. This finding contrasted with the factors associated with the 10 sudden infant deaths from which Clostridium botulinum had been isolated. All these 10 infants had been artificially fed for the months preceding the death.

Obviously, the toxin from this bacteria is so potentially lethal that should it be created in the gut of the infant, sudden fulminant death will occur. It is unlikely, however, that it will account for more than a few cases of sudden infant death. On present evidence, it should not be considered as a serious contender in Europe.

Congenital infection
As we showed in Chapter 7, there is substantial evidence to support an association between maternal infection during pregnancy and subsequent sudden infant death. Nevertheless, there is no clear particular type of infection responsible for the association, with positive reports for urinary tract infection, influenza, and vaginal infection.

Clear laboratory evidence of an infection acquired from the mother was produced by Helen Potencz from Romania. She reported an investigation of 8 sudden infant deaths occurring in a small area over a period of three weeks. Evidence from the post mortems of these infants indicated that 7 had evidence of cytomegalovirus infection. The author noted that the children had, in five instances, obtained this infection from the mother, and in two of them it was possible that the infection had been obtained from the breast milk. Five of the 8 mothers were unmarried. Dr. Potencz speculated that congenital infection of this type might be responsible for some cases of sudden infant deaths, although as she pointed out in most of the instances which she investigated the strict definition of sudden infant death could not be upheld. There was sufficient evidence of severe disease at post-mortem to make the strict definition of sudden infant death untenable.

Postnatal Infection
Factors from the epidemiological studies on sudden infant death have indicated that viral infections may be important. For example, it is well known that certain of the respiratory viruses are strongly associated with the winter months. It is also true that infants who are members of large families are more likely to come into contact with infections of various types, and a similar association has been reported for children from low social classes. Early studies in the 1960's made little progress in affirming or refuting the idea that viral infection might be associated with sudden infant death. The reasons for a lack of

achievement in this field lay mainly in the fact that techniques in identifying viruses were relatively crude at this stage. Subsequent studies found more evidence of viruses in infants who had died suddenly and unexpectedly, but it must be remembered in all these studies that many infants have viral infections during their early months. Viruses may be present without actually causing the death.

In 1970, an American study showed that 37.5% of sudden infant deaths had had viruses isolated compared with only 16.2% of children dying from other causes. A point of interest in this study was that respiratory syncytial virus and the influenza viruses were not detected. From Britain, however, the respiratory viral infections were more in evidence. Urquhart and Grist studied 72 sudden infant deaths in Glasgow and compared the viral isolations with 34 cases of explained deaths. They found that 42% of the sudden infant deaths and 29% of the other deaths had evidence of viral infections. A wide range of viruses were identified, the biggest group being the entero viruses and the adeno viruses. A similar study from Newcastle-upon-Tyne examined 49 sudden infant deaths. From 13 of these, viruses were isolated from the lungs. These included 6 infants with respiratory syncytial virus and 2 with influenza, but in all 13 cases only small amounts of virus could be found. There were no controls for this study, but the authors noted that all sudden infant deaths with viral isolations from the lungs had histological changes which supported the view that some bronchiolitis was present.

Subsequent studies have confirmed that the commoner viruses have continued to be isolated from cases of sudden infant death. Nevertheless, these viruses have been isolated in less than half the deaths, and even where they have been isolated, the quantities of virus have been relatively small. This supports the hypothesis that in some cases the cause of death might in fact be a hypersensitivity of the infant to the virus. Of course, by definition, an overwhelming viral infection would be identified at post-mortem and the infant would not have been classified as a sudden infant death.

Other evidence to support a link between respiratory viral infections and sudden infant deaths lie in the epidemiology of both. The respiratory syncytial virus, for example, is the major cause of admission for respiratory disease to children under 5 years of age in Britain. The age at which the child is likely to be admitted with the disorder is between 1 and 3 months, thus tying in with the known epidemiology of sudden infant deaths. As with sudden infant deaths, infants resident in cities were more likely to have the disease than those living in rural areas, and the incidence was lowest in social class I (similar, of course, to the sudden infant death rate). The ratio of boys

to girls was 1.4:1, identical to that often found for sudden infant deaths. Children with respiratory syncytial virus infections were more likely to have older siblings, as found with sudden infant deaths. Respiratory syncitial virus infections occur during winter rather than summer months, as do sudden infant deaths. Although these findings are striking, it is likely that infections with other viruses would show some similar patterns. Indeed, we have already indicated that the age distribution of botulism and other enteric infections is similar to that found with sudden infant death.

Vaccination
It has also been suggested that in some cases of sudden infant death there might be an association with immunisation. The first dose of triple vaccine is normally given at about three months of age, the time at which sudden infant death is most prevalent. Because of this, there will always be a number of cases where immunisation will precede the death, just by chance. Certainly it is well documented that infants who have had the vaccine are more likely to run a high temperature and even to have convulsions within the 24 hours immediately afterwards. The evidence for a long term effect, however, is far from convincing. As far as sudden infant deaths are concerned, there is no statistically convincing evidence of an association. Taylor and Emery looked at the immunisation history of 26 sudden explained and unexplained deaths. Only one (4%) had been vaccinated within 3 days of the death compared with 2 (4%) of 52 controls.

Infection or Allergen?

In conclusion, therefore, although some of the evidence does support an association between sudden infant death and a mild viral infection, the correspondence is certainly not one-to-one. In other words it is unlikely that a particular virus is responsible for all, or even the majority, of sudden infant deaths. Nevertheless it does seem possible that the pathway to a proportion of sudden infant deaths may be an anaphylactic shock in reaction to an infection of some kind, to which the infant has already been sensitised. The topic certainly warrants further research, and will be discussed again in Chapter 26. Meanwhile we shall describe ways in which the management of the death could be altered to cause the least possible distress to the parents, and discuss the prospects for future prevention.

Part IV

Reaction to the Death

Chapter 17

Bereavement

There is no suggestion here that the pain and sense of loss that occurs following a sudden and unexpected death of a baby can in some magical and therapeutic way be made to disappear – it cannot. However those undergoing such an experience can be aided and supported through the period of bewilderment, confusion and sense of failure if both they and those around them understand some of the normal psychological processes by which such an experience is assimilated.

In this chapter we first take a general look at some of the studies done over the last decade on the impact of sudden infant death on families. The way in which a family works through its grief may be hindered by the reactions of members of the public, especially those in authority. Chapters 19 to 22 will report the results of a large study of parents who contacted the Foundation for the Study of Infant Deaths – which examined the management of 713 sudden infant deaths over an eight year period.

Bereavement through loss of a child has, until recently, received less study than bereavement through widowhood or a child bereaved of a parent. Gorer has suggested that the loss of a child is likely to be 'the most distressing and long lasting of griefs'. Recent surveys in the USA have indicated that the grief and distress following an unexpected, unexplained death is often more severe than after a death which is anticipated or understood. The immeasurable personal heartache at the loss of a child is compounded by the circumstances: parents feel wholly responsible when an apparently normal baby, whose symptoms of illness, if any, were not considered serious, dies at home.

A mother's confidence in her mothering ability may be shattered, especially if it is her first child; a father too may experience feelings of frustration and futility; he may fear that a genetic factor on his side was to blame or wonder perhaps whether the infant care had been

good enough. The coroner's enquiry and police involvement needs to be tactfully handled to avoid adding to the parents' distress by making them feel under suspicion. The uncertain reaction of neighbours and friends can increase the parents' sense of isolation.

Grief is a succession of painful feelings in response to a loss. Although reactions vary widely according to an individual's social, emotional, cultural and spiritual resources and previous life experiences, grief tends to follow a pattern in which the initial phase is one of numbness and disbelief. The state may vary considerably in its duration. At this time parents need comforting and practical advice and help.

This phase of shock gives way to the phase of yearning and searching, and of emotional release. Parents may experience a strong desire to hold and touch their baby. Intense and unbearable sorrow and loneliness may be accompanied by irrational feelings and outbursts of anger, which are sometimes directed against a doctor, health visitor or person who had recently tended the baby and sometimes inwardly as self-accusation and overwhelming remorse. The intensity of guilt feelings may be closely related to the cause of death: if this is unknown or parents have anxieties about possible causes, they need a kind explanation from someone able to answer their questions.

Gradually the pining and searching phase dissolves into defeat; a period of depression and apathy succeeds in which a parent may feel utterly exhausted, unable to summon any enthusiasm and finding every task requires an effort. Relatives may become frustrated and friends give up at their apparent inability to promote a parent's recovery. Continued support is needed from someone who understands the bereaved person's need to go on working through their grief and talk about their loss.

In their own time, the bereaved will emerge into the fourth and final phase of acceptance and recovery. The stages of grief may overlap, and some individuals may progress more slowly than others. Although painful and difficult, the expression of grief is necessary before recovery and growth can occur.

With tactful management and good support many parents come through with greater maturity and stronger relationships, but for others tension and unresolved grief may cause psychological problems and can threaten marital harmony which may lead to separation, divorce and even suicide. In addition, relationships with grand-parents, and surviving and subsequent children, may be disrupted.

A recent study by Suzan Lewis, looked at 36 mothers who had had a sudden infant death and who subsequently had an infant who was

under the age of 3 months. A matched control group were similarly contacted and both groups were given questionnaires designed to test levels of anxiety both at the time of the initial contact and 12 months later. Feelings of guilt were still very much in evidence following the birth of a subsequent baby, and many mothers made comments like 'I must have been a very bad mother', or 'I am determined to do everything I can for this baby'. Other mothers regretted various factors such as not having breast fed their baby, having worked during pregnancy, having left their baby outside in the cold, having shown too much concern for the eldest sibling, or having gone out the night before the death. Interestingly but not surprisingly, given that no clear explanation was available, mothers were not consistent in their blame and would speak with conviction first of one and then another action which they felt caused or contributed towards the death.

Parents also blamed doctors and health visitors, either for their actions or inactions. Moreover strong feelings were most frequently described in relation to the visits of various personnel immediately after the death. Reports from the parents concerning these visits varied from that of considerable sympathy from the police, to those who felt allegations of cruelty were being made. Mothers living in the poorer social circumstances more often, although certainly not always, reported police harassment. Later, there was sometimes insight into the fact that statements made by the police under such circumstances were open to many interpretations. In many studies, mothers have reported having changed in important ways since bereavement. In this particular study there was a marked decrease in self-confidence and parents often felt a loss of control over their lives which could lead to anxiety, depression and a lapse into a state of 'learnt helplessness'.

In a study of 112 parents in America who had all experienced a sudden infant death, John DeFrain and his colleagues showed that from their subjective ratings, the immediate consequence of the death was a profound decrease in personal happiness and in family organisation. Figure 31 shows that although the measure of family organisation had returned to pre-death levels by 9 months, it was nearly three years before the level of personal happiness had recovered.

Suzan Lewis looked at the problems parents had with a subsequent baby, and found that most mothers admitted to 'cot watching' whereas others made a conscious attempt not to yield to the temptations to touch and look at their babies too often. This feeling of anxiety and concern over the subsequent baby had decreased by the time the babies were 15 months old. Nevertheless, these mothers were still considerably more anxious than a control group of mothers.

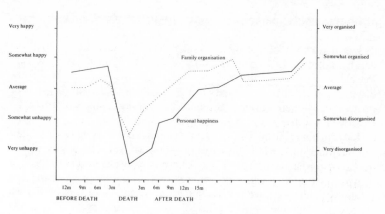

Figure 31

Mean levels of personal happiness and family organisation in relation to death (from DeFrain et al, 1982).

The disruption caused by the death was illustrated in a study by Robert Steel in Ontario, Canada. He contacted 337 families in which there had been a sudden infant death. Replies were received from 45% or 152. Of those who replied 45% had moved house after the death of the infant, 31% having done so directly because of the death. Of those who moved 24% did so within a few days, 38% within weeks and another 38% within months.

A suggestion that marital disharmony also resulted was reported from Australia by Cornwell and colleagues. A follow up was undertaken of 17 consecutive sudden infant deaths in Sidney, Australia. Drop-outs from the study included a family who moved after the first interview and another where there was a serious marital rift. Four parents refused follow up after two interviews, which left only 11 families to complete the study. One third of the marriages in the remaining group were described as encountering serious trouble and there was considerable anxiety concerning the remaining children with two mothers rejecting their subsequent children altogether. This pattern appears to be atypical though.

In an earlier study by DeFrain, fifty percent of the parents suffered physiological and psychological problems after the death, including trouble with sleeping, loss of appetite, difficulty getting up in the morning, feelings of nervousness and irritability. For most parents, however, their relationship with their spouses, other children and grandparents was generally strengthened in the long run. It was

obvious that these parents tended to turn to their own families first for support.

The behaviour of the other children within the families after the death studied by DeFrain was said by 78% of parents to have changed. Problems included nightmares, bed wetting, school problems, discipline problems, increased crying, blackout spells and being over protected by their parents. Similar findings have been reported by Cornwell and her team in Australia.

A disturbing finding from the Australian study was that at least half the medical practitioners involved 'did not see the plight of the bereaved parents as within their sphere of professional activity'.

Apart from one study in Inner North London by Watson, the parental reactions have not before been documented for the British scene. The design and methodology of the survey of parents contacting the Foundation for the Study of Infant Deaths is described in Appendix 2, and the results are discussed in the next four chapters. It is not a study of bereavement but rather a survey of the management of sudden death in infancy with a view to suggesting ways in which the tragedy can be better handled and parents given appropriate support.

Chapter 18

Management Immediately After the Death

Place of Death

The majority (86%) of the 713 sudden infant deaths in the Foundation Study occurred while the baby was at home or when visiting friends or relatives. A further 5.5% of deaths occurred in a car and 5% in a public place, either while shopping or at an institution such as a childminders'. Only 3% of the deaths occurred on the way to hospital or within 24 hours of admission.

Several babies were observed to die and three died in their parents' arms.

'At 8 p.m. the baby woke to be fed one hour early. She seemed very hungry and started to feed. She made a funny little noise which I thought meant there might be some wind. I helped her to get rid of the wind, then she made three tiny little gasps and her arms dropped and her colour drained.'

One baby died while on an apnoea alarm despite immediate attempts to resuscitate.

'He was a happy, seemingly healthy little boy six weeks old. At about 8.30 in the morning I went to the bathroom to brush my teeth after getting up, first making sure he was all right. Ten seconds later the respiration monitor which the baby was on sounded off and I rushed back to the bedroom where he was. I tried to suck him out with a special tube and tried mouth to mouth and cardiac massage but all was in vain.'

The initial response and the way in which parents summoned help varied enormously. To scream for help was a common reaction of mothers, some of whom became hysterical; many parents attempted mouth to mouth and nose resuscitation and a few cardiac massage but without success. Some tried to telephone for their GP and/or an ambulance, several ran to neighbours for help or to use their telephone, some took their babies by car to the nearest doctor, health centre, hospital or even police station. A few mothers rushed their

baby to their maternity hospital since that was the only hospital they knew.

> 'I ran the ten minutes to the Health Centre. Luckily all the doctors were there and as soon as they caught sight of her they all rushed into a surgery with her. They were in there for half an hour before they told me she was dead.'

Many parents commented on the sympathy and sensitive practical help of those involved in giving immediate help; their doctor, the ambulance and casualty staff, the police or coroner's officer, but as we shall see others experienced difficulties.

General Practitioners

Two per cent of parents gave unsolicited praise for the doctor's handling of the immediate crisis.

> 'My GP handled the whole situation in a very sensitive manner.' 'I found my own GP, the doctor on call and Health Visitor very helpful. I cannot say how appreciative I am of their kindness, sympathy and understanding.'

Parents reported difficulty in contacting a doctor or were critical of his attitude in 7% of occasions. There were four reports of the doctor declining to come to a 'dead' baby, usually suggesting it would be better to take the baby straight to a hospital; in a further five, the GP came only reluctantly after repeated requests. Although a doctor does not have a legal duty to attend after a death, failure to help parents at these moments of crisis caused acute distress. The following are examples of criticism of the doctor's immediate response:

> 'I had my baby in my arms and realised something was wrong. I was on my own with my two babies. I tried giving him the kiss of life but got very tired so rang for my neighbour. I continued the breathing but the baby died. My neighbour continued giving kiss of life while I rang our local practice. They told me to take the baby to hospital. I was furious and demanded that they contact the doctor who was in the surgery at the time. After a second phone call they decided to treat it with urgency and a doctor arrived about 20 minutes later.'
> 'I picked him up – he was bluish and limp like a doll. I called my husband who immediately tried to give the baby the kiss of life while I rang our doctor; but he wasn't much help saying that the ambulance was the best thing.'
> 'Immediately I found her dead (2.30 a.m.) I rang the ambulance and they came to our house in 7 to 10 minutes. They confirmed she had died 2 hours before. They rang our doctor and he was not on duty so they contacted a locum, but he refused to come out and said we should go to the hospital.'

Other criticisms referred to the unsympathetic attitude or hurtful comments of the doctor who confirmed death.

'The doctor came and looked at R. She called the police, offered us tranquillizers which we refused, and left. I've not seen her since.'

'The doctor completely ignored me when here and asked the Health Visitor many questions which upset me terribly, and it was dreadful when she asked if either I or my husband had hurt the baby in any way.'

Ambulance Service

In 482 cases, 68% of the total sample, an ambulance was called. The majority of parents found the ambulance staff efficient and helpful: 'The ambulance men were very calming and extremely kind.' 'The lady ambulance attendant wrapped T. in a shawl, cuddled him and said she would take good care of him.' However, 6% of these parents described difficulties they experienced. Half of these concerned delay in the arrival of the ambulance, sometimes because of difficulty in finding the address; the others related to inconsiderate handling of the baby, ambulance service rules concerning carrying dead bodies, not allowing the mother to accompany the baby in the ambulance, or failure in communication. The following are examples:

'My husband got up at 5 a.m. and looking at the baby saw he was alive but finding it difficult to breathe. The doctor came immediately and tried everything, but nothing worked. An ambulance had been called from about 20 miles away, but it got lost and arrived nearly an hour later just as the baby died.'

'They snatched my baby letting her hang and plonked her on a settee, and moved away saying nothing. I gently picked her up.'

'The ambulance men made a report but were not allowed to take the baby by their rules.'

'I begged them to let me travel in the ambulance with her, but they sent for a second ambulance and insisted I travel in that with neighbours.'

'I asked if I could go too but they said "No, go back to the house." We were surprised the ambulance left without a further word. After more than an hour of hearing nothing, my husband phoned the local hospital where we presumed they had gone. The baby had been taken there but the hospital did not know who she was nor whom to contact. They told us to come at once.'

Accident and Emergency Departments

Of the sample of 713 families, 60% lived in urban and 40% in rural areas. Among the urban families, two thirds (67%) of the deaths were confirmed at a hospital and one third (33%) by a doctor in the

community. In the rural areas the proportions were reversed, in 65% a GP confirmed the baby's death and in 35% the baby was taken to hospital. There were no differences between the two time periods.

Thus, although 97% (692) of the 713 deaths occurred outside hospital, because of the preponderance of urban families in the sample, in more than half (54%) the death was confirmed at hospital. As already stated, nearly 3% were admitted alive. In a further 3.5% resuscitation was attempted on arrival. In 78% of the cases confirmed at hospital, at least one parent, sometimes accompanied by siblings, went to the hospital.

This illustrates, especially in urban areas, the important role of Accident and Emergency staff in receiving the distraught and stunned parents and in initiating further support for the family by informing a member of the paediatric team. They should also notify the family's general practitioner, the health visitor and the community health department.

About 11% of parents who went to hospitals went out of their way to comment on the helpful and kind response of the casualty staff.

'We rushed the baby to casualty in our own car. Attention was immediately given to the baby and we were taken to a private waiting room and given tea; nurses stayed with us and asked us what had happened. The doctor came in soon after and confirmed the baby was dead, and advised us that it appeared to be a cot death as there seemed no apparent cause. We were advised that the police would have to be called and support was given until they arrived. The police drove us home and delayed their questions until the local police arrived. We feel that everything was explained and that we were helped to the best of everyone's ability.'

'The casualty staff were extremely helpful with explanations and answering questions. We were asked if we wanted to hold him. I kissed him and held his hand. They always referred to the baby by his name, and they contacted our doctor and church.'

'The senior paediatrician came and talked to us; the whole casualty staff were superb and very comforting.'

In 10%, however, adverse criticisms were made of the way parents were looked after or of hurtful comments made by members of the casualty staff indicating inadequate knowledge of sudden infant deaths or lack of understanding of the needs of bereaved parents. For example, the mother or parents were left alone, staff were uncommunicative or made inappropriate remarks, parents were not allowed to see or hold the baby, there was failure to try to make arrangements for the baby's baptism, no-one made sure that parent(s) and any accompanying children had transport to take them home, and they were not given the available literature on sudden infant deaths.

The following comments illustrate these:

'I was left alone for 2½ hours in a claustrophobic room.' 'The hospital gave us no help and left us to the police entirely.' 'The doctor who confirmed death did not even speak to us, and the sister in charge was very unsympathetic.' 'A casualty nurse asked why I didn't check on my children during the night and seemed hostile.' 'They took the baby away, before my husband, who joined me at the hospital, had a chance to see her.' 'I asked if the baby could be baptised but no-one could tell me.' 'When we arrived in the ambulance, the hospital was unco-operative in arranging seating or transport home.' 'I felt a lot more care could have been given to my other daughter and myself, especially as I was physically suffering from shock.'

Seeing or Holding the Baby after Death

For some parents, the desire to see their baby again, to express their love and say goodbye, is overwhelming. It also helps them acknowledge the reality of what has happened.

'I was very anxious to see A. again and kept saying this to the student nurse but felt she thought I was being hysterical. I insisted, and felt quite at peace after this.' 'We wanted to see and kiss him after he'd died. We both found it a help to do so.'

The questionnaire asked parents whether they wished to see and/or hold their baby again after death was confirmed. Sixty-eight percent in the 1974–9 period and 77% in the 1980–1 period replied affirmatively. The proportion who were offered the opportunity to do so rose only marginally from 62% in 1974–9 to 68% in 1980–1, indicating insufficient awareness of the comfort parents may derive from this.

The proportion of parents who did not want to see their child again fell from a third (32%) to less than a quarter (23%) in the two time periods. A few later regretted this. 'Within days of the funeral I had a desire to hold her and regretted not seeing and holding her at her death.' Others were deterred from doing so by officials or relatives, or by the police who did not want the body touched before the post mortem – 'When I made a move to pick her up, I was pulled away.' This attempt to leave the body undisturbed or to protect the mother from the sight of death is quite unrealistic, since in nearly all sudden deaths resuscitation has been attempted and when death has been confirmed at home many mothers have cuddled their baby for a long time before the body is taken away – 'After the doctor left, and while waiting for the police, I hugged my baby and cried and cried.' 'I held him all the time at home until the undertakers came.'

Some parents were given the opportunity to see their child later, in

the mortuary or undertaker's Chapel of Rest, and were comforted to see the baby looking so peaceful –

'I asked and saw him two days later in the mortuary. I took him off the attendant and had a cuddle and kiss and chat, and said sorry and goodbye to my baby.' 'I wanted to hold my baby very much after he died; this upset my husband. I went to the Chapel of Rest to see him before the funeral and felt enormous relief for having done so.'

A few parents, however, found the change in appearance after the post-mortem distressing – 'She was almost unrecognisable when we saw her at the undertakers; she was mangled, discoloured, bruised and distorted.' Pathologists and mortuary technicians need to remember that parents may wish to see the baby again. Occasionally the undertaker brought the baby to the parents' home for the night before the funeral, but in some cases a charge of £15 to do this was more than the parents could afford.

Table 14

Proportion of parents offered the opportunity of seeing and/or holding their dead baby; Foundation Study.

OPPORTUNITY	1974–9	1980–1
Satisfied: wanted to and given opportunity	153 (44.9%)	197 (56.3%)
Unsatisfied: wanted to but not given opportunity	77 (22.6%)	74 (21.1%)
Opportunity offered but declined	58 (17.0%)	41 (11.7%)
Opportunity not offered, but not wanted	53 (15.5%)	38 (10.9%)
ALL KNOWN	341 (100.0%)	350 (100.0%)

Table 14 indicates whether those that wanted to see or hold their baby after death was confirmed were given the opportunity to do so. Over 14% of parents in each period (two thirds of the unsatisfied parents) commented on problems they had experienced in relation to seeing or holding their baby after death had been confirmed. For some parents, the obstacles put in their way of paying their last respects caused great anger and additional distress. The importance attached to this was expressed by the following mother.

'I would just emphasise again the importance I feel of being able to hold your baby and say goodbye. After your baby has been taken to hospital and

death finally confirmed, up until that moment everything has been absolutely terrible and nightmarish. Quite honestly, I just couldn't bear the last memory of my child being when I saw him lying face down on his mattress. I knew he was dead before I picked him up, and thinking of that still makes me feel a terrible panic and inadequacy; but I can snap myself out of these terrible feelings by thinking of the very beautiful experience of our last hold of him dead, and that leaves us both with a strange and beautiful peace and contentment. I think it should be standard practice to ask parents if they want to hold their dead child, and then if the parents do not wish this they can just say no and there would be no fuss.'

Suppression of Lactation

Although the questionnaire did not ask about breast-feeding, 17 mothers in 1974–9 and 16 in 1980–1 spontaneously complained that they had received inadequate advice or medication to stop lactation, and commented on the great physical pain and emotional distress that engorged breasts caused them.

'I had very bad advice about cessation of breast-feeding which added acute physical discomfort to my distress.' 'My breasts were very painfully engorged for over a week and this was physically and psychologically terribly difficult to bear.' 'When I asked my doctor for tablets to dry up my milk, he refused and did not give me advice about drinking less fluid. Consequently, I was in great pain for 4/5 days after and in great discomfort for about 2 weeks.' 'I had a lot of trouble and pain getting rid of my milk. I would have liked to give it for premature babies.' 'I contacted a local milk bank (the day the baby died), as I had been breast-feeding and did not know how to relieve the discomfort. My doctor offered no help. I expressed my milk and filled 4 bottles, which made me feel I'd helped someone, and gave me something else to think about.'

Several mothers commented on what a psychological help it was to donate their breast milk to a 'milk bank' for premature babies.

Chapter 19

The Coroner's Investigation

For many parents the referral of their baby's death to the Coroner*
and the involvement of the police, albeit often acting on the Coroner's
behalf, comes as a surprise. It is associated with the need to record a
cause of death certified by a medical practitioner or Coroner.

The Births and Deaths Registration Act 1953 provides that the
death and cause of death of every person dying in England and Wales
must be registered by the Registrar of Births and Deaths for the sub-
district in which the death occurs. A registered medical practitioner
who attended a patient 'during his last illness' is required to sign a
Medical Certificate of Cause of Death 'true to his knowledge and
belief' and is also required to give to a qualified informant a written
notice of the signing of the certificate to be delivered to the registrar.
This is the usual procedure in deaths occurring as the result of illness.
When death has occurred suddenly and unexpectedly for no obvious
reason, however, or a doctor has not attended during the last illness, or
has not seen the patient within the 14 days before death, the doctor or
registrar would refer the death to the Coroner.

The Coroner is obliged by law (The Coroner's Act 1887 as
amended) to inquire into any 'sudden death of unknown cause' as well
as into deaths which appear to be 'violent' or 'unnatural'. The Coroner
is authorised to make inquiries and to arrange a thorough post-
mortem examination by a suitably qualified pathologist able to
distinguish natural from unnatural sudden death. The Coroner, to
whom the report of the post mortem examination is essential for
establishing the medical cause of death, is thus responsible for
choosing and paying the pathologist, whose report is then the property
of the Coroner.

In dealing with sudden infant deaths the Coroner has a multiple

---

* In Scotland sudden deaths are investigated by the Procurator Fiscal.

responsibility: (i) to ascertain so far as possible the medical cause of death, (ii) to satisfy himself, by autopsy and inquiries into the circumstances, that there is no reason to suspect that death was violent or unnatural, (iii) to supply the Registrar with a certified cause of death, and (iv) to dispose of the inquiry in a way which best serves the public interest.

In practice, nearly all reports and inquiries are dealt with initially by a Coroner's Officer, rather than the Coroner himself. The majority of Coroner's Officers are serving policemen seconded to assist the Coroner. In many parts of the country, especially in rural areas, the Coroner's Officer arranges for the local police to make the preliminary investigation.

In practice, the police are often called to a sudden infant death much sooner, sometimes by parents themselves who do not know to whom to turn to for help, sometimes by neighbours who try to summon a doctor, the ambulance and police. If there is any hope of reviving the child, the police assist with resuscitation – 'At the time of death the police were marvellous.' In many counties the police are automatically informed when 999 is dialled and an ambulance requested. It is this arrangement that can give rise to difficulties, especially if the uniformed police or Criminal Investigation Department officers turn up at the home with no other information than that a sudden death has occurred. Sometimes they arrive before the ambulance, or before the parents have returned from hospital –

'Two uniformed policemen arrived with the ambulance, at which point I was verging on hysteria. They questioned me and told me not to touch the cot; at once I was made to feel like a murderer or child abuser by their attitude.' 'A uniformed policeman was at our house when my husband and I got back from hospital. We were horrified to think that he had been searching while we weren't in.'

The questionnaire asked parents to describe the Coroner's investigation and police visits. The way in which the investigation was carried out and the extent of police involvement varied enormously. In only four instances, all in the period 1974–9, the death was registered without a post-mortem examination; the GP had issued the medical certificate of cause of death. For a relatively small proportion of cases (17% in each period) neither the police nor the Coroner's Officer visited the home; in these instances statements were made either at the hospital or the Coroner's office. For the majority (83%) who had home visits, these ranged from one visit by a single plainclothes Coroner's Officer or policeman to repeated visits from several uniformed police and CID officers at the same time, who took photographs and finger prints, and treated the death with suspicion.

The police have to make their enquiries on the Coroner's behalf before the post-mortem findings are known; the manner in which they assess whether the death was from natural causes, or was unnatural and likely to necessitate an inquest, is crucial. The number of parents who gave unsolicited praise (19% in 1974–9 and 15% in 1980–1) was greater than those who complained (13% in 1974–9 and 7% in 1980–1), but the latter's distress and anger was deepfelt. Parents praised those who conducted their investigations with tact, sympathy and kindness.

> 'All police questions were relevant to the situation and asked in the kindest and most tactful manner. We cannot say enough about the kind behaviour and approach of the police in this matter.'

Gratitude was expressed to those who took the trouble to explain the reasons for doing things.

> 'The Coroner's Officer was kind and took extreme care in explaining the probable procedure, and gave us the Foundation's Information leaflet.'
> 'The policeman called several times during the week following the death keeping us informed of what was happening. This was very helpful because without him we would have had no idea of the procedures.'

Parents were also particularly grateful to those who gave advice about making funeral arrangements.

A major point in the early periods concerned the failure to be told about the Coroner's investigation or likely involvement of the police. Thus, 27% in 1974–79 replied that they had not been informed of the Coroner's duties. Among other adverse criticisms were (a) the attitude of the police, implying suspicion by asking questions straight away or in a manner which 'made us feel like criminals'; (b) their arrival in great numbers; (c) repeated visits; or (d) unannounced visits. The following descriptions illustrate some experiences:

> 'The arrival of 3 CID officers within half an hour of our son's death shocked us deeply. We felt that we ought to have been told to expect them and also that they could have left it until later in the day. We were both in a state of shock which they made much worse. I felt under suspicion and it upset me a great deal.'
> 'The police were unnecessarily harsh and kept on asking questions I couldn't answer for over an hour. I told them the same things over and over again but even then they sent in a woman police officer. I just couldn't stand any more questioning at that time, so they asked where I'd be later that day. They rang later to say they were sorry they'd bothered me and that they'd decided not to see me again.'
> 'Immediately after my return from hospital, two uniformed police arrived, hardly giving me time to break the news to my husband. They were unsympathetic and asked some very hurtful questions, even though foul play had been ruled out by the hospital casualty staff. These were followed

at half-hour intervals by two other pairs of uniformed police who said they had come to check our stories. It was almost unbelievable in the circumstances.'

'Two policemen visited at the time of death and two hours later a plain-clothes policeman came to take away the bedding. Photographers also came, to photograph the cot and the scene of death.'

'My husband and father were both taken to the police station and asked a lot of questions. My husband was brought home and made to re-enact the scene using a teddy bear. The police also interviewed the neighbours whom my husband had gone to for help. It was terrible what my husband went through when the baby died, but it was made worse the way he was treated by the police.'

Identification of the Body to the Police/Coroner's Officer

Identification of the body is required in the event of an inquest, but the identification is usually done formally before the body is taken away for autopsy, whereas the decision whether or not to hold an inquest is usually taken after the autopsy has been performed and other inquiries made.

The proportion of cases, however, in which identification was requested appears to have declined slightly from 42% in 1974–9 to 36% in 1980–1, although the number of inquests has not declined. In 1980–1, analysis showed that identification was requested in 42% of deaths confirmed in hospital and only 30% of deaths confirmed at home.

In about 63% of cases, identification was made by the father alone, in 18% by both parents together, and in 13% by the mother alone. In the remaining cases identification was by a relative or GP. There were no differences across the time periods.

Some parents commented on the distress caused by what they regarded as an unnecessary procedure; others were upset if it involved delay or extra travel:

'My husband identified our son, a procedure he found particularly upsetting, and, in my opinion, totally unnecessary.'

'Two uniformed policemen arrived at my mother-in-law's within an hour of us arriving home, and they questioned us for about an hour and examined the baby's cot. We then had to follow them to the city mortuary to make a formal identification. To this day I cannot understand why we had to go to identify the baby at the city mortuary as I had been with him when he was taken to the hospital. No explanation was given.'

Inquest

Inquests were held in 11% of deaths 1974–9 and 14% in 1980–1. Of the 38 inquests for which information is available, 25 (66%) were held within 2 weeks of the death, but 3 inquests were as long as 2 months later. Such delay can cause considerable distress.

In the case of sudden deaths, the Coroner has had a discretionary power, since 1926, to dispense with an inquest and to notify the Registrar of the cause of death reported by the pathologist, if he is satisfied by the inquiries and post-mortem examination that death was from natural causes. Most Coroners take advantage of this, although it was apparent that some Coroners still hold inquests as a matter of routine. Very rarely parents ask for an inquest in order to have their name cleared in public. The ordeal of inquests has been described in detail by John Emery. A few parents in the survey commented on their upsetting experiences:

'I found the inquest to be particularly horrific when the Coroner asked the pathologist if there were any marks on the baby's body implying mistreatment. I felt he could have asked this in private. I found the whole experience distressing.'

'The inquest was the biggest trauma. There were 4 members of the press there and events leading up to G's death were sensationalised in at least one local paper, which was very distressing.'

There were two further matters which received repeated complaints from parents and which the police are in a position to ameliorate.

Complaints about Press Reports of the Baby's Death

About 5% of parents in each period complained about sensationalised or inaccurate reports of their child's death published in the local paper without the parents' prior knowledge or permission. Many parents resented, in particular, misleading descriptions of the cause of death, and the fact that the press had learned the cause of death from the police before the parents themselves had been told:

'One of the most upsetting factors was that the local newspaper printed details of E's death on the front page, copying exactly the police report, which ended "no suspicious circumstances". This was printed without the courtesy of ringing to see if we would mind ... When I rang the editor, he would not print the true cause of death: cot death.'

'The intrusion of the press who had heard the result of the post-mortem before us was ghastly. They came to interview me next day. I was so angry that I rang the Coroner's Officer who told me that the police had told the

press ... The police Inspector told me they had to inform the press and could only ask them not to pester bereaved parents.'

'The worst thing was that her death was on the front page of our local paper without our knowledge or consent. It was a terrible shock to us and our parents to see it reported in such a nasty way.'

The Press may report a post-mortem finding lawfully only if the Coroner has authorised it; the Coroners' Rules 1984 (S.I. 552), rule 10(2) states 'Unless authorised by the Coroner, the person making a post-mortem examination shall not supply a copy of his report to any person other than the Coroner.'

Retrieval of Baby's Clothes or Linen

In each period 2% of parents complained about the failure to return, or the difficulty they had in retrieving, the baby's clothes or bedding after the post-mortem examination:

'We had difficulty in retrieving E's clothes; it took a fortnight to trace them.' 'We asked the Procurator Fiscal if we could have her clothes back and were told to collect them from the station. By then it was 8 weeks after the death and we were horrified at their state; they were mouldy and smelt awful.' 'For some reason I expected our baby's clothes to be returned to us, together with his blankets and mattress, which were taken by the police. The contents of the pram, only, were returned 17 weeks later by the police. I had to contact the hospital mortuary who said our son's clothes were probably at the undertakers. I promptly rang the undertakers who told me that if no-one enquires they dispose of clothes about a month after the death.'

Parents may be told about clothes and bedding but fail to remember in their state of shock. It would seem sensible to record the parents' instructions in writing.

The Post-Mortem Findings and Registered Cause of Death

There were more comments and suggestions for improvement concerning notifying parents of the post-mortem findings and explaining the registered cause of death than for any other aspect (42% of all suggestions). This illustrates the importance that parents attach to hearing the post-mortem findings as soon as possible and from someone who is able to explain the medical terminology:

'The worst time was the wait between losing our little boy and finding out his cause of death when I blamed myself and asked myself endless questions.'

The speed with which parents are informed of the initial findings has increased over the whole period. Whereas only 13% were informed on the day of death or next day in the first years, this had risen to 35% by 1980–1. About 10% in both periods did not hear until at least a week after the death; a few of these waited for between 6 weeks and 5 months. The microscopic findings, of course, are not likely to be available until several weeks later. A few parents complained of the delay in hearing the initial findings if they had to wait for an inquest. Many parents commented that they 'need to know as soon as possible what caused their baby's death' and that they should be told automatically and should not have to ask.

Parents were asked by whom they were told the autopsy results and cause of death. In all periods, between 55% and 60% were informed by the Coroner or Coroner's Officer or police; only 12% of parents were informed by their GP. Nearly 10% in 1980–1 learned of their baby's cause of death from the Registrar of Deaths. There was a substantial decrease in the proportion of parents who had had to ask in order to learn the cause of death, from 15% in 1974–9 to 4% in 1980–1. Some parents learned from the undertaker, and in one case from the local newspaper. 'The cause of death was not shown to us till we had taken a letter which the undertaker gave us to the Registrar, which she showed us.'

About 40% of parents claimed that they were given no explanation of the post-mortem findings or the cause of death by a medically qualified person. In 58% the GP had given an explanation, but in 16% of these the 'explanation' was given before the post-mortem findings were known on the assumption that the cause of death was 'sudden infant death'. This is very unsatisfactory.

> 'If the death of a child occurs in any family, it is vitally important that the family doctor or medical unit explains the cause of death or explains about cot death. We count ourselves very lucky to have been explained things properly. It will never answer the question "why did he have to die?" but it does offer some comfort.'

Parents suggestions included:

(1) That all parents should be told in advance of the procedure and arrangements for informing them of the cause of death. 'Parents should be kept informed as to what is happening to their baby. We weren't told where our baby was until 4 days later, and were kept in terrible suspense not knowing when the autopsy would be carried out.'
(2) That there should be no undue delay in undertaking the post-mortem examination, in accordance with the 1984 Coroners' Rules, Rule 5, 'Where a Coroner directs or requests that a post-mortem

examination shall be made, it shall be made as soon after the death as possible.'

'The main problem we all found very worrying was the fact that P's post-mortem was not done until 6 days after death. Surely this is far too late and nothing is going to show up. Also it was very upsetting for the whole family, not only ourselves, to be kept waiting to know why P had died.'

(3) That parents should be told the post-mortem findings giving the cause of death as soon as they are available and without having to ask.

'The 5 days of waiting for the post-mortem result were absolute hell because I was made to believe I'd killed her as the ambulance men told me she'd suffocated. Two days after she'd died I 'phoned the hospital for the result of the Coroner's post-mortem and they said they couldn't tell me. Looking back it was a nightmare and I don't think parents should be treated like this. As soon as the post-mortem is carried out, parents have a right to know the results.'

'It seems very wrong that everyone else, the Registrar, the undertaker etc., knew the cause of death before us parents. We still have not seen the certificate.'

(4) That the family's GP, paediatrician or other medically qualified person should volunteer an explanation of the post-mortem findings, preferably after consulting with the pathologist.

'I think the GP should be present when parents are told the result of the post-mortem as the Coroner's Officer had no medical qualifications and could not explain anything we wanted to know.'

(5) That a copy of the post-mortem report should be shown to parents, or at least made available to their GP. Parents in England as well as Scotland felt very strongly about this. Parents in England and Wales are entitled under the 1984 Coroners' Rules, although there may be a small fee of about 55p a page.

'Scottish law does not permit parents or the GP to have a copy of the post-mortem report, the explanation of which is essential to remove doubts and confusion in the parents' minds.'

Registering the Death

The 1953 Births and Death Registration Act requires not only that the death and cause of death of every person dying in England and Wales must be registered by the Registrar for the sub-district in which the death occurs, but also stipulates that, except when an inquest is held, the death has to be registered by personal attendance of a 'qualified informant' within 5 days of death. The period for personal attendance

can be extended to 14 days if the informant sends the Registrar within 5 days written notice that the Medical Certificate of Cause of Death has been signed by a doctor.

When a death is referred to a Coroner, the Registrar of Deaths cannot register the death until he receives *either* a Certificate after Inquest from the Coroner (which should be given within 5 days of the inquest) which records the medical and circumstantial causes of death, enabling death to be registered without personal attendance of the informant, *or* what are known as Pink Forms A or B: 'Notification to the Registrar by the Coroner that he does not consider it necessary to hold an inquest'. Form A is used when, following discussion with the doctor, the Coroner has decided that no post mortem examination is necessary; the cause of death for entry in the register is taken from the Medical Certificate of Cause of Death issued by the doctor. Form B is used after a post-mortem examination and certifies the cause of death as reported by the pathologist. The last, as has been shown by the small number of inquests, is the most common practice after a sudden infant death.

70% of the deaths were registered within 5 days, 25% between 5 and 14 days and in 5% registration was completed over two weeks after the death. In over 40%, the Registrar of Deaths was the same person with whom the parents had registered the baby's birth.

Relatively few parents (2%–3%) commented on difficulties they experienced over registering the baby's death, but there were many different points of concern. These included confusion over arrangements for obtaining the certificate from the Coroner and taking it to the Registrar, and the distress caused by registering the death with the same Registrar as the birth –

'The registration of death had to be made at the same place and with the same officials where weeks before we had registered the birth. Whilst waiting for 2 hours, we were with other people's crying babies being brought in for registration, which was most upsetting.'

The distance and time it took to travel to collect the certificate from the Coroner and register the death was frequently mentioned.

'I had to make two trips to the Coroner's office 14 miles away to collect the necessary certificate. The Coroner would not release it until the day before the proposed funeral. On this day the Registrar was not working and had to be fetched from home at 7.30 p.m.'
'It took us 4 hours to travel and find the Registrar's office.'

Several parents were upset by the manner or inappropriate remarks of the individual Registrar, for example:

'Better luck next time' and 'Cot deaths don't happen to babies over 6 months' and 'We haven't had one of these cot deaths for a long time'.

Registered Cause of Death

The 713 unexpected infant deaths in the sample, were registered in more than 35 different ways. For further analysis these have been divided into five categories:

Group I comprises those in which the main cause of death was given as Sudden Infant Death Syndrome; 66%

Group II comprises those in which the main cause was given as a recognised condition but coupled with Sudden Infant Death Syndrome e.g. Bronchial pneumonia/cot death, asphyxia due to regurgitated vomit/sudden infant death syndrome; 7.3%.

Group III comprises those registered as due to a recognised condition alone e.g. Bronchiolitis, bronchopneumonia, epiglottitis, tracheo-bronchitis, or cardiac abnormality. It is not possible to tell how many of these were genuinely due to these conditions or were fictionally attributed; 15%

Group IV comprises those deaths registered as due to a vague condition e.g. respiratory failure, cardiac arrest due to respiratory infection, or 'natural causes'; 8.7%

Group V comprises deaths registered as due to accidental causes such as misadventure, asphyxia, choking on vomit or inhalation of vomit; 3%.

Parents were asked whether they understood their baby's registered cause of death. About two thirds said they did, and about one third did not. There were no differences over time. Table 15 relates the negative answers (those who did not understand) to the registered cause of death. The figures express the percentage of each cause of death group which was not understood by the parents.

It can be seen that the causes least well understood were the 'recognised' conditions, and that there was less confusion if the death was merely registered as due to the Sudden Infant Death Syndrome. The figures indicate that many parents are confused when Sudden Infant Death Syndrome is coupled with a condition such as bronchopneumonia –

'The cause of death is still difficult to understand. We are not certain whether she died as a result of bronchial pneumonia or from some unexplained cause as it was also called a cot death.'

These findings of Table 15 are at variance with those of Watson,

Table 15

Proportion of parents who did not understand the registered cause of death 1974–81; Foundation Study.

	REGISTERED CAUSE OF DEATH	NO. DEATHS (N = 100%)	PROPORTION NOT UNDERSTOOD
I	Sudden infant death syndrome	470	29%
II	Recognised condition + sudden infant death syndrome	52	46%
III	Recognised condition	106	46%
IV	Vague condition	62	40%
V	Accidental	21	29%

who found that the term Sudden Infant Death Syndrome caused a higher degree of anxiety in parents in Inner North London than a recognised condition. Possibly the different views are accounted for by the different social composition of parents in the surveys and by better public understanding of the term Sudden Infant Death Syndrome with increased usage since Watson's study. Several parents whose child's registered cause of death was a recognised condition (Group III) felt especially guilty, and a consistently high proportion were unhappy with the cause –

'I personally find it very difficult not to blame myself for our baby's death. I feel, given the post-mortem result bronchopneumonia, there must have been something I should have recognised.'

'I visited my doctor to ask what viral pneumonitis meant, and he told me he doubted very much if she had died from this as there were no symptoms and, anyway, the hospital had written to him that it was a cot death.'

'The registered cause of death was bronchial pneumonia, but the hospital said it was a cot death. It is distressing enough when a child dies, but the shock for parents being told one thing by the hospital and another by the Coroner is obvious.'

The causes of death which also gave concern were those (Group V) attributed to inhalation of vomit or stomach contents, especially if the parents or doctor, as frequently occurred, had attempted resuscitation at the time of finding the baby. Several parents in the category said that, although they understood the meaning of the terminology of the cause, they did not accept it as the true cause of death –

'My GP was not happy with the official cause of death, "inhalation of stomach contents", believing he introduced vomit to the lungs whilst trying to revive my baby. Certainly we would have been happier with sudden death in infancy. The official cause given implied lack of care on my part.'

'Because of the small amount of sick found in the baby's lungs the Coroner first accused us of laying the baby on his back; but not being able to uphold that, he accused us of overfeeding the baby. After discussion with the doctor present "overfeeding" could not be agreed upon and, therefore, "accidental death" was written on the certificate. We feel the whole inquest was brushed over. Is our Borough totally ignorant of cot death?'

As described earlier, many parents attempt resuscitation and cardiac massage on finding their baby apparently lifeless, and this may frequently disturb the stomach contents.

In at least 3 cases in the sample the initial cause of death was later changed as a result of representations made by parents and their doctor or paediatrician. In two cases the death was initially attributed to a heart condition, e.g. ventricular fibrillation and cardiomyopathy.

'The pathologist telephoned me 6 weeks later to say that after further tests he and our GP agreed on a revised cause of death – viral attack.'

In one case the initial cause of death was attributed to a hereditary condition. Six months later and after all the surviving members of the family had been tested for the abnormality with negative results, the consultant contacted the pathologist who retracted his initial finding and gave a revised cause of death, 'cot death syndrome'.

Chapter 20

Funerals and Administrative Problems

When a death is referred to a Coroner, either the Coroner's officer or the police arrange for an undertaker, at the Coroner's expense, to remove the body from where death has been confirmed to a mortuary for a post-mortem examination. The Coroner arranges this with a pathologist of his choice. In order to issue the correct certificates the Coroner will need a decision from the parents early on as to whether the baby is to be buried or cremated.

As soon as the post mortem is completed the Coroner can send the 'Certificate for Cremation – Form E' to the Registrar together with Pink Form B 'Notification to the Registrar that he does not consider it necessary to hold an inquest'. If parents choose burial, then the Registrar of Deaths issues the Disposal certificate for burial. If the Coroner decides to hold an inquest, at conclusion he completes a 'Certificate after Inquest' which records the medical and circumstantial causes of death, which is sent to the Registrar within 5 days of completing the inquest. The Coroner issues the 'Burial Order – Form E'/Coroner's Certificate for Cremation and may do so after opening an inquest to allow the funeral to take place. The two major problems which sudden infant death parents face in relation to the funeral are how to set about arranging it and paying for it.

Arranging the Funeral – Funeral Directors/Undertakers

Only those parents whose babies died between 1974–9 were asked in some detail about making arrangements for the funeral. Of these, 19% replied that they received no advice about how to arrange a funeral, while others sought advice from relatives (18%) or a variety of officials (Coroner's Officer/Police 19%; Minister of Religion 16%; Funeral Director 15%). As few as 4% of parents had obtained advice from the medical profession.

A few parents commented on the difficulty of having to decide so soon on burial or cremation –

'We would have liked more time to consider burial plans, as we were asked for a definite decision on the day of death.'

Some parents had been upset by the manner in which the undertakers had taken the body to the mortuary,

'I found the manner in which the baby was removed from the house very distressing and the image of her being put into what looked like a black tool box which was not quite big enough continues to haunt me. I was in the bedroom when this was done. The man did not speak a word to me from the time he entered the house to the time he left. He asked the police when he arrived where the body was. I did not employ him to take care of the funeral arrangements.'

Ninety seven percent chose different undertakers for the actual funeral. Eighteen percent selected a firm of Funeral Directors from a list shown them by the police or coroner's officer, 21% took the advice of relatives or friends, and 12% the advice of their Minister of Religion, 12% used a firm already known to the family, 10% chose the nearest and 7% the only one in the district, in 4% grandparents made and paid for funeral arrangements, in 1% the Department of Health and Social Security arranged and paid; 3% chose Funeral Directors on the advice of health professionals and the remainder chose from advertisements.

In view of the difficulties which many parents face in paying for the funeral, it was disappointing to learn that over 50% of parents received neither an estimate of the cost nor an explanation of the costs incurred

'The undertaker did not explain anything about how much it would cost and charged us for a special coffin and lots of other things that we did not ask for.'

Funerals – Minister of Religion

Over 80% of the 1974–79 sample said they had wanted a funeral service. The following comments illustrate its psychological importance –

'We wanted a funeral to say goodbye ... to make myself believe.' 'We felt tremendous relief after the service.' 'After the funeral we accepted she had really gone.'

'The funeral was distressing but a useful psychological landmark after which we could attempt to return to normal.'

Six percent of parents, however, said they would rather not have attended. Some were atheist parents who said they were embarrassed by the service. Parents in one case could not bear to go to the funeral, so the undertaker went in their place.

About 4% of parents were able to arrange a special or non-religious service.

'We decided not to have a service in church.' 'We arranged our own non-religious service.' 'We had reading and prayers at home and committal prayers at the cremation.' 'We had a family burial service at the graveside and a thanksgiving service in church.' 'The Vicar agreed to a funeral service at home as more personal and relevant for a baby.'

Two problems which several parents encountered concerned their desire to have the dead baby baptised, and ignorance about sudden infant death amongst Ministers of Religion. The following quotations illustrate these difficulties.

'We were very upset when we were arranging the funeral to find that because our baby had not been baptised, the service couldn't be held in church. However, the day before the service our minister informed us that he would break all rules and hold the service in the church, instead of by the graveside.'
'The vicar was a tower of strength. He arranged a special service of baptism for babies who died before being baptised. It gave us tremendous peace of mind to know that the baby had been officially baptised before burial.' 'The Parish Minister was unhelpful and disbelieving about sudden infant death syndrome so far as to suggest we were dabbling in black magic.'

The parents' own Minister of Religion conducted the funeral in 55% of cases: in a fifth (21%) the Minister of Religion waived his fee or donated it to charity which in view of the high cost of funerals, was a much appreciated gesture.

Amongst the parents surveyed, the Minister of Religion played an important role not only in advising about funeral arrangements, but also giving continued psychological and spiritual support. It would help the Minister if the doctor or Health Visitor liaised closely with him.

Funeral Costs

The current size of the funeral bill and speed with which it has to be paid imposes a great strain on many families. In some cases, 'The Funeral Director asked for full payment at the first interview.' Although several Funeral Directors offer a 10% discount if the bill is prepaid or settled within a few days, families in greatest need are least able to take advantage of such reductions. The financial worry and

debt incurred adds greatly to their distress at a very harrowing time.

Parents of young children are at an expensive stage of life and will have recently incurred a lot of extra expenditure for the new baby. Few parents at this stage have a large income; most have no savings, and many have no stable financial background. There is no 'charitable' source of assistance to help pay for funerals for the majority of deaths in this age group, nor are children of this age likely to be covered by an insurance policy or have any estate.

In the survey 88% of parents gave the total cost of their baby's funeral, and 35% gave details enabling mean average costs for a simple, basic funeral and other necessary disbursements to be calculated.

The average total costs paid in 1981 were £145 for a burial (excluding cost of headstone which averaged an additional £210), and £105 for a cremation, excluding cost of cremation certificate fees which are not charged in coroner's cases. Equal proportions of parents chose burial and cremation. Individual costs varied greatly. In 1981 the total cost paid varied from as little as £45 for a simple cremation to £410 for a burial; in addition 6% of parents paid for a headstone, gravestone or memorial tablet costing between £100 and £400.

A few parents resorted to a simple disposal: burial in a communal grave without the presence of the parents, the system chiefly used in the past for stillborn babies. There are no mourners, no cars, no church service and only a rough wooden coffin.

Death Grant

The death grant is related to national insurance contributions, for a child under 3 years of age it is currently only £9. This represents only 6% of the average cost of an infant's burial and 9% of a cremation. Not surprisingly, the overwhelming majority of parents (90%) criticised the death grant as grossly inadequate, describing it as 'insulting', 'derisory', 'not worth going through the trauma to collect it'.

About 5% of parents also complained of the procedure to collect it.

'We received a copy from the Registrar which is an application for a claim form. Why not just one form at such a difficult time? I'm only claiming £9 for heaven's sake and the time spent by clerks filing all this bumf must cost more than that.'

'The claim for the death grant does not indicate the amount. If we'd known it was only £9 we would not have gone through the distressing procedure for claiming it.'

'The death grant is a waste of time; it should either be abolished or be substantially more.'

'There should be some way of dealing with the D.H.S.S. other than sitting in a long queue and then having to explain everything. The clerks were tactless and constantly referred to our baby as "it", and were generally slow and unhelpful.'

'Considering the pain involved in claiming the grant, it should cover 50% of the cost or nothing.'

About 6% of parents did not claim the death grant, and another 2%, for whom relatives had registered the death and dealt with funeral arrangements, said they were unaware there was a death grant until they filled in the Foundation's questionnaire. Some self-employed parents were upset to find they were not eligible for the death grant.

Advice Leaflet

As many as 17% of parents 1974–7, 10% in 1978–9 and 5% in 1980–81 suggested that there should be a leaflet given to the parents immediately following an unexpected death giving guidance on the Coroner's procedure, registration of the death, how to set about making funeral arrangements and the legal/administrative/financial matters that may have to be attended to. Comments up to 1979 included:

'Bereaved people need advice immediately after a death to explain all that needs to be done ... I suggest some kind of leaflet giving advice about coroners, registration, funerals, cremation, etc. The legal issues could be briefly explained. The lack of knowledge amongst professionals astounds us.'

'Perhaps a leaflet could be issued by the GP or other person confirming death explaining all the procedures and the matters which have to be attended to.'

In August 1979, after consultation with various organisations concerned, the D.H.S.S. published just such a leaflet, entitled *What to do After a Death*. Some parents in the later period 1980–1 referred to this helpful pamphlet, which they had acquired when they went to register the death. Several parents commented however, that they needed the advice sooner.

Other D.H.S.S. Administrative Problems

Two further problems which numerous parents complained about concerned overstamping the Child Benefit Book and confusion over entitlement to free Dental Treatment and Prescriptions.

Child Benefit Book

Many parents were upset by having their Child Benefit Book returned with each page overstamped with the reduced amount but still with the dead baby's name on the front.

'The Child Benefit Book was returned with each token overstamped with the reduced amount and with the baby's name still on the front. I found this most disturbing as a constant reminder every time I draw the allowance.'

Other complaints concerned the length of time it took for the administration to return the book which contained the allowance for the other surviving children, during which time the mother was unable to draw any payments.

'The Child Benefit Book contained allowances for all the children and when this book had to be returned, all payments ceased. Some alternative arrangements should have been offered at once.'

Entitlement to Free Dental Treatment and Prescriptions

Six parents complained that they were charged for dental treatment following their baby's death, although this was within a year of the baby's birth.

'I was surprised that my free prescriptions and free dental treatment stopped as I was under the impression that this should continue for a year following giving birth.' 'On visiting the dentist after my baby's death, I was told that treatment was no longer free.' 'I had to pay for full dental treatment after my baby died.'

None of these mothers should have been charged for dental treatment, since the D.H.S.S. rules have always entitled mothers to free dental treatment for a year following the birth of a baby irrespective of its survival. There was confusion however, since entitlement to free drug prescriptions for a year after delivery did cease on the death of the baby. In 1981, however, the D.H.S.S. changed the rules and allowed free prescriptions to the mother for a year after giving birth in line with free dental treatment.

There had been many complaints from mothers at the withdrawal of free prescriptions, so the new rules will be welcomed.

'My wife's prescription exemption certificate had to be returned although her circumstances had not changed and she needed more medication than if the baby had lived.'

Chapter 21

Support for Parents

The death of a child is a poignant tragedy in most circumstances but the effect can be devastating and long lasting when it is neither anticipated nor understood, and parents are unable to resolve their feelings of responsibility and self-reproach. Informed support, kind explanation and counselling at this time is invaluable in helping parents to understand why their baby died and to share and work through their grief.

The Health Professionals

Sudden infant deaths however do pose problems which sometimes hinder professional support being given. The doctor and health visitor may be very distressed by the baby's death; some health professionals do not feel capable of helping in such a harrowing situation, because of their own sense of failure or fear of death. The relationship between the parents and primary care team may become 'strained', particularly if the doctor or health visitor had recently been consulted about the baby's death, since in their grief, parents may blame or vent their anger on those who had been involved with the baby.

Further difficulties arise when neither the GP, the Health Visitor or other community staff hear immediately of the death. The routine system of notification of deaths in weekly returns from the Registrar of Deaths to the Health Authority and thence to community health staff may take up to 2 weeks, or longer if an inquest is held which postpones registration of the death, or if the baby is taken to a hospital (and death confirmed) in a different district. The delay has been reported in some cases as being 2, 3 or 4 months. Even a delay of a week or more occasionally resulted in the health visitor calling on families unaware that the baby has died.

'The health visitor came to do a regular check on the baby. She was monosyllabic when told what had happened; she left and never returned.'

General Practitioner

In the survey 71% of parents in each period replied that they had been given support by their family doctor, the majority (90%) of whom had been in touch within 2 days of the baby's death. The other 29% of parents indicated that they had received inadequate support from their GP: 10% had no contact with their GP at all, a further 14% had only received help after they had told their GP of their baby's death or had made an appointment seeking his help, and a further 5% had not seen their doctor again after the baby's death had been confirmed.

Parents felt very upset at this apparent lack of interest.

'Our GP did not make any sort of contact whatsoever. We had no members of the medical or nursing profession or a health visitor call or contact us after the night of our son's death.'

When asked how support could be improved, 11% of parents praised the GP.

'Our GP came to us immediately and again after the post-mortem and told us the result and gave us an explanation about the findings. The Health Visitor arrived an hour after the baby died and stayed 4 hours, she visited every day for the next ten days and then periodically. The GP and health visitor could not have acted with more kindness and efficiency.'

'My own GP could not have been more helpful. He had attended a symposium on cot death 2–3 years ago and seemed genuinely concerned to make us understand we were not to blame and to be as open as possible with us. He visited me at home occasionally since to see how I am. He showed me the post-mortem report after it had been sent to him, although it was not for viewing by a "third party". Why is this? Surely as the child's parents we are entitled to see the post-mortem report?'

'We were fortunate in that our GP or health visitor called nearly every day, or whenever we asked them to, so we were able to resolve any feelings of guilt we had. They were constantly reassuring, answered all our questions at length and listened to all our worries.'

Most of the 29% of parents who felt they had received inadequate support from their GP made suggestions for improving support. These fall mainly into seven categories.

(a) Doctors should get in touch with the bereaved parents as soon as possible to offer support.

'I feel sure our GP would not have visited us if I had not asked him to see me. Immediate help is essential.'

(b) Doctors should not offer medication as a substitute for counselling.

'We both felt that a talk with our GP would have helped greatly. All the support he offered was a prescription for tranquillisers which we both refused to take. We have not seen him since.'

(c) Doctors should have a better understanding of grief and the likely feelings and fears of bereaved parents.

'Our doctor was very unsympathetic; he didn't want to hear any details of her death and cut off the conversation when I tried to talk about her and said in a roundabout way that cot deaths were a rather unimportant medical problem and that I should forget about her as soon as possible. I left him feeling almost despairing.'

(d) Doctors should obtain details of the post-mortem findings and be able to explain the cause of death.

'The GP should have a copy of the post-mortem report so that he could tell us exactly what was found.'

(e) Doctors should be better informed about sudden infant deaths or refer parents to those who are.

'The doctor seemed ill-equipped to deal with the questions we wanted answers to and merely said, "It's just one of those things." He had not heard of the Foundation nor read any literature on cot deaths.'

(f) Doctors should give parents information on sudden infant death, preferably in written form as soon as possible, including advice about legal procedures and arrangements for funeral. They should put parents in touch with the Foundation who can offer to put them in contact with other formerly bereaved parents.

'Any woman who loses a baby suddenly and unexpectedly should be visited as a matter of course by her doctor the following day and the doctor should give her information about the Foundation and the "Information for Parents" leaflet. I personally feel it is most important that this source of help is made immediately available, at least within 24 hours, the optimum time being the following day. I believe the longer one is left to flounder alone with overwhelming feelings of sorrow, guilt, incomprehension and fear at this stage, the longer the ultimate healing process will take.'

(g) The support from a doctor, health visitor, social worker or bereavement counsellor should be continued for as long as may be necessary.

'We desperately needed to talk about the tragedy months after it happened. The initial help we received was excellent, but the grief, bewilderment and most of all, for me, guilt, goes on.'

Health Visitors

In each period over 75% of the families surveyed had received visits from their Health Visitor after their bereavement. (In only 6 cases had the Health Visitor called unaware that the baby had died.) In a further 3% the Health Visitor had attempted unsuccessfully to give support; the mother had been out and the Health Visitor did not try to call again, the parents had moved address, or in a few cases the Health Visitor wrote but did not attempt a visit. In another 3% the Health Visitor visited after a request from the parents to do so. In 17% of cases in each period, however, the parents had no contact with a health visitor at all after their baby's death.

Like many people who have not received training in bereavement counselling there is sometimes a reluctance to visit at all or a wish to defer the visit to avoid intruding on grief.

In all 38% of mothers who had seen a Health Visitor described the visit(s) as 'very helpful' and a further 23% as 'helpful'. Only 17% said the visits were 'not helpful' and the remainder made no comment. Overall the proportion of mothers who found the visits very helpful or helpful increased over time, 40% in 1974–7 to 65% in 1980–1. However, when the evaluation is related to the interval from death to when the first visit was made, the proportion of mothers who found it very helpful or helpful was considerably higher (66%) among the 85.5% of parents who were visited within the first two weeks. When the first visit was made after 2 weeks, however, only a small proportion of visits (26%) were considered helpful or very helpful.

These trends indicate that the value of Health Visitor support is improving and that it is very important to visit early, if possible, within 24 hours of the baby's death to give practical help and emotional support, and again within a week to make an early assessment of the parents' reactions and the support they are receiving from relatives and the community.

The comments of parents, illustrated below, endorse these interpretations and include suggestions for improving the value of the Health Visitor's support; by visiting early, by being better informed about sudden infant death, by being able to answer questions and give advice and comfort, by avoiding misleading information and by helping parents with their surviving children.

Parents expressed great appreciation of good support.

'I cannot speak too highly of the health visitor. She helped a great deal when M was alive with his feeding and has been marvellous since he died coming two or three times a week. She has been so helpful, comforting and understanding.'

'The health visitor and GP were and still are wonderful. The health visitor visited every other day and usually stayed 2 hours and let me talk which was a great relief.'

Parents were upset by failure to call.

'My health visitor refused to come on the grounds of being too upset.'

'We were angered by the health visitor's failure to call, especially as we have a toddler who is as much her responsibility as I and who could have been suffering all manner of neglect as a result of our grief.'

'The health visitor called three weeks later, which was too late. She was very keen to point out that the clinic hadn't missed anything when we had been.'

'The health visitor arrived 2 days after the funeral. I finished up comforting her and showing her her "Information for Parents" leaflet as this was the first cot death for her.'

'After our baby's death we were left in limbo with no information or guidance of any kind. Our health visitor was kind but totally lacking in information, assuring us that our twin was not at any risk when we knew that this was not so and that she was at increased risk. She was unable to tell us anything about cot deaths at all.'

A few parents, particularly those whose babies had died very young turned to their Midwife for comfort as someone who knew their baby well and could give reassurance. Parents who were visited by the midwife in place of the Health Visitor were included in the proportion who were given support.

Replies from 353 parents in 1980–1 showed that 57% of parents were supported by both their GP and Health Visitor, a further 40% by either their GP or Health Visitor (or Midwife), and only 3% were not visited by either. Parents felt very abandoned and angry when no support was forthcoming.

'After our son's death no one contacted us from any of the services. We felt so alone. If it wasn't for the fact we had a daughter aged three and a wonderful family who helped us financially and morally and a wonderful brother who is a teacher who found out about cot deaths and told us the facts, we would know nothing and would not be as strong about it as we are.'

Most helpful after death

Parents were asked to indicate which persons were of most help in giving support after their child's death; more than one set of people could be indicated.

In all periods relatives, which included husband/wife and grandparents, were understandably the prime source of comfort; about 72% of parents claimed that relatives were amongst the most helpful. Close friends came next (55%). The next most valuable sources of help were the Minister of Religion (about 47%), the General Practitioner (42%) and the Health Visitor (35%), followed by neighbours (34%) and the Coroner or his officer or police (24%). Other professionals were mentioned by 16%. They included Midwives, Paediatricians, Social Workers and Funeral Directors.

These ratings differ in order from those in Inner North London, although in both surveys relatives scored highest; it is likely that the order will vary according to the nature of the district – inner city, urban, rural, and the social background of those surveyed.

There was little difference over time in these figures apart from an increase in score gained by Health Visitors from 21% in the period 1974–77 to 35% in 1978–9 and 37% in 1980–81. This illustrated the growing value parents found in their bereavement counselling.

Paediatricians did not score highly in the survey since very few parents had apparently seen a paediatrician. Of the 29 parents in 1980–1 who mentioned seeing a paediatrician, 17 (58%) indicated that he was amongst those who gave greatest support.

Paediatricians who are well informed about cot deaths can be enormously helpful as the following quotations show.

'We asked the coroner if we could talk to a paediatrician and he put us in touch. The paediatrician explained to us in detail about cot death and talked to us at length; he was very helpful and reassuring.'

'About 2 months later after our surviving twin's six month check up, my husband and I saw the consultant paediatrician who put at rest our lingering doubts about the cause of the other twin's death. This was the most useful practical conversation of all but we would have welcomed the opportunity for discussion with him earlier.'

'We wrote to the paediatrician and he came to our house and gave us as much information as he possibly could. He was marvellous but by this time three months had elapsed and our guilt had become almost unbearable. He certainly alleviated a great deal of our guilt complex.'

'I feel that much help is needed after the initial shock has gone in. We needed to discuss the baby's death and the effect it may have on future pregnancies and children with a paediatrician.'

Two parents' experiences however were not so beneficial.

'What shocked me most was the uncaring attitude of everybody from the police to the paediatrician who was supposed to put our minds at rest. The only comment or suggestion was "It's best all forgotten, go home and have another baby", which did nothing to help us understand our son's death.'

'The paediatrician was not able to help as he did not have full details of the post-mortem report.'

Parents turn to a paediatrician as someone they expect to be well informed about sudden infant deaths, who can explain the post-mortem findings in detail, help parents to understand their baby's death and discuss their anxieties about surviving and future children. Most parents are grateful to have an opportunity to talk about these aspects a few weeks after the baby's death when the shock has worn off and further questions have come to mind, but this should not take the place of immediate explanation of the post-mortem findings and registered cause of death as soon as they are known. This should be done by a GP or paediatrician. Some parents found waiting for 6 weeks or 2 months much too long; indeed one commented on the pain it caused to relive the nightmare some months later when they had begun to readjust and establish a new pattern of living.

An arrangement in some districts which works well is that the General Practitioner makes an appointment for parents to see a paediatrician a few weeks later which the parents can cancel if they do not want to keep it.

Use of tranquillisers and sedatives in bereavement

Pressures are put on doctors to prescribe, yet grief cannot be cured by drugs and may indeed become complicated or prolonged by them. From the questionnaires it became apparent that two-thirds of parents (65%) took drugs after being offered them or requesting them. A further 12% were prescribed drugs, but did not use them. Twelve percent were not offered drugs, and 11% were offered them but refused.

Of mothers who used drugs, 73% in the first period and 88% in the later period said they were of help. Thirty-three fathers in the first period and 73 in the second had also taken drugs; half and three quarters of these respectively said the drugs were of help.

When asked for how long the mothers used the drugs, 46% indicated they took them for less than one week. Thirty-four percent used them for between one week and one month after the baby's death, while 20% said that they were on drugs for more than one month –

some for several months, but the questionnaires were returned too soon to indicate for how long.

Analysis of the type of drugs prescribed in 1980–1 indicates that of the 244 prescriptions, 52% were mainly sedatives and 45% were tranquillisers.

Comments were mostly from parents who thought that taking drugs was not the best way of coping with grief and that they merely postponed the pain of grief. Several stopped taking them after one dose because they felt 'unreal and drugged'.

'We preferred not to take drugs as we did not wish to dull the sensations of pain and grief.'

'My doctor and I felt that drugs would not help; it would delay returning to normal.'

The parents who were angry at being prescribed drugs appeared to be those who were given insufficient explanation and support by their GP and who were prescribed drugs as a substitute for counselling.

'My GP was no help at all and did not explain anything. All he gave me was drugs to drug me up, and I'm still on them 3 months later.'

In 2 cases at least the mothers reported that their husbands had removed the drugs.

'The doctor gave me a large amount and my husband took them from me as he thought I might do something silly.'

'Doctors shouldn't give depressed mothers tranquillisers as they only deepen the problem. I almost took an overdose one day as I was so depressed. I just wanted to be with V. My husband came home early and threw the rest of the bottle away and forced me to be sick to bring up the pills I had taken.'

Several parents commented that they refused or stopped taking tranquillisers but were grateful for sleeping tablets to help them sleep at night. Three parents admitted that they did not take drugs but turned to drink instead.

Clinic Appointments

There was a decline over time from 12% to 5% in the proportion of parents who received clinic appointment cards for immunisation, developmental assessment or hospital follow-up for the 'deceased' child. (Here we have included only appointments arriving ten days or more after the baby's death.)

Since identification of a death relies on the Registrar's returns,

which in some circumstances can be up to 3 months after the baby's death, those health professionals initially involved should ensure that notification of the child's death is speedily passed by telephone to the Community Health department, child health clinic, hospital out-patient departments if necessary and to the Family Practitioner Committee, so that the dispatch of appointment and Medical Cards can be stopped.

Interest in the baby's prior health

A small number (3% to 4%) suggested that greater professional interest should have been taken in their baby's health prior to his death. In some cases parents wanted to give information about their baby to help find the reasons for sudden infant deaths and thus spare others the grief they had suffered.

'We felt very strongly that we wanted our experience to be put to some use. It was a great disappointment to us that never at any time has anybody shown interest in our case.'

Others felt that the baby had been 'different' and wanted to explore further what could have been wrong in order to put their minds at rest:

'No one seemed very interested in what happened prior to the baby's death. The doctor, health visitor and police all said we could have done nothing to stop it happening, but I feel he was different over the previous 24 hours.'
'I wanted someone to ask questions about my baby's health prior to death practically immediately so that any symptoms or irregularity could be remembered.'

Some were quite shocked that so little enquiry was made into the medical aspects of the baby's death.

'It is hard to accept that in this day and age, a healthy happy beautiful baby can die without a major enquiry taking place.'
'When these deaths are the mystery that they are, we cannot help but feel that as much as possible should be done to try to establish why the babies die.'

Some parents commented on the benefit of filling a questionnaire.

'It has helped us so much to read of the research being done and has eased the feeling of isolation to feel that I have done something positive just filling in the questionnaire.'

Watson has commented that taking a medical history can be a therapeutic experience when done by an experienced interviewer who is really sensitive to parental feeling and able to give support in their bereavement at the right time. Giving information, however, should not take the place of receiving support.

'I have received a letter from a clinic doctor doing research into sudden deaths who is coming to interview me tomorrow. Bearing in mind she is coming for information she could have come to help me when the baby died 4 months ago as she is from my clinic.'

Some suggestions for Counselling

The counsellor's role is to be the compassionate listener whom the parents trust and who is sufficiently knowledgeable about babies and bereavement to answer questions about the cause of death, give reassurance on many aspects of infant care, and to help the family express and share their grief. Before supporting others, a counsellor will need to have thought through and come to terms with her own attitudes to death.

Explanation of cause of death: Many parents find it difficult to accept their baby's death when they do not know how or why it died. They need an explanation for themselves and to give relatives and neighbours. If, however, the baby was found to have a recognisable disease that can be fatal, such as pneumonia, the parents may be distraught that they failed to obtain effective treatment in time. It can be explained that an infection can overwhelm a baby very rapidly. Parents are often relieved to hear that sudden infant death is a recognised medical problem in many parts of the world and that such deaths have occurred to the children of nurses, doctors and paediatricians and in hospitals and children's homes.

Many parents decide for themselves what caused death and have a deep fear they allowed the baby to suffocate; they may have had theories suggested by friends or press reports; by being asked to describe all that happened and what she feels a mother can express her fears and misconceptions can be dispelled.

Reassurance concerning blame and guilt needs to be given in the presence of both parents and anyone else caring for the baby; a babysitter, childminder or grandparents may need separate counselling as well. It may be helpful to mention that parents often blame themselves and sometimes each other, thus giving the family a chance to reveal or deny such feelings. The counsellor should be prepared for expressions of anger and bitterness directed towards the medical or nursing profession and recognise these as signs of normal grieving and not necessarily calling into question their competence.

Many parents are frightened by the intensity of their emotions and have unrealistic expectations of how soon each will recover. While people need privacy and time to grieve on their own, most mothers sooner or later feel an urge to talk repeatedly about the baby and need

to work through their grief long after other members of the family have come to terms with the death. A father often tries to repress his emotions sometimes to the extent of refusing to talk about the baby. He can become frustrated at his inability to console the mother who may be upset at his apparent lack of caring. The counsellor can help parents to understand that people grieve in different ways and for different lengths of time.

A comforter may want to cry too; this is natural and there is nothing wrong with sharing sorrow so long as the comforter remains a source of strength and does not lose control.

Parents may require guidance on the emotional needs of siblings or want to meet someone else who has come through a similar loss. These needs are considered in a later section.

All parents fear the tragedy recurring to future children. Although sudden infant deaths have been known to recur in a family, it is very rare. If parents ask, it is important to give reassurance while not misleading them: the experience in Britain is that of every 500 subsequent babies born, at least 496 will happily survive. The risk of recurrence is no greater than the risk of having a stillborn child in the general population. It is helpful where possible to reassure parents that the post-mortem findings did not reveal any hereditary cause but that they deserve special attention with the next pregnancy and child.

The next baby needs to be regarded as a new personality and not a replacement, so it is advisable for parents to complete mourning the child who has died before embarking on another pregnancy. Some parents want another baby straight away; others fear they are going to be advised not to have any more children and some sadly are too frightened to try. The topic can be helpfully discussed and guidance given, and then the timing of future children left to parental choice unless there are medical considerations. Special help will be needed for parents who have been voluntarily sterilised and for those few mothers who are already pregnant and whose grieving may be suspended until after the subsequent baby's birth. The counsellor should look out for avoidance of mourning, prolonged grief or a delayed reaction. Bereavement may revive memories of previous loss or emotional crises which were inadequately resolved. There may be special difficulties for adoptive or foster parents, where the natural parents may need counselling too, as do emotionally isolated parents and unmarried mothers. The prolonged help of a clergyman, social worker or psychiatrist may be necessary.

Bereaved persons cannot be rushed into recovery and many parents appreciate the continued support of their health visitor, clergyman or befriender over a long time. Sometimes however it is necessary to give

parents permission to stop grieving. Intense grieving after the death of a baby is likely to last several months and may recur throughout the first year and especially at anniversaries of the baby's birth and death. Many mothers say that it takes six or seven years before they can recall the loss without pain.

The aim of counselling is to help parents understand their baby's death, identify their fears and misconceptions, share and work through their grief until they can come to terms with their loss and face the future with confidence again.

Difficulties experienced by parents in telling others of their baby's death

Parents were asked whether they found any special difficulties in telling others of their baby's death and whether other people's reactions were understanding.

About a third of parents in each period said they found it very difficult to tell others. The three most common difficulties mentioned were because they did not understand why the baby had died (several said they gave other people copies of the Foundation's 'Information for Parents' leaflet to explain); because they felt guilty and bitter about the death; and because they felt confused by the registered cause of death. For example,

> 'We tell people it was a cot death and not that the death certificate says pneumonia/bronchitis. People would think he was ill and I had not looked after him.'

Two parents said they found it particularly difficult because a previous child had also died.

Comments from other parents were that although it was not especially difficult it was very painful telling others, or that it became more difficult as time went on; some parents felt a compulsion to talk and others said that by telling other people they were able to convince themselves of the tragedy.

Society's reaction to a cot death

Parents were asked whether they thought other people's reaction was one of understanding. There was substantial change over time. For deaths in the period 1974–77 only 19% were able to reply 'yes', compared with 48% of parents in the period 1978–9 and 76% in 1980–1. These figures presumably reflect the publicity and public education that have taken place over the past decade. Although the proportion of parents who encountered problems or found the reaction hurtful fell from 42% in 1974–7 to only 13.6% in 1980–1, it was noticeable that the problems which arose through not

understanding what sudden infant death or cot death was, or from misconceptions about possible causes, were chiefly amongst the grandparental generation or single people.

The following are examples of the kind of reaction which parents considered hurtful or not understanding listed in order of the frequency with which they were mentioned – never heard of cot death; did not understand what a cot death was; could not accept that no reason for the death was found; thought cot death was due to suffocation/smothering or choking; embarrassment, acting as if nothing had happened; avoiding or ignoring the parents; pretending the baby never existed; refusing to talk about the baby; tactless remarks implying the mother had been negligent; malicious gossip that the parents had 'murdered the baby'; fearing that it might happen to them.

Other hurtful attitudes mentioned by a few parents included; that to have another baby would solve everything; denial of the loss of the twin 'at least you've got one left'; being told to forget the baby; the assumption that cot deaths were due to young inexperienced mothers living in poor social conditions; that a cot death meant that something was wrong with the make of the cot or the manner of putting the baby into it; expecting the bereaved parents to support them.

The following quotations from parents illustrate the reaction.

'I have been particularly hurt by some people's reaction in that they avoid me or say "hello" and rush past. I realise that this is due mainly to embarrassment on their part; but if more publicity was given about SIDS I feel sure people would be less worried about seeing me.'

'The worst are people who will not let you talk and try to shut you up or ignore you at the mention of anything to do with C.'

'The problem I found was that people seemed oblivious to sudden death in infancy. I knew it existed but I suppose it is one of those things that you think will never happen to you. Several people said silly things like "Well, babies choke easily", "their covers soon go over their faces" and "they suffocate"; and someone even said to me that at least I still have two healthy children. It annoys me that people should think that just because S was only 10 weeks old we should get over his death as if we had only lost a £5 note or something.

'My vicar's wife told me that when they lost their baby twenty years ago in similar circumstances – the baby had seemed quite healthy – the Coroner had asked her whether she had suffocated the baby.'

'A lot thought that cot deaths meant strangulation or suffocation or choking on vomit. We wanted everyone to know that there was nothing we could have done.'

Changes in Family Circumstances

The Foundation survey asked parents what changes in family circumstances associated with the cot death bereavement they had made, if any.

The proportion who stated they had made no changes in their family circumstances as a result of the baby's death rose slightly over the two periods from 32% in 1974-9 to 40% in 1980-1. Analysis of the 1980-1 replies indicates that 40% made one change, 16% two changes, 2% three changes and one family indicated 4 changes.

The most frequent change noted was the mother's return to work or a part-time job, 33% in each period; the next two most common changes were moving house 23% in 1974-9 and 15.5% in 1980-1 and planning another pregnancy 9% in each period. The number who changed their doctor (as a consequence of cot death and not the house move) was about 5% in each period. Other changes made by between 2.5% and 5% of parents in each period included the father changing his job, moving furniture or redecorating, or a pre-planned house move which helped.

Other consequences which a few parents commented on were that their marriage had suffered or broken up, or the father had lost his job because he had taken time off to comfort his distraught wife, the employer having refused compassionate leave. Another distressing problem mentioned by 5 couples, was the need for reversal of sterilisation which had usually been performed shortly after the baby's birth a few weeks or months previously.

Some parents have later attributed the failure of their marriage and the need to make other changes to their inability to grieve properly over the baby's death.

'My marriage broke up after 18 months. I met another man, moved house, and changed my doctor. If I had grieved at the time I would not be in this state of depression now.'

Information for Parents

The parents were asked whether, when and by whom they were given the leaflet, 'Information for Parents Following the Sudden and unexpected Death of their Baby'. By definition, of course, all parents in this study had contacted the Foundation.

Although the questionnaires were returned to the Foundation anonymously it is possible for there to be a bias in commenting on the value of the leaflet, nevertheless over 92% in 1974-7 and over 95% subsequently replied that the leaflet had been helpful or very helpful.

While over 60% of parents received the leaflet within a week of the

baby's death, it is disheartening that even in 1980–1 over a third of parents received the leaflet from the Foundation or another voluntary organisation which they had had to contact themselves. Several parents commented how distressed they were to learn later that their doctor or Health Visitor had had the leaflet at the time of the baby's death but had not given it to the parents.

'Months later my health visitor told me she did have a leaflet, but did not like to give it to us as she did not think it would be helpful.'

Many parents commented on how helpful the leaflet had been not only for themselves to refer to repeatedly but also to show to relatives and friends as an explanation of the baby's death. Many however asked that the leaflet should be given to parents sooner.

'It was very important and reassuring to have an explanation of cot death in print for us, our family and friends.'

'We found the Foundation's information pamphlet very useful, but it should reach parents immediately.'

'I just wish we had been given the leaflet at the time of death.'

'The most important facet of all we have gone through was receiving the information from the Foundation without which I would have been in a more confused, distraught and guilty frame of mind. I cannot express how beneficial it was to me.'

'I cannot begin to tell you how much the leaflet meant to us both. We kept reading it and referring to it time and time again, and still do.'

A few parents commented however that they were given the Health Education Council leaflet 'The loss of your Baby' written for parents following a stillbirth or neonatal death, which 'obviously was not much help' or 'was of no use or help'. It is important that health professionals take care to give the appropriate information.

Local Support Groups

Many parents suggested that they should have been told about or put in touch with the Foundation or with a local parent support group who offer support from formerly bereaved sudden infant death parents. Many parents wanted to be able to talk to other parents who had experienced a cot death.

'Since I have made contact with your Foundation I have begun to come to terms with his death.'

'We feel the main thing is to make parents aware of the Foundation so they realise they are not alone.'

'My wife and I both feel that we needed the help of someone who actually knew what it was like to lose a baby or child as soon as possible.'

'I found a visit by a parent who had experienced a cot death to be one of the most beneficial visits. She knew how I felt and I could look at her and think, she has come through it.'

'We wish someone from the Foundation could have got on to us the first or second day while the families were gathered together.'

'There should be more liaison between the Foundation and every hospital. Having left the hospital knowing my child was dead, there was no one to comfort my husband and me.'

The Foundation's Role in Supporting Parents

Between five and six hundred new cot death families a year contact the Foundation's office. Parents will find the Foundation's address on the leaflet 'Information for Parents following the Sudden and Unexpected Death of their Baby' which it is hoped they will have been given by the coroner, coroner's officer, police, GP, Health Visitor or Accident and Emergency Department.

Newly bereaved parents telephone, write to, or visit the office. Sometimes they telephone within hours of finding the baby dead; more usually contact is made days or weeks later. A few are so stunned or distressed they want someone to talk to them; others are desperate or grateful for a sympathetic listener. Many want to know about cot deaths and research, while a few express feelings of anger at their baby's death.

The Foundation's role is to respond to each individual's need, to be prepared to listen, to ask about the baby and what happened, and to be able to give explanation, reassurance, counsel or advice in answer to a wide variety of questions.

The Foundation writes to all parents personally enclosing further copies if needed of the 'Information for Parents' leaflet and copies of the twice-yearly Newsletters commenting on research findings. Those who want further detailed information are referred to appropriate articles or books.

Many parents are keen to give information to help research and the Foundation invites them to complete a medical/epidemiological questionnaire enquiring into the history of the pregnancy and health of the baby and family. The Foundation also offers to put parents in touch with formerly bereaved parents or support groups, Friends of the Foundation, who offer an individual befriending service. Over half accept this offer at once or a few months later. Befrienders provide

empathy, credibility, unlimited time, an opportunity to share tumultuous emotions, reassurance that reactions are 'normal' and hope for recovery. The Foundation would hesitate to ask any parent to befriend others until at least a year has elapsed since their own tragedy and would take care in selection and matching. The befriender has to be a source of emotional strength. Many Friends of the Foundation are active also in disseminating information locally about sudden infant deaths and raising funds for the Foundation's research programme. Such constructive outlets can help mothers and fathers overcome their frustration by doing something positive in memory of their child, and by taking part in community activities again, can break down the sense of isolation that surrounds many bereaved people.

The Foundation also sometimes assists in obtaining, through their GP, further professional help from a paediatrician, a psychiatrist or child psychologist. An increasing proportion of time is spent in giving reassurance and advice to parents expecting or caring for a subsequent baby. The Foundation has published a leaflet, 'Your Next Child', describing commonly felt anxieties, and the green card 'When to Consult a Doctor About Your Baby', designed to help parents identify potentially serious symptoms of illness, which is welcomed by many as practical advice which any new mother is reassured to have.

Chapter 22

Children's Reactions to Death

Children, like adults, vary widely in their reactions to death, but even very young children are likely to be upset at the loss of a baby and by their parents' distress. A child's temperament and his relationship to the baby as well as to his parents will influence the way he reacts. Parents may be so desolated by their grief that they find it difficult to comprehend their other children's needs. It is important for them to listen to and observe their other children who may express their feelings vocally and/or in behaviour. It may be helpful to understand how children's perceptions of death change with age.

Babies are mostly affected by their parents' emotional state and mood, although a twin is likely to miss the other. Toddlers, 1–3 years, cannot understand the permanence of death; they may be puzzled by the baby's disappearance and ask repeatedly about his coming back. Since they do not easily distinguish fact from fantasy, they may believe they were responsible in some way, especially if they tried to wake the baby or are accused of having done something to the infant. They may also be upset by their parents' lack of interest in them and may regard it as rejection, and may revert to infantile behaviour to attract attention. Toddlers and even older children may express their feelings through play.

Pre-school children, 3–5 years, will still ask about the baby's whereabouts and when he will return. Some may still think of death as temporary and reversible. At this age of magical thinking, children believe that their thoughts and wishes influence events and they might be frightened and remorseful at perhaps having been jealous or angry at the baby's arrival or having wished the dead baby would go away or was 'dead'. Their parents' preoccupation with the dead baby may be perceived as confirmation of their guilt. Upset by their parents' grief, they may try to comfort their parents in the same way that they have been previously comforted. Children of this age are perhaps the most

vulnerable. The memory of the events will be lost but the memory of their feelings may remain subconciously and re-emerge on a future occasion of loss or grief. Those who are able to act out their feelings in play or even in difficult behaviour may be more fortunate than those who become very good or withdrawn. The former are more likely to receive parental or professional attention for their distress.

Primary school children from the age of 6 onwards are beginning to understand the permanence of death. Intelligent children or those who have experienced the death of someone close or of a pet may understand at a younger age. Children aged between 6 and 8 may try to sort out their ideas by playing at funerals or organising elaborate burials of any small dead animal or pet in the garden. Children of this age benefit from taking part in a family mourning, since the fantasy is often more frightening than reality. Some children may not show how upset they are; they may find the pain too great and repress their feelings. There is a danger of interpreting their apparent lack of feeling as callousness. This way of reacting needs to be recognised since these children are liable to be overwhelmed by grief over some minor incident later on.

From 9 to 10 years old the irreversibility of death begins to be grasped and children realise they too will die some day. By the age of 11, a child usually perceives the finality of death in an adult way. Teenagers search for the meanings or value of their own lives and the life that has gone.

Problems with Surviving Children

The Foundation questionnaire asked parents if their other children had any grief problems.

In 537 families in the sample, there were surviving children, the majority of whom were aged between 1 and 11 years. There were a few families with teenagers or adult step-children and one family whose 16 month old son died unexpectedly 12 weeks after their infant daughter was born.

Over 60% of these families in 1974–9 and 50% of 1980–1 replied that they had problems with their surviving children's grief reactions although most of these were of short duration. The others commented that no problems arose or that their children showed the expected sorrow but adjusted well.

Problems reported in toddlers were mostly behavioural expressions of loss and insecurity, and included reversion to infantile behaviour and baby talk, regression in toilet training, nightmares, insomnia,

refusal to be left alone; they needed extra love, cuddling and reassurance that they too would not disappear. Some of the very young one and two year olds repeatedly searched for the baby, while some of the 2–4 year olds acted out the tragedy, sometimes with their toys. One nearly 3 year old rejected her favourite teddy bear saying it was 'dead' and never played with it again.

Some of the 3 to 5 year olds were fearful that all babies would die or that they would suddenly disappear or that their parents would go away. This resulted in the child being unwilling to let his parents go out of his sight.

'Since Q died our other son who is 4½ won't leave me alone. He follows me from room to room and has started to come into our bed in the middle of the night. For the first time in 2 years he won't go to playgroup. He told me he wanted to stay at home to look after me.'

A few of the 3 to 7 year olds became aggressive and naughty or cheeky.

Some children became severely withdrawn. One 2 year old sister was in the bedroom when the baby was found.

'For the next 4 days including the funeral she was well behaved but very quiet and would not talk about her brother. On the fifth day after 16 hours' sleep, she was still comatose and hardly responding. She was admitted to hospital for 2 days' observation; with nothing physically wrong, her condition was attributed to reaction. After this she started to talk about her brother.'

Others talked out their grief.

'Our 4 year old kept running up to people, even ones we didn't know, and telling them that her baby brother had died, usually adding that he had been squashed. This continued until our GP had a very kind but firm word with her.'

Amongst primary school age children the sort of problems reported were that their school work suffered, that they were frightened to ask questions; some would only talk to outsiders and would ask them questions, while others would not talk about the tragedy to anyone outside the immediate family.

Some of the more difficult problems seemed to arise when the parents delayed telling the siblings that the baby had died or would not come back, when the sibling had shared the baby's room, been present when the baby was found or had accompanied it to the Accident and Emergency Department. Some young children refused to let their mothers do things for them or comfort them, or developed phobias about doctors and hospitals.

'Our daughter, who was 19 months at the time, woke with night terrors and wanted to know where the baby was. She would refuse to have me comfort her. I believe this was because she saw me rush off with R. and not bring him back. For up to six weeks after, she used to tell me he was crying. We are only now after six months getting to grips with each other again. On my part, I felt I withdrew emotionally from her, being afraid to love her too much.'

Five families commented that they helped their children by taking them to see the baby again.

'We took our five year-old to the Chapel of Rest where he kissed the baby.'
'Our 8 year-old daughter was very frightened at the time about burial or cremation and had horrifying ideas about putting S. in the ground. We asked her if she would like to see her sister. After first refusing violently because she thought she would look horrible, she changed her mind and came with us. It was a very refreshing experience; she talked to S. as she had always done. It helped her greatly and cured her horrific ideas of death as it was such a beautiful sight and a lasting memory for her. We parents also found great solace in going to see S. It helped greatly in the week between the death and the funeral.'

Fifteen parents (3% of those with other children) described severe physical grief reactions such as the development or worsening of asthma, eczema, hay fever, nervous dermatitis or rash, psoriasis, or stammering which persisted for several months. One 9 year-old developed phobic reactions (obsessive handwashing) 3 months after the death.

'Our 12 year-old developed eczema all over his face and a nervous cough, our 5 year-old suffered delayed shock, chest trouble and had an epileptic fit for the first time, our 3 year-old screamed at playgroup and cried for the baby every day. The trauma on the family is terrible.'

More than half the mothers of twins commented on difficulties with the surviving twin, some as young as 8 weeks old. Reactions included being very unsettled for a few weeks, losing weight, and in one 24 week old twin not sleeping at all for the ensuing 48 hours. Some twins had problems adjusting to the excess of breast milk; two mothers said they found it very difficult to nurse the surviving twin for a day or two.

'I feel that people undergoing bereavement for the first time need additional help. Having C. the twin to look after wasn't really a comfort. I was terrified to do anything for her and felt very inadequate and I don't think anyone appreciated I would feel that way. Also C. was the small baby at birth and we had worried a lot about her, but D. was so well we hadn't worried over her. I felt guilty that I had been concerned for the wrong baby. I feel very strongly that having twins you have no time to adjust before

having another baby. Others thought that having the twin would help. It does now, but for the first couple of weeks it just adds to the strain.'

Two parents appeared to be helped by having the surviving twin admitted to hospital for observation for a few days.

Twelve parents commented that their grief caused problems in relating to their surviving children.

'At first I did not want anything to do with my other daughter aged 3.' 'I tended to resent my other daughter (aged 2) for a short while.' 'I did not want to handle my other baby (3 months) at first. I felt she, who was younger, should have died and not my older son (aged 16 months). My husband, however, was very protective, bringing the baby into our room at night.'

A few parents commented that they sought help from their Child Guidance Clinic with persisting problems. Many sought the help of their GP or Health Visitor; and several who had not been visited by their Health Visitor felt that she ought to have called for the sake of the toddler alone. 'I think more care should be made either by the GP or Health Visitor that any surviving children are not suffering. I found it very hard, and still do, to cope with my little girl (18 months). At first I did not want to be bothered even to change her nappy. Now it only happens occasionally when she gets on my nerves.'

Suggestions for Helping Other Children After a Baby's Death

If parents find it difficult to give time to their other children, they should ensure that someone whom the child knows or a professional person experienced in helping distressed children is available for the child to talk to about his feelings or to help the child understand these through play. It is easier for a child to talk if the parents talk both between themselves and also with their children.

Though it may be tempting to send children away to protect them from the distress, this is likely to be perceived by the child as 'rejection', so if it is at all possible children should remain with their parents.

The question is often asked whether children should go to the funeral. In general it is better that they do, although parents usually know best what is right for their child. If children of 6 or over want to go to a funeral, parents should be encouraged to let them go. The service may be a great help to them.

Parents sometimes ask what to tell their children. If parents don't know what they believe about death, it is better for them to be honest and to say that 'we don't really know'. The role of the professional is not to tell parents what to say but to help them sort out what they

think. It is wise for parents to avoid giving an explanation in which they do not believe themselves, and sensible to avoid those which may create more confusion, guilt and fear; for example, to say that 'to die is to go to sleep and not wake up' may cause sleeping problems in a young child. Children need to be told the truth in a way suited to their age and level of comprehension.

A few children will become difficult; it is their way of expressing their feelings. They may become 'good' or withdrawn, indicating they are finding it difficult to express their feelings. Parents are welcome and should be encouraged to make use of a child guidance clinic: it is better to seek help, if needed, early on. Often just a few visits enable the family to talk more easily.

Parents should be encouraged to talk about the baby who has died and to share their sorrow with their surviving children, without burdening them with unrealistic expectations and concerns. They must take care that, in their tendency to idealise the dead baby, they do not make their other children feel inadequate. 'It is always difficult to compete with a little angel': if the dead baby is seen as too wonderful, the other children may feel it is hopeless to try to keep up with it.

It is very important to recognise that children grieve, although they may express their feelings in a wide variety of ways. Some may find it very difficult to cope with the pain of their feelings. By watching children and listening to them, parents can better understand and respond to their individual needs, and can encourage them to share their feelings within the family.

Part V

The Way Ahead?

Chapter 23

Prediction

Given strong epidemiological patterns, such as those demonstrated by sudden infant deaths, it is possible to assess the risk that any particular child should die in this way. This might be of use in allaying the fears of parents or doctors, or it can be employed to identify a group of infants at relatively high risk, for research or intervention purposes. There are two methods of scoring for risk: that known as the Sheffield Multistage Scoring System, and our own system published here for the first time.

The Sheffield Multistage Scoring System

The first version of this scoring system was published in 1974 by Carpenter and Emery, based on the results of a retrospective survey by Protestos and his colleagues. They had compared factors related to 94 sudden infant deaths with 135 control infants, and produced a set of scores based on factors identifiable at birth. Later, with a larger series of deaths (195), these scores were refined, and further factors which could be identified by the health visitor in her first visit were added. The scores are shown in Table 16 below.

Although all these items of information should be available at the time when the infant is discharged from maternity hospital, the last four items of information were only collected in Sheffield, when the infant was one month of age. Carpenter and his colleagues have therefore considered the score as taking place in two stages. In essence, they state that any infant scoring 754 or more points is at 'high-risk', one scoring between 600 and 753 points is at 'medium risk', and an infant scoring less than 600 points is at 'low risk'. The authors also suggest that medium risk infants should become high risk if they are admitted to hospital at any time, but low-risk infants do not become high-risk if admitted to hospital.

Table 16

The Sheffield Multistage Scoring System (from Carpenter et al, 1977).

ITEM	SCORE
Mother's age	$10 \times (50 - \text{age in years})$
Previous pregnancies .... none 0	
one 21	
two 43	
three 64	
four 85	
five 107	
six 128	
seven 149	
eight 171	
nine+ 192	
Duration of second stage of labour <5min 127	
5–14min 100	
15–29min 72	
30min–2hr 45	
>2hr 18	
NA/NK 76	
Mother's blood group .... O, B, AB 44	
A 0	
Birthweight .... <2000g 93	
2000–2499g 78	
2500–2999g 62	
3000–3499g 47	
3500–3999g 31	
4000–4499g 16	
4500–5500g 0	
Twin 103	
Feeding intention .... Breast only 0	
Other 38	
Urinary infection in pregnancy 54	
Cyanotic/apneoic attacks in maternity hospital 237	
Difficulty in establishing feeds .... Yes 83	
No 0	
NK 36	
State of repair of home .... Excellent 9	
Good 43	
Average 78	
Fair 112	
Poor 147	
Interval from last live birth....	
– if less than 100 months	$2 \times (100 - \text{no. months})$
– if 100 months or more 0	
– if no previous livebirth 128	

(scores to be added together)

There are several defects in this scoring system as applied to the generally recognised sudden infant death since the scores were developed in relation to all deaths that occurred unexpectedly, the only cases excluded being due to congenital malformations – in other words, deaths for which a positive cause had been identified were included. It is not easy to ascertain how much bias might be introduced. Certainly there are factors in the score for which we have shown in earlier chapters that there is little justification. These include the mother's blood group, and the length of the second stage of labour. It can also be seen from the results, that the authors have assumed that associations are always linear. Thus, with mother's age, the score assumes that the difference in risk between infants of mothers aged 32 and 37 is of the same order as that found between mothers aged 17 and 22. The evidence produced earlier shows that that is unlikely to be true. Similar assumptions are made in regard to birth order, birthweight and grouped lengths of the second stage of labour.

The justification for any scoring system, however, lies in its ability to predict, and for this purpose one needs to use a different set of cases from those used to develop the score. The Sheffield system has now been used on a variety of different places including Southampton, Birmingham, Newcastle-upon-Tyne and Sheffield itself. In general the scoring system will identify about half of the sudden infant deaths as being at high risk, but will find approximately a quarter of all births as having been in this category. In other words, in an area with 6000 livebirths a year, 1500 would be considered at high risk. Seven of the 14 sudden infant deaths would have been in the high-risk group.

Use of Relative Risks

Another method of scoring involves the use of the relative risks that were first described in Chapter 6. A relative risk of 1 implies a risk that is average for the population. In developing a scoring system, it seemed to us to be important to concentrate on those factors for which there is strong epidemiological evidence, confirmed by two or more studies in different areas. The factors and their scores are listed in Table 17. Scores should be multiplied together to give an estimate of the composite relative risk.

We present below two examples, in order to show how the scoring system should be used, and how the results may be interpreted.

Example A   Mr and Mrs Jones are of social class III (he is a car mechanic), and are both in their early twenties. This was their first baby. The pregnancy had been uneventful, apart from a bout of 'flu in the first month. Mrs Jones smoked about 15 cigarettes a day. Their

Table 17

Relative risks to be used multiplicatively to create a score.

HUSBAND'S SOCIAL CLASS:

I & II	0.7
III	0.8
IV	1.1
V	1.9
Other	1.6
No husband	2.3

MOTHER'S AGE	BIRTH ORDER	
<20	1st	1.3
	2nd	2.9
	3rd+	7.0
20–24	1st	0.8
	2nd	1.3
	3rd	1.8
	4th+	3.0
25–29	1st	0.3
	2nd	0.6
	3rd	1.0
	4th+	1.4
30+	1st	0.2
	2nd	0.4
	3rd	0.6
	4th+	0.9

INTERVAL FROM LAST PREGNANCY TO THIS CONCEPTION

Less than 6 months	2.0
6 months or more	0.8
No previous preg.	1.0

DATE OF L.M.P.

Known by mother	0.9
Not known	1.9

SMOKED DURING PREGNANCY

None	0.6
1–19 per day	1.3
20 or more	2.6

INFECTION DURING PREGNANCY

Yes	2.0
No	0.9

MATERNAL DRUG ADDICTION

Yes	5.0

MOTHER TOOK BARBITURATES

Yes	2.5

MONTH OF DELIVERY

March–June	0.8
July	0.9
Aug–Dec	1.2
Jan–Feb	1.0

SEX OF INFANT

Boy	1.1
Girl	0.9

GESTATION

<35 wk	3.9
36 wk	2.1
37 wk+	0.9

BIRTHWEIGHT

<2500g	1.9
2500–2999g	1.2
3000g+	0.8

MULTIPLE BIRTHS

Singleton	1.0
Twin	2.7
Triplet	5.7

CONGENITAL DEFECT PRESENT

Yes	2.0

PREVIOUS SUDDEN INFANT DEATH

Yes	3.0

baby boy was delivered in August after a gestation of 36 weeks. He weighed 2650g.

The scores to be multiplied together are as follows:

0.8 (social class III)
0.8 (1st baby to mother aged 20–24)
2.0 (infection in pregnancy)
1.3 (mother smoked 1–19 cigarettes a day)
1.1 (boy)
2.1 (gestation 36 weeks)
1.2 (birthweight 2500–2999g)

Multiplying these scores together gives a composite score of 4.6. This implies that Baby Jones is over 4 times the risk of sudden infant death as compared with the other babies in the population.

This can be made more realistic by calculating the daily risk that he incurs during his first year of life. In Table 3, on page 33, we listed the risk to an infant of risk 1.0 in a population where the incidence was about 2.5 per 1000 (i.e. similar to that found in most English speaking areas). A baby with relative risk 4.6 would have a greater daily risk of death, and this can be calculated by dividing the figures on the right of Table 3 by 4.6. Thus the risk to baby Jones in the first four weeks of life will be 1 in 35,826 per day, and for the next four weeks they will be 1 in 17,913. In other words, even when the infant has such a high relative risk, no betting man would dream of laying odds on a sudden infant death occurring. The risk is still exceptionally small.

Example B   Jane Gordon's fiancé was killed in a car crash during the early part of her pregnancy. She had never smoked. She was 28 years old when she gave birth to this her third child. There was a gap of four years between this and her previous children. She was not sure of the date of her last menstrual period and she gave birth to a girl weighing 3,250g in March.

The scores to be multiplied together are as follows:

2.3 (no husband)
1.0 (aged 25–29, 3rd baby)
0.8 (6 months+ since last pregnancy)
0.6 (non-smoker)
1.9 (date of LMP not known)
0.8 (March birth)
0.9 (girl)
0.8 (birthweight 3000g+)

Multiplying these scores together gives a composite score of 1.2. Thus

baby Gordon's risk of sudden infant death is only slightly above the average.

The advantage of a scoring system of this type is that it can be added to when further risk factors are identified. Nevertheless it should be remembered that no risk assessment system is perfect. The system will give an estimate of the chances. The scoring system described above has now been tested on a different population base from that from which the various scores were derived. Analysis of the 33 sudden infant deaths in the 1970 British cohort study showed that 70% had a score of two or more, compared with 43% of 46 explained deaths and 18% of 313 random controls (giving a sensitivity of 70% and specificity of 82%). This may be compared with the validations of the Sheffield score by Oakley and Harris and their colleagues where the sensitivity was between 45 and 60% and the specificity was between 67 and 86%. (Generally, risk assessments aim to obtain simultaneously the highest possible sensitivity and specificity.) We should be interested to hear from anyone else with information who could work out the relative risks both for infants who actually died and for a random sample of the population at risk. In this way, one can test the feasibility of using the system.

As we pointed out at the start of this chapter, a scoring system is only of interest if it can be used. There is an implied assumption in most treatises on risk assessment that identification of high risk infants will assist in the prevention of the condition. But are there ways of preventing sudden infant death? This is a topic which raises much argument and which we shall endeavour to address in the next chapter.

Chapter 24

Prevention

Introduction

There are several different lines of approach to assess whether sudden infant death may be preventable but bald assertion does not hold a place in scientific argument. For example, there have been publications which have implied that an adverse social or medical factor present in the history of the infant may have been responsible for the death. They have assumed that such deaths are therefore preventable. They may, of course, be right, but their argument is not convincing. We have pointed out the fallacy in such a method throughout this book.

In this chapter, we shall examine the more specific claims that have been made for methods of prevention and discuss clues from epidemiological studies.

Primary Prevention – Epidemiological Evidence

It has been pointed out before that a statistical association does not prove causation. We have listed in Table 17 on page 193 the factors that are epidemiologically associated with sudden infant death. It is obvious that some of the factors could be eliminated – but that does not mean that the incidence of sudden infant death would decrease. For example, one could suggest that no woman should conceive again within 6 months of her previous delivery – or that no woman should smoke. Either may reduce the numbers of sudden infant deaths, but it is also feasible that such measures would make no difference – the original associations may have indicated that the *temperament* or *knowledge* of the mother who conceived rapidly or of the mother who smoked was the factor that was really associated with the elevated risk of sudden infant death.

Nevertheless, given the epidemiological clues that are available, can

we afford to ignore them on the grounds that they might not be as straightforward as they would initially appear? Decisions should weigh the possible harm that might be done against the potential benefits.

Legislation is not possible, but health education could make some progress. From the figures available it would seem possible that the numbers of sudden infant deaths could be reduced if:

(a) Mothers did not smoke, either during the pregnancy or after the child was born.

(b) Women postponed child-bearing until the age of 25 or so.

(c) Family planning methods were used so that conceptions did not follow too rapidly upon one another.

(d) The dangers to their children of their own drug addiction were impressed upon young women.

If these factors really did have a causative role to play, the incidence of sudden infant death would be reduced to 40% of the current rate by using these simple measures.

Secondary Prevention – Appreciation of the child's symptoms

The difficulties in assessing whether sudden infant deaths have symptoms prior to death which could have alerted the health team and the parents have been stressed. Certainly, after the event, parents will recall slight alterations in behaviour, and minor symptoms, but all young infants tend to have frequent changes in temperament and abnormal symptoms. This was brought to the fore in a study carried out by Jane Pattison and her colleagues in Newcastle-upon-Tyne. They persuaded 44 mothers to keep a health diary for eight weeks for their normal young infants. On average, symptoms were present on 75% of the days covered, for each baby!

Whether or not there are abnormal signs or symptoms prior to the true sudden infant death as opposed to the death for which there is a medical explanation must remain moot. Nevertheless, there is an argument for:

1. Trying to indicate to mothers exactly what symptoms in babies should be taken seriously.

2. Making access easier to the primary health care services for mothers of babies who develop symptoms and are within the sudden infant death age band.

3. Indicating to general practitioners that children falling within this age group should be kept constantly under review whilst they have symptoms.

The Foundation has produced a set of recommendations which are reproduced below:

— SOME SUGGESTIONS —
WHEN TO CONSULT A DOCTOR ABOUT YOUR BABY

* *IF YOU THINK your baby is ill even without any obvious symptoms CONTACT YOUR DOCTOR*
* *IF YOUR BABY shows any of the following symptoms especially if he has more than one*
  YOUR DOCTOR would expect you to ask for advice

ALWAYS URGENT
- a fit or convulsion, or turns blue or very pale
- quick difficult or grunting breathing
- exceptionally hard to wake or unusually drowsy or does not seem to know you

SOMETIMES SERIOUS
- croup or a hoarse cough with noisy breathing
- cannot breathe freely through his nose
- cries in an unusual way or for an unusually long time or you think your baby is in severe pain
- refuses feeds repeatedly, especially if unusually quiet
- vomits repeatedly
- frequent loose motions especially if watery (diarrhoea). Vomiting and diarrhoea together can lead to excessive loss of fluid from the body and this may need urgent treatment
- unusually hot or cold or floppy

* *Even if you have consulted a doctor, health visitor or nurse, IF BABY is not improving or is getting worse,*
  TELL YOUR DOCTOR AGAIN THE SAME DAY.

Appreciation of methods of care

Although, as we have shown in Chapter 14, very few sudden infant deaths can be attributed to hypernatraemia, it is sensible to ensure that feeds are made up according to the manufacturers' instructions.

Similarly, although it has not been proven that sudden infant deaths are caused by either hyperthermia or hypothermia, it is prudent to

advise parents how much clothing and wrapping to use on an infant. Many modern synthetic materials are impervious to liquids and therefore do not allow the normal evaporation of sweat from the surface of the baby's skin. As this is the major way a baby has of decreasing his or her temperature, the actual material of the baby's clothes or wrapping may have a significant effect.

Another possible problem is when a baby who is suitably wrapped for cold weather is brought inside into a heated room – say in a pram – but no wrappings and garments are removed.

As a general guideline – after the first couple of months – the amount of clothing and wrapping for an infant can be best judged by what the adult would feel comfortable in under similar temperature conditions.

In general, first ensure that the young baby's room be kept at an even temperature of about 65° F (19° C) both day and night. Babies need to be well-wrapped until about one month of age after which they become better at keeping themselves warm. It is sensible to protect the baby, including his head, from draughts; the hood of the pram should be used if there is a chilly wind.

In cold weather a baby can lose heat quickly, even in a cot or pram. A method of checking whether the baby is warm enough, or too hot, is to put one's hand beneath the covers and feel the actual skin of his body. If the baby is too hot he will feel hot and sweaty to the touch, and may be thirsty.

Fresh air is good for a healthy baby, but probably not so important when he has a cold or the weather is foggy or cold. In hot weather it is important that the baby should not get too hot; he should be kept out of direct sunlight, with the pram hood down and a sun canopy.

Whether or not these measures would be responsible for prevention of true sudden infant death, is still to be debated. Nevertheless, these measures might help prevent one or two deaths that would have been 'explained'.

Health Visitor Intervention

An interesting experiment took place in the early 1970's in Sheffield. Using the scoring system similar to that shown in Table 16, Carpenter and Emery at birth identified those at high-risk of explained or unexplained sudden infant death. Half of this group were randomly chosen for intervention.

The intervention comprised two clinical examinations of the baby, one made within 48 hours of birth, the other at 5 weeks of age, together with 10 visits to the home by specially appointed health visitors in the

first 20 weeks of life. Of the 922 infants who were at high-risk, but in which there was no intervention, 9 unexpected deaths occurred. Among the 837 infants where intervention was offered, 5 unexpected deaths occurred. The difference, though suggestive, was not statistically significant. Interestingly, three of the five deaths occurred among the 210 infants for whom participation in the scheme had been refused by the parents.

Controversy has existed ever since the results have been published concerning whether there is or is not a preventive role for the health visitor. The Sheffield participants felt so strongly that intervention worked that they were convinced that continuation of the trial was unethical: all high-risk infants are now given special attention by the health visitors. Unfortunately this means that there is no valid means of evaluation of the results. At the Royal Statistical Society in 1982, Carpenter presented his reasons for thinking that the intervention has succeeded in reducing the number of post-neonatal deaths in Sheffield, but there was considerable discussion concerning the validity of his argument. Information published subsequently by him has suggested that the reduction in deaths may be in the 'explained' rather than the 'unexplained' sudden infant death.

Thus, although there are many reasons for thinking that frequent health visitor attendance is helpful to the mother, there is no conclusive evidence yet that such visits prevent 'unexplained' sudden infant deaths. Nevertheless scoring and intervention schemes depend on first, the accuracy of the scoring system which may need to be adapted to the special features of infant mortality in each area, and second, on the commitment of the community health staff, and especially the health visitors involved. Modified schemes are currently being tried out in several areas.

Apnoea Alarms

The use of apnoea alarms at home to monitor an infant's breathing is controversial. In the absence of conclusive scientific evidence of their value and in the light of increasingly recognised parental need for special support with babies in certain circumstances, the Scientific Advisory Committee of the Foundation for the Study of Infant Deaths issued this statement in 1981:

'In recent years, alarms called respiration or apnoea monitors have been developed to monitor a baby's breathing movements. A bell rings and a small light flashes if breathing movements cease (apnoea) for more than a chosen period, usually 20 seconds. Some monitors use a sensor placed beneath the baby's mattress, others use a small capsule attached to the baby's abdomen with sticking plaster.

Breathing stops when a person dies, and if anything can be done to save a child at that moment, an apnoea alarm may make this possible. It is not, however, always possible to revive a child by the time breathing movements have stopped. There is also the danger that, even if resuscitated, serious brain damage may already have occurred.

The problem is complicated by the knowledge that some apparently normal infants have natural pauses in their breathing when asleep, and then start to breathe again spontaneously. The significance of these pauses is not understood. The alarm sounding during a temporary pause may interrupt the baby's normal sleep rhythm and it is not yet known whether this is undesirable.

Limitations of the equipment: the apnoea alarms currently available for home use are designed to monitor breathing movements of the chest and/or abdomen and do not immediately detect a blocked airway since the muscles controlling breathing movements can go on functioning for some time even though no air is reaching the lungs.

The monitors occasionally also give false alarms. Sometimes they fail to detect shallow breathing and ring the alarm although the baby is quite all right. The alarm will also sound if the equipment becomes detached from the baby.

On the other hand, instances are known of the monitor picking up the heart beat or other baby movements and failing to detect that breathing movements have stopped.

The value of using apnoea alarms to prevent unexpected infant deaths is not yet established. The extent if any to which prolonged apnoeic spells are the underlying cause of death in otherwise healthy infants is not yet known. Only a small proportion of babies who have died unexpectedly have had a proven history of apnoeic spells. There is therefore insufficient evidence to recommend the widespread use of apnoea alarms for normal babies to prevent cot deaths.

There are however certain groups of babies for whom as part of their management and for a variety of reasons paediatricians may wish to recommend an apnoea monitor for use at home. These may include:

(a) babies born prematurely who sometimes seem especially susceptible to prolonged apnoea and whose breathing may still be irregular, when otherwise clinically well,

(b) babies who have been found apnoeic (not breathing) and cyanotic (looking blue), sometimes called "near miss" cot deaths. There are of course many different reasons for these so-called "near miss" events such as pneumonia, seizure, disturbed body chemistry and regurgitation as well as breath holding attacks, airway obstruction and other breathing disorders for which careful examination should be made,

    (c) some subsequent siblings (brothers and sisters) of cot death babies who may be at slightly increased risk and whose parents need some kind of extra support.

Paediatricians and physiologists researching in this field recommend that if a baby is to have a monitor for use at home the parents must first discuss their baby's and their needs with a paediatrician who is able

    (i)   to examine the baby and select the most suitable kind of monitor
    (ii) to train the parents in resuscitation methods (mouth to nose-and-mouth or bag and mask) to enable them to cope should the baby be found apnoeic and cyanotic, and also
    (iii) to arrange for a support system, available 24 hours per day, seven days per week in the event of the equipment breaking down and needing immediate replacement or other crisis which may include temporary admission to hospital.'

There are major problems concerning false positive alarms – i.e. the alarm going off although the baby is perfectly well, and false negative episodes – when the baby has ceased to inhale but the alarm has not gone off.

The false positive alarm rate can be as high as 25–50% causing considerable parental fatigue with the consequent temptation to disconnect the alarm. False negative episodes can occur for two reasons, with the consequence that the alarm fails to trigger, although the baby has been apnoeic for a considerable time. The first is due to what is called cardiac triggering (the heart rate slows but the beats become louder). The second is obstructive apnoea, when the baby is making breathing movements of the chest wall although failing to take in any air. The alarm would only go off when all such movements ceased, by which time the infant may be brain damaged if not already dead.

David Southall recently reviewed the published studies on home monitoring and came up with some interesting information. Of infants who had had an episode of 'near-miss' cot death, 176 had been given a monitor and 7(4%) had died; of 455 infants who were not on a monitor, only 5(1%) had died. As he stressed, caution must be used in interpreting these figures since the two groups were probably not comparable. Nevertheless, it is difficult to persuade oneself that the monitors were *preventing* deaths.

Among 404 siblings of sudden infant deaths who were assessed by various authors, only 73 were given apnoea alarms, and one of these

died during monitoring. Among the 331 siblings who were not given apnoea monitors there were no deaths.

Thus the major advantage of apnoea alarms may lie only in their reassurance to the parents. Sarah Stewart-Brown, a doctor who had had a previous sudden infant death described graphically her feelings of relief when her next child was put on an apnoea alarm. There is no clear way of assessing the value of these instruments other than by a randomised controlled trial. Meanwhile, as the Foundation's Scientific Committee's statement emphasises and Hamish Simpson concludes in his review of the problem, 'the scientific basis for home monitoring is (at present) imprecise'. It is not yet known whether monitoring saves lives. Both authorities however, also recognise that while some parents want to care for their subsequent children entirely normally, others are so anxious they are desperate for an aid which, despite acknowledged limitations, spares them continual 'cot watching'. Each family should be treated individually and offered support appropriate to their needs and wishes. It may be that other systems of support, including close health supervision with monitoring of weight gain, may prove more acceptable to some families. Meanwhile, until the apnoea theory is confirmed or refuted, the psychological needs of parents must remain paramount.

If the ideal monitor – able to detect central and obstructive apnoea, bradycardia, alveolar hypoventilation, hypoxia and hypoxaemia – and with facilities to record, becomes available in the future, it may be possible to clarify the role of home monitoring. If such a machine *is* produced it is vital that it be evaluated appropriately.

Conclusion

Until we know the cause(s) of sudden infant death, attempts at prevention might seem to be like shooting at a target in the dark. Although experience has shown that sometimes in medicine the incidence of a disease can be reduced without accurate knowledge of causation (which may come subsequently), it may appear more profitable for the moment to concentrate some activity on determining causation. Nevertheless, we can improve the attitudes to, and management of, sudden infant deaths as and when they occur. Suggestions as to how this might be done are produced in the next chapter.

Chapter 25

Amelioration

The Foundation study showed how much parents appreciated prompt and well-informed professional support and explanation after the unexpected death of their baby, in addition to the sympathy of family and friends. The survey set out to examine criticisms and problems. From the findings, it is possible to draw conclusions and to make a number of recommendations concerning future management.

Conclusions

(i) Although failure of communication, tactless investigation and absence of professional support was reported in a minority of the deaths surveyed, the numbers were not negligible and the experience caused unnecessary distress and psychological trauma to the parents and their surviving children.

(ii) The system of notification that a baby has died should be improved to ensure that the family's GP and Health Visitor are immediately informed. The key to effective support both initially and longer term is speedy communication between those initially concerned – Accident and Emergency staff, H.M. Coroner, General Practitioner, Community Health Services, paediatrician and the Foundation for the Study of Infant Deaths (or local Parent Support Group), so that there is informed support immediately available for all parents.

(iii) A copy of the post-mortem findings should be made available to the GP who should take responsibility for ensuring that an explanation is given to the bereaved parents by a medically qualified person.

(iv) There has been considerable increase in public awareness of sudden infant deaths over the decade 1971–1981. The efforts of the

Foundation to inform professionals and the public have been worthwhile, but there is still much to be done in this respect. As one sad parent concluded in 1981: 'This seems greatly improved since our last baby died 9 years ago.'

It is worth recalling, at this point, that the Foundation's study was heavily weighted with parents from social classes I and II. The fact that so many difficulties were experienced by parents that were probably better able to work the system implies that stories from the parents from reduced circumstances, especially the single unsupported mothers, may have been even more horrific than those we have quoted. There is obviously no room for complacency.

Recommendations

1. *Ambulance Staff*
Insight into the special problems associated with sudden infant death in infancy is required of Ambulance and other emergency staff, so that compassion and common sense can be applied from the start. Ambulance staff should always remember the need for considerate handling of the dead baby in the parents' presence; there should be flexibility in applying their rules concerning carrying dead bodies or allowing one or other of the parents, if they wish, to accompany the baby to hospital.

2. *Hospital Accident and Emergency Staff*
Sudden death in infancy should be considered during medical and nursing training so that Accident and Emergency staff are as well informed about such deaths as they are about non-accidental injury to children. Suggested guidelines for receiving babies found unexpectedly dead and initiating support for the parents are printed below.

SEQUENCE OF ACTION IN ACCIDENT & EMERGENCY DEPARTMENT

Infant arrives moribund or dead.

1. Verification of death should be made in the Accident Department rather than in the ambulance.
2. If resuscitation is attempted or while the baby's condition is being evaluated, a brief history of the baby's health and recent events should be taken from an accompanying parent.
3. Every effort should be made to provide a room or privacy for the distressed parents.

4. Ensure that a suitable person is looking after the baby's brothers and sisters who may have come with the parent(s).
5. If only one parent is present and agrees, contact the other parent or relative.
6. INFORM (i) a member of the paediatric department.
7. INFORM (ii) hospital chaplain if parents request a dying child to be baptised or wish for his support.
8. Review information briefly before breaking the news that the baby is dead. Parents will need privacy in which to express their grief.
9. After an appropriate interval, inform parents of the need for a post-mortem examination to establish the cause of death, which will be arranged by the coroner.
10. Unless there is a history of diagnosed illness, obvious signs of injury or the parental attitude arouses suspicion, explain to the parents that the death appears to be a cot death (also called sudden infant death syndrome).
11. Explain to parents that it is the coroner's duty to investigate all sudden deaths of unknown cause and that they will be asked to make a statement to the coroner's officer or police who may visit their home and may take the baby's bedding for examination to help establish the cause of death. This does not mean that anybody will be blamed or that an inquest will necessarily be held.
12. INFORM (iii) hospital social work department. Someone should remain with the parents until they leave.
13. INFORM (iv) coroner's officer and explain whether death appears to be natural or unnatural.
14. Offer parents an opportunity to see their baby and let them hold him before the baby is taken to the mortuary. The infant should be clothed and made as presentable as possible.
15. If identification of the body to the coroner's officer or police is required, a member of staff or hospital chaplain should accompany the parents to the mortuary.
16. Offer parents copies of the leaflet INFORMATION FOR PARENTS FOLLOWING THE SUDDEN AND UNEX- PECTED DEATH OF THEIR BABY, which gives the address and telephone number of the Foundation for the Study of Infant Deaths (see below).
17. Discuss with the parents arrangements for continued support.
18. INFORM (v) family doctor
          (vi) health visitor
          (vii) social worker if already involved with the family.

19. The mother, if breast-feeding, will need immediate advice on suppression of lactation.
20. Ensure that the parents have suitable transport to take them home.

Prompt *communication* from a hospital Accident and Emergency Department to the paediatric department, GP and Health Visitor, and from the Coroner's Office to the GP and a designated person in the Community Health Service is needed to eliminate any risk of the GP or Health Visitor not knowing quickly of a baby's unexpected death, and to enable professional support to be given immediately to all parents.

3. *The General Practitioner*

GPs should get in touch with the bereaved parents as soon as possible after a sudden infant death to give support. They should ensure that the parents are given an explanation of the post-mortem findings and registered cause of death by a medically qualified person. In some districts, a paediatrician who takes a special interest in sudden infant deaths may offer to do this. The GP Check List for Unexpected Infant Deaths is available for doctors managing a sudden infant death for the first time.

Check List – GP Support for the Family
(adapted from the Check List produced by the Foundation)

1. As soon as you hear of the baby's death, contact the family to express sympathy, by a home visit if possible. Early support prevents later misunderstandings.
2. Unless there is obvious injury, a history of illness or the parental attitude arouses suspicion, tell the parents it appears to be a cot death but that a post-mortem examination will be necessary to establish the cause of death. If death remains unexplained, it may be registered as sudden infant death syndrome. Some parents want to see or hold their child after death is confirmed but before the body is taken to a mortuary.
3. Explain the coroner's duty, the possibility of an inquest, and warn parents that they or relatives may be asked to identify the body. Advise the parents that they will be asked to make a statement to the coroner's office or police, and that bedding may be taken for examination to help establish the cause of death. If necessary, give advice on registering the death and

making funeral arrangements. Coroner's officer may need to know parents' choice of burial or cremation.

4. If considering offering parents a drug to alleviate the initial shock, it is known that many do not want anxiolytics or anti-depressants, but prefer something to induce sleep.

5. If the mother was breastfeeding, give advice on suppression of lactation; prescribe medication and advise her to leave the breasts alone except to empty them once a day if an easy method is available.

6. Take particular note of siblings. Remember that twin babies carry extra risk of cot death and that a surviving twin may need hospitalisation for observation. Give guidance on emotional needs of siblings, who may be neglected or over-protected; reassure parents that older children are not at risk.

7. Advise parents of likely grief reactions such as aching arms, hearing the baby cry, distressing dreams, and strong positive or negative sexual feelings, but reassure them that these and other symptoms such as loss of appetite and sleeplessness are normal and temporary. Anger, sometimes directed towards the GP, guilt and self-blame, especially on the part of the mother, are common grief reactions for which the doctor should be prepared.

8. Offer parents copies of the Foundation's Information for Parents leaflet.

9. Make sure that parents have a relative or close friend very near them during the 48 hours after the death, and offer explanation to them and to the minister of religion. Make sure the family's health visitor and other members of the primary care team know of the baby's death and are prepared to give continued support.

10. Arrange a subsequent meeting with the parents to discuss the cause of death. Make sure the coroner informs you of the initial and final post-mortem findings and consult with the patholo-gist if any clarification is needed.

11. Offer parents a later interview with a paediatrician both for themselves and the siblings. An independent opinion is mutually beneficial to the parents and GP, restoring parental confidence in the primary care team and sharing some of the load of counselling particularly concerning future children.

12. Parents who have lost a baby unexpectedly will need extra attention and support with their subsequent children from their obstetrician, paediatrician, general practitioner and health visitor.

When notifying the coroner or police of a sudden infant death, it is helpful if the doctor could indicate if he thinks it is a natural death. (A thorough post-mortem examination is needed to establish the medical cause of death.) It lessens the trauma for parents if the doctor or A & E staff can explain gently to parents the coroner's duty and the role of the police.

4. *Management by the Police, Coroner and Pathologist*

Most officials perform their delicate task very sympathetically. However, the parents, although 'stunned' at first, are acutely sensitive, and a careless remark imputing blame, a suggestion as to what may have caused death, or a manner implying suspicion that the parents may have injured their child is likely to be long remembered and may cause agonising and unnecessary guilt. In this regard the manner in which the coroner's officers and police conduct their enquiries is crucial,

(i) There should be greater public understanding of the responsibilities of the Coroner and the role of the police in relation to sudden deaths;

(ii) Police training should give greater consideration to handling unexpected infant deaths, so that they carry out their delicate task of distinguishing between natural and unnatural death with tact, recognising that in this age-group natural sudden deaths vastly outnumber deaths of children from non-accidental injury;

(iii) Police should consider the circumstances in which the CID involvement is necessary. They should take into account the impression of the doctor who confirmed death and, where possible, the autopsy findings;

(iv) Parents should be kept informed of procedures and progress;

(v) Consideration should be given to the circumstances in which identification of the body is required, and how this can be arranged with minimum extra stress. Inquests should be held only when necessary;

(vi) Police or undertakers should ensure that the parents are asked whether they would like the baby's clothes returned, and should make a written note of the parents' instructions;

(vii) Coroners and police need to take steps to prevent the 'most distressing' and 'inaccurate' press reports of a baby's death being published without the parents' prior knowledge or permission.

Coroners should be encouraged to use the services of a paediatric pathologist wherever this is possible. Paediatric pathology referral centres should be designated regionally with whom pathologists chosen by the coroner should be encouraged to cooperate. These recommendations are in accordance with the Brodrick Report on Death Certification and Coroners.

'The term "cot death" is used to describe the circumstance in which a baby is found dead with no obvious explanation of the cause of death ... It is clearly in the interests of medical science, and hence of children and their parents generally, that "cot deaths" should be investigated from the medical aspect as fully as possible. ... The investigation of a cot death often involves difficult problems of interpretation and ... it may require knowledge and experience only possessed by pathologists who have specialised in paediatric work. It could best be carried out in a hospital with a special interest in paediatric pathology and with good facilities for microscopic work. ...

In the investigation of a "cot death", a good clinical history is almost as important as a good post-mortem examination. Where the death is reported to the coroner by a doctor, his report should contain a good deal of the necessary information, since he will need personally to have considered the circumstances of the death in order to arrive at the decision whether or not to report it to the coroner. If the report does not contain all the necessary information, or if the death was reported by someone other than a doctor, the coroner will need to make his own enquiry into the circumstances leading up to the death. ... We hope that the peculiar poignancy of the "cot death" situation will encourage the coroner to make imaginative use of all sources of information. ... A coroner should consider with the greatest care whom he should ask to visit the home and attempt to obtain from the parents relevant information about the history of events leading to the death.'

Post-Mortem Findings. Suggestions for improvement in the handling of the post-mortem findings and registered cause of death included the following,

(i) There should be no undue delay in undertaking the post-mortem examination, in accordance with the 1984 Coroners' Rules.

(ii) All parents should be told in advance of the procedure and arrangements for informing them of the post-mortem findings and cause of death as soon as they are available.

(iii) The Coroner should inform the GP or, if the family is not registered, a specified community doctor or paediatrician of the post-mortem results at the same time as informing the family.

(iv) The family's GP, paediatrician or other medically qualified person should explain the post-mortem findings to the parents, preferably after consulting the pathologist.

(v) A copy of the post-mortem report should be shown to parents, or at least be made available to their GP. If considered properly interested persons by the Coroner, they are entitled to a copy under the 1984 Coroners' Rules, although there may be a small fee per page. Rule 57 provides (1) A Coroner shall, on application and on payment of the prescribed fee (if any), supply to any person who, in the opinion of the Coroner, is a properly interested person, a copy of any report of a post-mortem examination ... or special examination, or of any notes of evidence, or of any document put in evidence at an inquest.
(2) A Coroner may, on application and without charge, permit any person who, in the opinion of the Coroner, is a properly interested person to inspect such report, notes of evidence, or document.

(vi) Coroners and pathologists should avoid misleading or confusing registered causes of death.

5. *Paediatricians and other health professionals*
Each Health Authority should review its local procedure and have a definite plan for speedy notification of unexpected child deaths and the provision of support. The person best able to co-ordinate the information is likely to vary in different places but could be a community paediatrician.

The Health Visitor and/or midwife should contact the parents as soon as possible. The Health Visitor should liaise with the Minister of Religion, and local Parent Support Group if there is one, or social worker for some families, to ensure that long term support is available to parents who need it.

The use of structured interviews by health professionals enquiring into the baby's history and the family's health can be a therapeutic experience for the parents, and may be valuable for understanding factors contributing to the baby's death. The interviewer needs preparation and sensitivity to the feelings of the bereaved.

The Foundation's leaflet 'Information for Parents following the sudden and unexpected death of their baby' should be given to parents as soon as possible, when unnatural death is discounted. Parents should be told about the Foundation and thus offered the opportunity to be put in touch with formerly bereaved parents who could help them.

One *paediatrician* in each health district should take a special interest in sudden death in infancy. Paediatricians should arrange to

be notified promptly of any unexpected infant death by Accident and Emergency staff, mortuary attendants, and coroner's officer, for example. Paediatricians can assist with the immediate management and comfort of parents whose babies are brought to A/E departments. They can liaise with the family's GP or Community Health staff, and offer to explain the post-mortem findings to parents, especially those not registered with a GP, after consultation with the pathologist. They can arrange a consultation for a few weeks after the baby's death to consider any microscopic post-mortem findings, discuss future children and the risk of recurrence, advise on genetic counselling, if necessary, and to answer parents' further questions which may help restore their relationship with the GP if it is strained. Paediatricians should offer to see the mother during a subsequent pregnancy to discuss arrangements for examining the baby and other post natal care according to the baby's and the parents' needs.

All parents who have lost a baby need extra attention and support from their obstetrician, midwife, paediatrician, GP and Health Visitor through a subsequent pregnancy and when caring for the next child. The leaflet 'Your Next Child' and the green card 'When to consult a doctor about your baby' may help.

6. *Funeral Directors*

Undertakers help with certification and registration; they should give full information about the services offered, including a written estimate of all charges, remembering that most parents find the expense of a funeral a great burden. These should not be exceeded without permission. Undertakers should handle the baby caringly when in the parents' presence, and make sure they have parents' instructions concerning the return of the baby's clothes.

All officials and professionals who are likely to be involved with bereaved relatives should make sure they have copies of the DHSS pamphlet 'What to do after a death', and remember to offer them early on. Thus, the leaflet should be available to Coroners, Coroner's officers, police, doctors, mortuary attendants, Emergency and Accident Departments of hospitals, Medical Social Workers, Health Visitors and Funeral Directors. Registrars of Death should remember to offer the leaflet to relatives – some parents saw copies on display but were not offered one.

7. *Ministers of Religion*

Ministers should consider using an adapted baptism service for babies that have died. They need to liaise closely with health professionals in giving continued support to the bereaved.

8. *Helping Bereaved Parents*

As has been shown earlier, bereaved parents turn to their relatives and friends for comfort and help. Many people, however, are embarrassed by an untimely death they do not understand or perhaps are scared for their own children's sake, and so avoid the bereaved or make inappropriate remarks. The Compassionate Friends, an organisation of bereaved parents has published a helpful list of Do's and Don'ts to guide people about helpful and unhelpful reactions.

HELPING BEREAVED PARENTS –
DO's and DON'Ts

DO's	DON'Ts
DO let your genuine concern and caring show.	DON'T let your own sense of helplessness keep you from reaching out to a bereaved parent.
DO be available ... to listen, to run errands, to help with the other children, or whatever else seems needed at the time.	
DO say you are sorry about what happened to their child and about their pain.	DON'T avoid them because you are uncomfortable (being avoided by friends adds pain to an already intolerably painful experience).
DO allow them to express as much grief as they are feeling at the moment and are willing to share.	DON'T say how you know how they feel (unless you've lost a child yourself you probably don't know how they feel).
DO encourage them to be patient with themselves, not to expect too much of themselves and not to impose any 'shoulds' on themselves.	DON'T say 'you ought to be feeling better by now' or anything else which implies a judgement about their feelings.
DO allow them to talk about the child they have lost as much and as often as they want to.	DON'T tell them what they *should* feel or do.
	DON'T change the subject when they mention their dead child.
DO talk about the special, endearing qualities of the child they've lost.	DON'T avoid mentioning the child's name out of fear of reminding them of their pain (they haven't forgotten it!).
DO give special attention to the child's brothers and sisters – at the funeral and in the months to come (they too are hurt and	DON'T try to find something positive (e.g. a moral lesson,

DO's	DON'Ts
confused and in need of attention which their parents may not be able to give at this time).	closer family ties, etc.) about the child's death.
DO reassure them that they did everything that they could, that the medical care their child received was the best or whatever else you know to be *true and positive* about the care given their child.	DON'T point out at least they have their other children (children are not interchangeable; they cannot replace each other).
********	DON'T say that they can always have another child (even if they wanted to and could, another child would not replace the child they've lost).
Prepared by: Lee Schmidt Parent Bereavement Outreach Santa Monica, California.	DON'T suggest that they should be grateful for their other children (grief over the loss of one child does not discount parent's love and appreciation of their living children).
	DON'T make any comments which in any way suggest that the care given their child at home, in the emergency department, hospital, or wherever, as inadequate (parents are plagued by feelings of doubt and guilt without any help from their family and friends).

Children's grief needs to be acknowledged. Parents may need help in understanding children's perceptions of death at different ages, and the variety of ways in which children may express or cope with their feelings.

9. *Practical and Administrative Problems*
Steps should be taken to ensure that:

(a) Sufficient medical advice is given to assist the suppression of lactation in mothers who were breast-feeding at the time of their baby's death. Some mothers may like to donate their milk to a premature baby 'milk bank'.

(b) All clinic appointments for the deceased child are cancelled immediately, and that the Family Practitioner Committee, hospital as well as the Child Health Clinic are informed.

(c) The DHSS should issue a new Child Benefit Book instead of returning the old one overstamped with the dead baby's name still on the front.

(d) It should be quite clear to all that a mother is now entitled to free dental treatment and free drug prescriptions up to a year after the baby's birth despite the baby's death.

(e) The 'grossly inadequate' death grant of only £9 for an infant under 3 years old needs urgent review, as does the complicated and distressing procedure for claiming it.

Chapter 26

The Unsolved Mystery

Introduction

Before tackling the possible solutions to the problem, it is essential to ask first the question of whether there is likely to be a solution. In 1976 John Emery wrote 'we are dealing with a whole range of diseases and social situations ... any attempt to find a cause for sudden infant death is due to disappointment.'

Is this really true? Are there really so many different causes that our efforts are useless? The very strong epidemiological patterns, consistent in different countries, may indicate one or two specific factors associated with large numbers of sudden infant death. True the solution might lie in blanket terms, such as 'infection', 'allergic reaction', 'vitamin deficiencies', 'congenital defects', but that is not to detract from the validity of such a solution.

Again, we may ask is there such an entity 'sudden infant death', i.e. a death where nothing in the history or at post-mortem can satisfactorily explain the reason why the infant died? Here we are in the area of subjective assessment – but the fact that the majority of paediatric pathologists are able to answer 'yes' and in the English-speaking world, using this definition, the incidence figures obtained are remarkably similar, supports the assertion.

The aim of this chapter is to use the epidemiological patterns that we have found as possible clues in the search for the reasons why sudden infant deaths occur.

From the findings described in Part II of this book, it is obvious that there are several factors which appear to be strongly associated with sudden infant death. These include the age and sex of the infant, the season of birth, the number of older siblings, the age and socio-economic circumstances of the mother, whether she smoked during pregnancy and subsequently, whether she was addicted to opiates.

Other factors of importance include short gestation, growth retardation and the presence of congenital malformations.

Season

Various profound changes in temperature, wind, humidity, baro-metric pressure and hours of sunshine obviously vary with the month of the year. That the changes in the weather effect the functioning of the body is obvious to anyone with disorders of the joints – from rheumatism to an old fracture. Biochemical changes are known to occur within the whole population: these include decreases in urinary excretion of calcium in the winter as well as a decrease in both serum and plasma 25-hydroxyvitamin D and increase in plasma transferrin. The first three of these changes are the direct result of lack of sunshine – but others may be found as a consequence of the seasonal variation in foodstuffs – especially vegetables and fruit.

The temperature itself appears to be associated with outbreaks of influenza. A study in the United Kingdom showed that though influenza epidemics almost invariably occur during winter months, the prevalence of influenza is lower when the weather is relatively mild. Deaths from pneumonia in all age groups in Britain have been compared with daily mean temperature, humidity and rainfall by Dr. Bull. He showed statistical associations with cold weather a week before death, with low humidity a week before death and high humidity and high temperature on the day of death. The association was strongest among the elderly though.

As far as infants are concerned, a team at Newcastle-Upon-Tyne investigated all emergency hospital admissions of infants for respiratory infection. During the 6 year study, 2% of children were admitted with bronchiolitis associated with the respiratory syncytial virus. There were marked epidemics with the incidence being highest in the winter, associated with little sunshine and low temperatures. The other viruses in the survey included parainfluenza viruses (with peak incidences in the summer), and influenza viruses.

In Cardiff, the number of sudden infant deaths occurring in each week were compared, over a 10-year period, with isolations of influenza A in the population of Cardiff. The authors found a positive association, but did not publish enough evidence for the reader to be able to assess whether the association could have been merely due to the fact that both tend to occur more often in the winter.

Interaction between climatic factors and infection is taken one step further in the study of air pollution. It has long been established that bronchitis in childhood was more prevalent in areas with high

concentrations of air pollution. There is now an interesting suggestion from Los Angeles implicating air pollution in sudden infant death. Hoppenbrouwers and his associates compared the pattern of deaths over a 4 year period with various pollution measures. They showed, not that the days of death were days with more pollution, but rather that the deaths were preceded by periods of high pollution – occurring 7 weeks earlier. They showed that the risk for the month of birth corresponded to atmospheric pollution levels present at conception and the months prior to and after delivery. In addition they found the infants born in an area of high atmospheric carbon monoxide levels died younger.

Thus from the seasonal association that is shown for sudden infant death, many possible theories as to the underlying defect can be produced. These range from underlying biochemical deficiency (e.g. calcium, vitamin D), viral infection (e.g. influenza A, respiratory syncytial virus), hypothermia or long-term effects of atmospheric pollution. Crucial to any tenable hypothesis though, must be knowledge of when the seasonal effect works. Is it an association with the time of death or with the time of birth? Are we looking for deleterious seasonal effects during pregnancy or in the early days of the child's life? This is a problem with which statisticians may be able to assist.

Age and Sex Differences
Sex differences have been found in many types of childhood illness and behaviour. Even before they are born, boys are heavier than girls, but girls are physically more mature. In the early months of life, girls are reported as spending more time asleep, and boys to be more irritable. Certainly, in the pre-school period boys are more likely to have temper tantrums and be restless and unable to settle. Biochemical differences include increased red blood cell counts, haemoglobin and haematocrit in the first months of life – but possibly of more importance is the fact that baby girls are able to produce higher levels of antibodies to the common viruses.

A collaborative study in 10 centres of the United Kingdom recorded information on all children under 5 years of age admitted to hospital in the winter for respiratory disorders. As we mentioned previously, respiratory syncytial virus was the major cause, with a sex ratio among admissions with this infection of 1.4 (identical to that shown for sudden infant death on page xxx). The age distribution of cases bore a strong resemblance to that found with sudden infant death, as can be seen in Figure 32 below.

As we have already mentioned, the peak age for sudden infant death

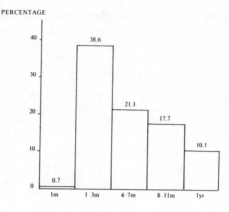

Figure 32

Age distribution of hospital admissions with respiratory syncytial virus (from Clarke et al, 1978).

coincides with the changeover from the antibodies received by the infant from the mother, and the development of the child's own immune system. This is the age at which infants are more likely to develop botulinism and salmonellosis. Other physiological changes are also occurring although these may be less well documented. They include changes in breathing and sleeping patterns.

Area Differences

We have shown that comparison of incidence between areas is difficult since definitions are inconsistent. Nevertheless, it is possible to state that the incidence of sudden infant death appears to be consistently higher in cities than in the surrounding areas – and that the incidence in Scandinavia and Israel appears to be substantially lower than in the English speaking world.

That cities tend to have more air pollution than other areas is obvious: probably this is responsible for the fact that the adult death rate from bronchitis is higher in residents of cities than other areas. A similar pattern has been shown for infections in young children, such as for the respiratory syncytial virus. Nevertheless, there are many other ways in which the city population differs: these include the proportion of mothers who are immigrants to the area, the prevalence of psychiatric disorder, the proportion of single mothers and, probably, the dietary composition and other habits such as smoking.

Several proposals have been raised as to the reasons for the lower

rates in Scandinavia. Two Swedish authors have suggested that it might be relevant that 99% of all children in Sweden are in contact with the child health services, having an average of 12 contacts with doctor or nurse in the first year of life. Another Swede wrote after spending two years as a general practitioner in Britain:

> 'It is not unusual to see housing conditions in industrial estates in the Midlands and North of England which are almost unbelievable by Swedish standards. ... The bedrooms are often damp and cold, with the only heat from a gas fire.'

Further possible relevant differences concern the lower proportion of mothers who smoke cigarettes in Scandinavia, the fact that the birthweight of the babies is considerably greater and atmospheric pollution less likely.

Maternal Age and Birth Order

We have shown that the younger the mother and the more children she already has, the more likely is the baby to become a sudden infant death. That is not to say that these deaths never occur among the first-born of mothers in their 30s, but they are less likely to do so. The increased risks in the infants of young mothers and large families offers clues as to possible reasons.

Young mothers are more likely to have poor housing, to move home frequently, to have unstable marital relationships and be psycho-logically unbalanced. Most of all, however, they are uncertain and inexperienced. Children of young mothers are more likely to suffer from behaviour problems – and are at increased risk of accidental injury.

The increased risk of sudden infant death in children of larger families points to other possibilities: on the one hand the mother of a large family has less time to devote to each individual child, with the result that particular signs of illness might not be spotted; on the other hand, the young child of a large family is likely to be introduced early to a variety of infections brought into the home by the elder siblings; yet again, the more children the mother has had, the poorer her nutrition in pregnancy and it may be that her immunological system is less competent.

Social Class

Classification of social class is a useful indicator to employ in epidemiological studies. Sudden infant death shows an increased

prevalence in social classes IV and V, but unlike many causes of death there is no steep trend from social classes I to II to III. Outcomes that show increasing prevalence with lower social class may indirectly implicate a variety of factors from maternal depression to poor maternal and infant nutrition, relative lack of education, poverty, poor housing and ignorance over health care. It has not yet been possible to determine which, if any, of these factors may be linked to sudden infant death.

Children of single mothers have been shown to be at markedly increased risk of sudden infant death. In general, this group are socially disadvantaged. There tend to be frequent household moves to inadequate rooms, often with over-crowding. Mothers tend to feel isolated and the incidence of depression is very high. They may respond to their circumstances by increasing the number of cigarettes they smoke, the amount of alcohol they drink or taking hard drugs.

Maternal Smoking

Mothers who smoke differ from non-smoking mothers in many aspects of their behaviour. They are more likely to book late in pregnancy, more at risk of failing to keep their appointments and less likely to know the dates of their last menstrual period. In addition, they are less likely to wish to breast feed, less likely to have their children immunised or to take them to the dentist. Thus, the association between maternal smoking and sudden infant death could reveal a psychological or behavioural factor.

On the other hand, there is a physical effect on the unborn child due to the constituents of the smoke inhaled by the mother. There is now incontrovertible evidence that this results in growth retardation of the fetus and an increase in the risk of perinatal death. In addition, as we have already pointed out, the mother's blood becomes deficient in vitamin C and the child's initial immunological defences are reduced.

In this respect, it is interesting to note that the sudden infant deaths that occurred within the first 12 weeks were more likely to include severely growth retarded infants and/or those of the mothers who had smoked heavily. It is possible that the cause of these deaths was an early infection in a temporarily immunologically incompetent infant.

Birthweight and Gestation

Associations with both growth retardation and short gestation can have a variety of interpretations. They can indicate adverse factors operating during the pregnancy. On the other hand, the young infant

affected in this way is more likely to be immunologically incompetent and liable to catch various infections. He is also more likely to have feeding difficulties and behaviour problems. Children of low birthweight are more likely to cry excessively, and to be admitted to hospital for correction of abnormalities that may have been due to difficulties experienced before the baby was born. These include squints and hernias.

Conclusions

On the whole there is evidence to suggest that some of the sudden infant deaths suffered an adverse period *in utero*. They were more likely to suffer the consequences of their mother smoking and smoking heavily, and even of their mother's heroin addiction or barbiturate ingestion. They were more likely, too, to have been *in utero* when she had an infection. Evidence that they were affected by their uterine environment lies in the fact that they were more likely to have been growth retarded, of short gestation or with mild congenital malformations.

The question of whether such a history predetermines their death or whether it merely increases their susceptibility to further adverse factors remains unanswered. It could be that a potentially fatal development has occurred, causing a defective condition which is not demonstrable using present methods of pathological detection.

Alternatively, the difficulties *in utero* might result in a particularly sensitive newborn – but sensitive to what? Given the evidence currently available we suspect that the infection aspect has more evidence for than against it – but in no way is the case clear cut enough to be didactic.

One might suggest that given money for research into sudden infant death, this may be one of the more promising avenues for investigation.

In all instances of disease and mortality there is variability between individuals. Even in an epidemic caused by a new virus, some will be affected to a major extent, some so mildly as to be almost undetectable and others will be unaffected. Yet in spite of an immense amount of knowledge the determinants of why one individual should become ill on a particular day and another not, are largely uncharted. Scientists tend to use the term 'multi-factorial' to cover the lack of knowledge – with the assumption that one is probably dealing with a number of different genes, various aspects of intra-uterine and extra-uterine life, including nutrition, and the natural environment on the day of death. With such a body of different influences it is easy to forget that the

individual would not have become ill unless he had 'caught' the virus.

Similarly, sudden infant death clearly has a 'multifactorial' component. That is not, however, to say that there may not be specific causes for the death.

This epidemiological search for clues has focused on factors which are statistically associated with increased risk of sudden infant death. Such an approach does not necessarily provide clues as to the cause of individual deaths. We recognise indeed that there are many sudden infant deaths to which these risk factors did not apply. Most studies, for example, show that over 80% of sudden infant death babies were neither low birth weight nor of short gestation, at least 30% of the mothers were non-smokers and the great majority of mothers did not take drugs (opiates or barbiturates) in pregnancy. About a quarter of sudden infant deaths are first children, and at least half of the deaths occur in families living in favourable social circumstances.

Meanwhile, the files are open. The puzzle remains. Speculation is invited but more hard facts are especially welcomed.

Further research is essential to find the reasons for and ways of preventing these unexplained tragedies to put an end to the anguish of parents losing a beloved child and not knowing why their baby has died.

Appendix 1

Sudden Infant Deaths in Oxfordshire and West Berkshire 1971-75

Information collected by the Oxford Record Linkage Study includes birth certificates, death certificates, information on pregnancies and deliveries, and all general hospital admissions to a population living in the Oxford Regional Health Authority. For the purposes of the present study we confined our attention to that part of the region included within the boundaries of Oxfordshire and West Berkshire. This area has a population of some 800,000 with about 14,000 births a year.

The information collected by the Oxford Record Linkage Study includes birth certificates of all infants born to women resident in this Area, regardless of the place of delivery, death certificates of all persons currently resident in the Area regardless of where they died, and death certificates of infants born in the Area but resident elsewhere at the time of death. For the present study two populations were considered.

(i) *Deaths among residents of the Area.* For this part of the study all children who died while resident in the Area were included. Details of all the deaths, including post-mortem reports and clinical information were obtained. In all there were 456 deaths to children aged between 1 week and under two years of age. Of these, 220 had been referred to a coroner, thus implying that the deaths had at least been sudden. Detailed examination of all available information by an experienced paediatric pathologist (Dr. Jean Keeling), resulted in the identification of 169 deaths attributable to the sudden infant death syndrome.

A comparison of the details of the place of death, time of death, age at death and seasonal variations has been analysed and described in Chapter 5.

(ii) *Deaths to infants born in the area.* The children who had died, regardless of where they died, but who had been born within the boundaries of Oxfordshire and West Berkshire to mothers who were resident in that area at the time were identified. Obviously, a large proportion of these deaths were identical to those in sample (i). Nevertheless, there were a substantial proportion who had moved out of the Area, with their parents, before they died. The death records were examined in a similar way to those in sample (i), and 167 sudden infant deaths to women resident in the Area at the time of the child's birth were identified.

Analysis of these data took place in two steps. Firstly, comparison of the social class, maternal age, birth order and hospital of delivery of the sudden infant deaths (the index infants) were compared with all other births in the Area. Strong differences were shown.

Further details of the index pregnancies, labour, delivery and the early neonatal period were obtained from the mothers' clinical obstetric case notes. In order to obtain comparable information on surviving children, we chose three matched controls for each sudden infant death. The matched controls were of the same social class, the same maternal age, the same parity, delivered in the same type of hospital, and born in the same year. Comparison of cases with controls was carried out using normal statistical methods. The results are described in Chapters 6 to 11.

Appendix 2

Retrospective Study of the Management of Sudden Infant Deaths: Parents of the Foundation for the Study of Infant Deaths.

This survey compares the management of sudden infant deaths in two time periods: 1974–79, and 1980–81. Its purpose was (i) to consider the scale and nature of criticisms of officials and health professionals handling cot deaths; (ii) to assess whether the present system of notification of sudden infant deaths to health authorities and community health staff was satisfactory; (iii) to see whether sufficient explanation is given by the medical profession and (iv) to evaluate the Foundation's welfare and information work in encouraging informed support for bereaved parents and in disseminating information.

As described in Chapter 4, parents were asked whether they would complete a questionnaire enquiring into the management of the baby's death and practical problems which arose thereafter. The 713 questionnaires in the sample relate to sudden infant deaths which occurred throughout Britain (95% in England and Wales, 5% in Scotland). Omitted were a further 9 questionnaires relating to sudden infant deaths in the first week of life, as were 19 questionnaires referring to adequately explained deaths (e.g. meningitis or accidental suffocation) or deaths occuring to British families overseas, such as the Armed Forces in Germany, Hong Kong and Australia.

Completion of questionnaires varied over the time period. In 1978, participation was invited from the 948 parents who had been bereaved in the period 1974–77 using the Foundation's newsletter. One hundred replies (10.5%) were received. Thereafter a personal invitation was made to those newly bereaved parents who contacted the Foundation for support.

Some 252 questionnaires were received from 610 parents (41%) whose infant had died between 1978 and 1979. For 1980 and 1981 there were 361 questionnaires from 975 parents (37%).

The main aim of the survey was to monitor the management of the deaths and the way these changed over the two time periods. There are no significant differences between the two time periods in the epidemiological factors recorded. The social class and birth order distributions were similar as was the seasonal and sex variation in the deaths. In four percent of each group the death had occurred in a twin. The distribution of age at death was similar in both studies, with median age at death 12.6 weeks in the earlier series and 12.3 weeks in the group of deaths in 1980 and 1981.

That there are biases in the overall response is not disputed. Nevertheless the two groups appear to be epidemiologically very similar to one another, thus permitting valid comparison between them.

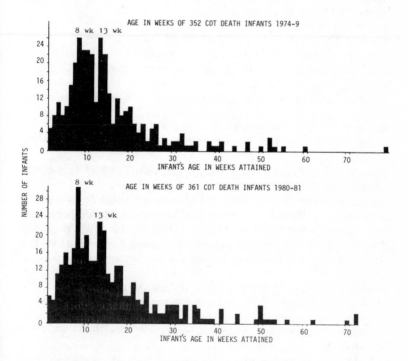

Figure 33

Comparison in age at death distribution between the two groups in the survey.

Glossary

Aetiology   The study of the causes of a disorder.

Apgar Score   A measure of the baby's asphyxia at birth. Normally taken at 1 and 5 minutes. Low scores denote severe asphyxia.

Apnoea   Cessation of breathing.

Atopy   A hypersensitivity to various substances.

Control Infant   A child who did not die during infancy.

Control Mother   Mother of a control infant.

Early Neonatal Deaths   Infants born alive but dying within 7 days of life.

Incidence   The number of sudden infant deaths per 1000 infants at risk.

Index Infant   An infant who became a sudden infant death.

Index Mother   Mother of one of the sudden infant deaths in the study.

Late Neonatal Deaths   Infants dying between 7 and 28 days of life.

Multiple Birth   Twin, triplet, etc.

Neonatal deaths   Infants born alive but dying within 28 days of life.

Non-Obstetric Disorder   A condition that occurred during pregnancy but was not directly related to the fact that the mother was pregnant.

Parity   Number of previous pregnancies resulting in either a livebirth or a stillbirth. (Pregnancies resulting in a miscarriage or abortion are omitted).

Perinatal Deaths   Stillbirths and early neonatal deaths.

Post-Neonatal deaths   Infants dying between 4 weeks and 1 year.

Post-Perinatal deaths   Infants dying between 1 week and 1 year.

Post-term   Gestation 42 weeks or more.

Pre-term   Gestation less than 37 weeks.

Prevalence   The proportion of sudden infant deaths occurring in the population.

Rate   (see Incidence).

Relative risk In this volume we have taken the risk to the whole population as 1.0 and measured the risks to sub-groups in relation to this (see page 44).

Second Degree Relatives First cousins, aunts, uncles, nephews, and nieces, grand-parents.

Sibling A brother or sister.

Singleton An infant who has not shared the uterus with another fetus (as opposed to twins, triplets etc).

Statistical significance A method of determining whether a result could have occurred by chance. Thus, 0.05 or 5% probability means that the odds are at least 1 in 20 against the finding occurring at random. When large numbers of items are being looked at it is thought wise to take a 'higher' level of significance, and 0.01 or 1% is preferred.

Stillbirths Infants born dead.

Sudden Infant Death A death which cannot be explained by history and for which no adequate cause can be found at post-mortem.

Sudden respiratory death Either a non-hospital death referred to a coroner with a respiratory cause of death, or a death with sudden infant death syndrome on the death certificate.

Term Gestation between 37 and 41 weeks.

Third Degree Relatives Second cousins, great aunts, great uncles etc.

Vital records Birth certificates and death certificates.

References

Chapter 2: A Perspective of Infant Deaths

Beckwith JB (1970) Observations the pathological anatomy of the sudden infant death syndrome. In 'Sudden Infant Death Syndrome: Proceedings of the Second International Conference on Causes of Sudden Death in Infants'. p.83, edited by AB Bergman, JB Beckwith, and CG Ray. University of Washington Press, Seattle.

British Medical Journal (1905) 2: 1586.

Paltauf A Von (1889) Wiener Klinische Wochenschrift. 2:880.

Savitt TL (1979) Journal of the Florida Medical Association. 66:853–869.

Templeman (1892) Edinburgh Medical Journal.

Werne J and Garrow I (1953) American Journal of Pathology 29:633–676.

Chapter 4: Introduction to Epidemiological Methods

Emery JL (1976) In Recent Advances in Paediatrics no.5, ed. D. Hull; Churchill-Livingstone, London. pp 203–220.

Chapter 5: Variation with Time, Place and Age of Infant

Incidence
Armitage J and Roffman BY (1972) Nebraska Medical Journal 57:213–7.

Asher I (1975) New Zealand Medical Journal 82:369–373.

Barkin RM, Hartley MR and Brooks JG (1981) Pediatrics 68:891–2.

Beal S (1972) Medical Journal of Australia 2:1223.

Beal SM (1983) In 'Sudden Infant Death Syndrome' ed JT Tildon et al, Academic Press, New York. pp 15–28.

Bell TJ, Sexton JS and Conrad SE (1975) Journal of South Carolina Medical Association 71:312–315.

Bergman AB et al. (1972) Pediatrics 49:860–70.

Biering-Sørensen F, Jørgensen T and Hilden J (1978) Acta Paediatrica Scandinavica 67:129–137.

Bloch A (1973) Israel Journal of Medical Sciences 9:451–458.

Blok JH (1978) American Journal of Public Health 68:367–72.

Borhani NO, Rooney PA and Kraus JF (1973) California Medicine 118:12–16.

Canby JP and Jaffurs WJ (1963) Military Medicine 613–616.

Clarke J et al. (1977) Archives of Disease in Childhood 52:828–35.

Eckert EE (1976) Medizinische Klinic.

Fedrick J (1973) British Journal of Preventive and Social Medicine 27:217–24.

Fergusson DM et al. (1978) Australia Paediatric Journal 14:254–8.

Fohlin (1974) in 'SIDS 1974' Ed. R.R. Robinson, Canadian Foundation for the Study of Infant Deaths, Toronto. pp147–150.

Froggatt P, Lynas MA and MacKenzie G (1971) British Journal of Preventive and Social Medicine 25:119–134.

Getts AG and Hill HF (1982) Developmental Medicine and Child Neurology 24:61–68.

Greenberg MA, Nelson KE and Carnow BW (1973) American Journal of Epidemiology 98:412:422.

Grice AC and McGlashan ND (1978) The Medical Journal of Australia 2:177–180.

Hilton JMN and Turner KJ (1976) The Medical Journal of Australia 1:427–430.

Houstek J et al. (1971) Ceslps: pvemske zdravotaletve 19:447–452.

Karlberg et al (1977) Monographs in Paediatrics No.9 Ed. F. Falkner Karger, BAsel 83–120.

Lewak N, van den Berg BJ and Beckwith JB (1979) Clinical Pediatrics 18:404–411.

Mason JK et al (1980) Journal of Epidemiology and Community Health 34:35–41.

Milligan HC (1974) Public Health London 88:49–61.

Murphy JF, Newcombe RG and Sibert JR (1982) Journal of Epidemiology and Community Health 36:17–21.

Naeye RL, Ladis B and Drage JS (1976) American Journal of Diseases in Childhood 130:1207–1210.

Naito J (1976) Quoted by Peterson DR (1980) Epidemiologic Reviews 2:102.

Peterson DR (1966) American Journal of Epidemiology 34:478–82.

Peterson DR (1972) American Journal of Epidemiology 95:95–98.

Petersson PO and Sydow G. von (1975) British Medical Journal 2:490.
Robertson JS and Parker V (1978) Lancet ii:1012–14.
Schneider H (1977) Gesundh-Wesen 39:642–649.
Standfast SJ, Jereb S and Janerich DT (1979) Journal of the American Medical Association 241:1121–1124.
Strimer, R, Adelson L and Oseasohn R (1969) Journal of the American Medical Association 209:1493–7.
Tonkin S (1974) in 'SIDS 1974' ed. R. R. Robinson, Canadian Foundation for the Study of Infant Deaths, Toronto, Canada pp. 73–75 & 169–175.
Valdes-Dapena M et al. (1968) Journal of Pediatrics 73:387–94.
Winter ST et al (1978) Forensic Science International 12:87.
Zachau-Christiansen B and Ross EM (1975) Babies: Human Development during the first year. John Wiley and Sons (New York).

Variation within Area
Barkin RM, Hartley MR and Brooks JG (1981) Pediatrics 68:891–2.
Fedrick J (1973) British Journal of Preventive and Social Medicine 27:217–224.
Froggatt P, Lynas MA and Marshall TK (1971) Ulster Medical Journal 40:116–135.
Getts AG and Hill HF (1982) Developmental Medicine and Child Neurology 24:61–68.
Hilton JMN and Turner KJ (1976) Medical Journal of Australia 1:427–430.
Spiers P, Schlesselman JJ and Wright SG (1974) American Journal of Epidemiology 100:380–389.
Spiers PS (1980) International Journal of Epidemiology 9:45–48.
Watson E (1977) Medical Science Law 17:183–186.

Age at Death
Fedrick J (1973) British Journal of Preventive and Social Medicine 27:217–224.
Froggatt P, Lynas MA and MacKenzie G (1971) British Journal of Preventive and Social Medicine 25:119–134.
Grice AC and McGlashan (1978) Medical Journal of Australia 2:177–180.
Jørgensen Y, Beiring-Sørensen F and Hilden J (1979) Acta Paediatrica Scandinavica 68:11–22.
McGlashan, ND & Grice AC (1983) Social Science and Medicine 17:885–8.
Strimer R, Adelson L and Oseasohn R (1969) Journal of the American Medical Association 209:1493–7.

Turner KJ, Baldo BA and Hilton JMN (1975) Developmental Biology Standard 29:208–216.
Ministry of Health (1965) Enquiry into sudden death in infancy. Reports on Public Health and Medical Subjects no. 113, Her Majesty's Stationery Office, London.

Time of Death
Froggatt P, Lynas MA and Marshall TK (1971) Ulster Medical Journal 40:116–35.
Peterson DR (1966) American Journal of Epidemiology 34:478–482.

Place of Death
Fedrick J (1973) British Journal of Preventive and Social Medicine 27:217–224.
Peterson DR and Beckwith JB (1974) Pediatrics 54:644–646.

Variation over Time
Beal SM (1983) In 'Sudden Infant Death Syndrome' Ed. JT Tildon et al, Academic Press, New York. pp. 15–28.
Biering-Sørenson F, Jørgensen T and Jørgen H. (1978) Acta Paediatrica Scandinavica 67:129–137.
Borhani NO, Rooney PA and Kraus JF (1973) California Medicine 118:12–16.
Carpenter RG and Shaddick CW (1965) British Journal of Preventive and Social Medicine 19:1–7.
Grice AC and McGlashan (1978) Medical Journal of Australia 2:177–180.
Houstek J, Holy J and Vanecek K (1973) Padiatri und Padologie 8:257–263.
Macfarlane A and Pharoah POD (1982) 'Studies in sudden infant deaths' Studies on Medical and Population Subjects, no 45 Her Majesty's Stationery Office, London. pp.1–8.
Robertson JS and Parker V (1978) Lancet ii:1012–1014.
Strimer R, Adelson L and Oseasohn R. (1969) Journal of the American Medical Association 209:1493–7.
Valdes-Dapena M (1977) Pathology Annual 12:117–145.
Peterson DR, Belle G van and Chinn NM (1979) American Journal of Epidemiology 110:699–707.
Peterson DR and Chinn NM (1977) Pediatrics 60:75–79.
Carpenter RG and Gardner A (1982) In 'Studies in sudden infant deaths'. Studies on Medical and Population Subjects. no. 45. Her Majesty's Stationery Office, London. pp. 23–31.

Variation with Season
Beal SM (1978) Lancet i:1257.
Farber MD and Chandra V (1978) Lancet ii:473.
Fedrick J (1973) British Journal of Preventive and Social Medicine 27:217–224.
Grice AC and McGlashan ND. (1978) Medical Journal of Australia 2:177–180.
Hoppenbrouwers et al (1981) American Journal of Epidemiology 113:623–635.
Kraus AS, Steele R and Langworth JT (1967) Canadian Journal of Public Health 58:364–371.
McGlashan ND and Grice AC (1983) Social Science and Medicine 17:885–8.
Peterson DR (1972) American Journal of Epidemiology 95:95–98.
Strimer R, Adelson L and Oseasohn R (1969) Journal of the American Medical Association 209:1493–1124.
Zoglo DP, Luckey DW and Fraiker AL (1979) Lancet ii:260.

Day of the Week
Beal SM (1983) In 'Sudden Infant Death Syndrome' Ed. JT Tildon et al, Academic Press, New York. pp. 15–28.
Borhani NO, Rooney PA and Kraus JF (1973) California Medicine 118:12–16.
Cameron AH and Asher P (1965) Medical Science Law 5:187–199.
Clarke J et al (1977) Archives of Disease in Childhood 52:828–835.
Emery JL (1959) British Medical Journal 4:925–928.
Fedrick J (1973) British Journal of Preventive and Social Medicine 27:217–224.
Froggatt P, Lynas MA and Marshall TK (1971) Ulster Medical Journal 40:116–135.
Hilton JMN and Turner KJ (1976) Medical Journal of Australia 1:427–430.
McGlashan ND and Grice AC (1983) Social Science and Medicine 17:885–8.
Macfarlane A and Gardner A (1982) 'Studies in sudden infant deaths'. Studies on Medical and Population Subjects no. 45. Her Majesty's Stationery Office, London. pp. 19–22.
Peterson DR (1966) American Journal of Epidemiology 34:478–482.
Richards IDG and McIntosh HT (1972) Archives of Disease in Childhood 47:697–706.
Standfast SJ et al (1983) In 'Sudden Infant Death Syndrome' ed. JT Tildon et al, Academic Press, New York. pp. 59–75.

Clustering of deaths on the same day
Coe JI and Hartman EE (1960) Journal of Pediatrics 56:786–794.
Fedrick J (1973) British Journal of Preventive and Social Medicine 27:217–224.
Froggatt P, Lynas MA and MacKenzie G (1971) British Journal of Preventive and Social Medicine 25:119–134.
Kraus AS, Steele R and Langworth JT (1967) 58:364–371.
Peterson DR (1972) American Journal of Epidemiology 95:95–98.

The Weather
Bonser RSA, Knight BH and West RR (1978) International Journal of Epidemiology 7:335–340.
Fedrick J (1973) British Journal of Preventive and Social Medicine 27:217–224.
Greenberg MA, Nelson KE and Carnow BW (1973) American Journal of Epidemiology 98:412–421.
Heaney S and McIntire MS (1979) Journal of Pediatrics 94:433–434.
Kraus AS, Steele R and Langworth JT (1967) Canadian Journal of Public Health 58:364–371.
Kraus AS, Steele R, Thompson MG and de Grosbois P (1971) Canadian Journal of Public Health 62:210–218.
McGlashan ND & Grice AC (1983) Social Science and Medicine 17:885–8.

Clustering in time and space
Bonser RSA, Knight BH and West RR (1978) International Journal of Epidemiology 7:335–340.
Chamberlain R and Simpson N (1979) 'The Prevalence of Disease in Childhood.' Pitman Medical Press, London.
Fedrick J (1973) British Journal of Preventive and Social Medicine 27:217–224.
Fedrick J (1974) British Journal of Preventive and Social Medicine 28:164–171.
Froggatt P, Lynas MA and MacKenzie G (1971) British Journal of Preventive and Social Medicine 25:119–134.

Chapter 6: Characteristics of the Parents

Social Class
Adelstein AM, Alberman ED and Barrett JC (1976) A collection of studies OPCS 33:43–60.
Adelstein AM, Macdonald Davies IM, Weatherall JAC and White GC (1982) Studies on Medical and Population Subjects no. 45 Her Majesty's Stationery Office, London pp. 40–50.

Biering-Sørensen F, Jørgensen T and Hilden J (1970) Acta Paediatrica Scandinavica 68:1–9.

Fedrick J (1974) British Journal of Preventive and Social Medicine 28:93–7.

Froggatt P, Lynas MA and MacKenzie G (1971) British Journal of Preventive and Social Medicine 25:119–134.

Kraus JF (1983) In 'Sudden Infant Death Syndrome' Ed. JT Tildon et al, Academic Press, New York pp. 43–58.

Lewak N, van den Berg BJ and Beckwith JB (1979) Clinical Pediatrics 18:404–411.

Mason JK et al (1980) Journal of Epidemiology and Community Health 34:35–41.

Naeye RL, Ladis B and Drage JS (1976) American Journal of Diseases in Childhood 130:1207–1210.

Office of Population Censuses and Surveys (1979) OPCS Monitor SH1 79/2.

Protestos CD et al. (1973) Archives of Disease in Childhood 48:835–841.

Standfast SJ et al (1983) In 'Sudden Infant Death Syndrome' Ed. JT Tildon et al, Academic Press, New York pp. 59–75.

Strimer R, Adelson L and Oseasohn R (1969) Journal of American Medical Association 209:1493–7.

Unemployment
Froggat P, Lynas MA and Marshall TK (1971) Ulster Medical Journal 40:116–135.

Kraus AS et al. (1972) Canadian Journal of Public Health 62:210–8.

Murphy JF, Newcombe RG and Sibert JR (1982) Journal of Epidemiology and Community Health 36:17–21.

Marital Status
Biering-Sørensen F, Jørgensen T and Hilden J (1970) Acta Paediatrica Scandinavica 68:1–9.

Chamberlain R and Simpson N (1979) 'The Prevalence of Diseases in Childhood' Pitman Medical Press, London.

Froggatt P, Lynas MA and Marshall TK (1971) Ulster Medical Journal 40:116–135.

Kraus AS et al. (1971) Canadian Journal of Public Health 62:210–218.

Kraus JF and Borhani NO (1972) American Journal of Epidemiology 95:497–510.

Standfast SJ et al (1983) In 'Sudden Infant Death Syndrome' Ed. JT Tildon et al, Academic Press, New York pp. 59–75.

Maternal age

Adelstein AM, Macdonald Davies IM, Weatherall JAC and White GC (1982) Studies on Medical and Population Subjects no. 45, Her Majesty's Stationery Office, London pp. 40–50.

Carpenter RG, Gardner A and Emery JL (1979) Archives of Disease in Childhood 54:406–407.

Fedrick J (1974) British Journal of Preventive and Social Medicine 28:93–97.

Froggatt P, Lynas MA and MacKenzie G (1971) British Journal of Preventive and Social Medicine 25:119–134.

Jørgensen T, Biering-Sørensen F and Hilden J (1979) Acta Paediatrica Scandinavica 68:11–22.

Kraus JF (1983) In 'Sudden Infant Death Syndrome' Ed. JT Tildon et al, Academic Press, New York pp. 43–58.

Lewak B, van den Berg BJ and Beckwith JB (1979) Clinical Pediatrics 18:404–411.

Naeye RL, Ladis B and Drage JS (1976) American Journal of Diseases in Childhood 130:1207–1210.

Peterson DR, van Belle G and Chinn NM (1982) Journal of the American Medical Association 247:2250–2.

Puffer RR and Serano CV (1973) Patterns of Mortality in Childhood. Pan American Health Association. pp. 238–240.

Standfast SJ et al (1983) In 'Sudden Infant Death Syndrome' Ed. JT Tildon et al, Academic Press, New York pp. 59–75.

Birth Order

Adelstein AM, Macdonal Davies IM, Weatherall JAC and White GC (1982) Studies on Medical and Population Subjects no. 45 Her Majesty's Stationery Office, London pp. 40–50.

Carpenter RG, Gardner A and Emery JL (1979) Archives of Disease in Childhood 54:406–407.

Fedrick J (1974) British Journal of Preventive and Social Medicine 28:93–97.

Froggatt P, Lynas MA and Marshall TK (1971) Ulster Medical Journal 40:116–135.

Jørgensen Y, Biering-Sørensen F and Hilden J (1979) Acta Paediatrica Scandinavica 68:11–22.

Kraus AS et al. (1971) Canadian Journal of Public Health 62:210–218.

Kraus JF (1983) In 'Sudden Infant Death Syndrome' Ed. JT Tildon et al, Academic Press, New York pp. 43–58.

Kraus JF, Franti CE and Borhani NO (1972) American Journal of Epidemiology 96:327–383.

Peterson DR, van Belle G and Chinn NM (1982) Journal of the American Medical Association 247:2250-2.
Standfast SJ et al (1983) In 'Sudden Infant Death Syndrome' Ed. JT Tildon et al, Academic Press, New York pp. 59-75.
Roberts J et al. (1984) British Medical Journal. In Press.

Height of Mother
Naeye RL, Ladis B & Drage JS (1976) American Journal of Diseases in Children 130:1207-1210.

Race
Armitage J and Roffman BY (1972) Nebraska Medical Journal 53:213-7.
Blok JH (1978) American Journal of Public Health 68:367-372.
Fedrick J (1974) British Journal of Preventive and Social Medicine 28:93-97.
Lewak N, van den Berg BJ and Beckwith JB (1979) Clinical Pediatrics 18:404-11.
Naeye RL, Ladis B and Drage JS (1976) American Journal of Diseases in Childhood 130:1207-1210.
Standfast SJ et al (1983) In 'Sudden Infant Death Syndrome' Ed JT Tildon et al, Academic Press, New York pp. 59-75.
Strimer R, Adelson L and Oseasohn R. (1969) Journal of the American Medical Association 209:1493-7.

Blood group
Aird I et al (1954) British Medical Journal 2:315-321.
Clarke CA (1961) In 'Progress in Medical Genetics' Vol. 1 Ed. AG Steinberg.
Carpenter RG, Gardner A and Emery JL (1979) Archives of Disease in Childhood 54:406-407.
Fedrick J (1974) British Journal of Preventive and Social Medicine 28:93-97.
Harris JDC et al (1982) Journal of Epidemiology and Community Health 36:162-166.
Oakley JR, Tavare CJ and Stanton AN (1978) Archives of Disease in Childhood 53:649-652.

Previous Pregnancy Loss
Fedrick J (1974) British Journal of Preventive and Social Medicine 28:93-97.
Jørgensen T, Biering-Sørensen F and Hilden J (1979) Acta Paediatrica Scandinavica 68:11-22.

Kraus AS et al. (1971) Canadian Journal of Public Health 62:210–218.
Peterson DR, van Belle G and Chinn NM (1979) American Journal of Epidemiology 110:699–707.
Protestos CD et al. (1973) Archives of Disease in Childhood 48:835–841.
Spiers PS (1976) American Journal of Epidemiology 103:355–361.

Date of last menstrual period
Fedrick J (1974) British Journal of Preventive and Social Medicine 28:164–171.
Kraus JF and Borhani NO (1972) American Journal of Epidemiology 95:497;510.
Wenner WH and Young EB (1974) American Journal of Obstetrics and Gynecology 120:1071.

Smoking in Pregnancy
Bergman AB and Wiesner LA (1976) Pediatrics 58:665–8.
Chamberlain R and Simpson N (1979) The Prevalence of Disease in Childhood. Pitman Medical Press, London.
Lewak N, van den Berg BJ and Beckwith JB (1979) Clinical Pediatrics 18:404–411.
Murphy JF, Newcombe RG and Sibert JR (1982) Journal of Epidemiology and Community Health 36:17–21.
Naeye RL, Ladis B and Drage JS (1976) American Journal of Disease in Childhood 130:1207–1210.
Schrauzer GN, Rhead WJ and Saltzstein SL (1975) Annals of Clinical and Laboratory Science 5:31–37.

Drug addiction
Chavez CJ et al. (1979) Journal of Pediatrics 95:407–9.
Finnegan LP (1979) Clinics in Perinatology 6:163–180.

Non-obstetric Disorders
Fedrick J (1974) British Journal of Preventive and Social Medicine 28:164–171.
Naeye RL, Ladis B and Drage JS (1976) American Journal of Diseases in Childhood 130:1207–1210.
Protestos CD et al. (1973) Archives of Disease in Childhood 48:835–841.

Chapter 7: Characteristics of the Pregnancy

Inter-pregnancy Interval

Fedrick J (1974) British Journal of Preventive and Social Medicine 28:93–7.
Kraus AS et al. (1971) Canadian Journal of Public Health 62:210–8.
Lewak N, van den Berg BJ and Beckwith JB (1979) Clinical Pediatrics 18:404–411.
Standfast SJ et al (1983) In 'Sudden Infant Death Syndrome' Ed. JT Tildon et al, Academic Press, New York pp. 59–75.

Planned pregnancies

Chamberlain R and Simpson N (1979) The Prevalence of Disease in Childhood, Pitman Medical Press, London.
Lewak N, van den Berg BJ and Beckwith JB (1979) Clinical Pediatrics 18:404–411.
Protestos CD et al (1973) Archives of Diseases in Childhood 48:835–841.

Antenatal Care

Jørgensen T, Biering-Sørensen F and Hilden J (1979) Acta Paediatrica Scandinavica 68:11–22.
Kraus AS et al (1971) Canadian Journal of Public Health 62:210–218.
Kraus JF and Borhani NO (1972) American Journal of Epidemiology 95:497–510.
Lewak N, van den Berg BJ and Beckwith JB (1979) Clinical Pediatrics 18:404–411.
Naeye RL, Ladis B and Drage JS (1976) American Journal of Diseases in Childhood 130:1207–1210.
Palmer SR, Wiggins RD and Bewley BR (1980) Community Medicine 2:102–8.
Standfast SJ et al (1983) In 'Sudden Infant Death Syndrome' Ed. JT Tildon et al, Academic Press, New York pp. 59–75.

Toxaemia

Fedrick J (1974) British Journal of Preventive and Social Medicine 28:164–171.
Naeye RL (1983) In 'Sudden Infant Death Syndrome' Ed. JT Tildon et al, Academic Press, New York pp. 77–83.
Naeye RL, Ladis B and Drage JS (1976) American Journal of Diseases in Childhood 1207–1210.

Haemorrhage, Anaemia and other disorders

Fedrick J (1974) British Journal of Preventive and Social Medicine 28:164–171.

Froggatt P, Lynas MA and Marshall TK (1971) Ulster Medical Journal 40:116-135.
Jørgensen T, Biering-Sørensen F and Hilden J (1979) Acta Paediatrica Scandinavica 68:11-22.
Lewak N, van den Berg BJ and Beckwith JB (1979) Clinical Pediatrics 18:404-411.
Naeye RL (1983) In 'Sudden Infant Death Syndrome' Ed. JT Tildon et al, Academic Press, New York pp. 77-83.
Naeye RL, Ladis and Drage JS (1976) American Journal of Diseases in Childhood 130:1207-1210.
Protestos CD et al. (1973) Archives of Disease in Childhood 48:835-41.

Pharmaceutical drugs
Naeye RL, Ladis B and Drage JS (1976) American Journal of Disease in Childhood 130:1207-1210.
Protestos CD et al. (1973) Archives of Disease in Childhood 48:835-841.

Chapter 8: Labour and Delivery

Place of birth

Chamberlain R and Simpson RN (1979) The Prevalence of Disease in Childhood. Pitman Medical Press. London.
Fedrick J (1974) British Journal of Preventive and Social Medicine 28:164-171.

Labour and Delivery

Fedrick J (1974) British Journal of Preventive and Social Medicine 28:164-171.
Froggatt P, Lynas MA and Marshall TK (1971) Ulster Medical Journal 40:116-135.
Hoppenbrouwers T, Zanini B and Hodgman JE (1979) American Journal of Obstetrics and Gynecology 133:217-220.
Jørgensen T, Biering-Sørensen F and Hilden J (1979) Acta Paediatrica Scandinavica 68:11-22.
Lewak N, van den Berg BJ and Beckwith JB (1979) Clinical Pediatrics 18:404-411.
Naeye RL, Ladis B and Drage JS (1976) American Journal of Diseases in Childhood 130:1207-1210.
Protestos CD et al. (1973) Archives of Disease in Childhood 48:835-841.

Murphy JF, Newcombe RG and Sibert JR (1982) Journal of Epidemiology and Community Health 36:17–21.

Season of Delivery
Beal SM (1983) In 'Sudden Infant Death Syndrome' Ed. JT Tildon et al, Academic Press, New York, pp. 15–28.
Bergman AB et al, (1972) Pediatrics 49:860–870.
Carpenter RG and Gardner A (1982) 'Variations in unexpected infant death rates relating to age, sex and season.' In 'Studies in sudden infant deaths'. Studies on Medical and Population Subjects no. 45. HMSO. pp. 23–31.
Geertinger P (1968) 'Sudden Death in Infancy' Charles T. Thomas, Springfield.
Hoppenbrouwers T, et al (1981) American Journal of Epidemiology 113:623–635.
Murphy JF, Newcombe RG and Sibert JR (1982) Journal of Epidemiology and Community Health 36:17–21.
Stewart A (1975) British Medical Journal 2:605–607.
Taylor WB (1982) International Journal of Epidemiology 11:138–145.

Chapter 9: Characteristics of the Infant in the Early Neonatal Period

Sex differences

Asher I (1975) New Zealand Medical Journal 82:369–73.
Beal S (1972) Medical Journal of Australia 2:1223.
Bergman AB et al (1972) Pediatrics 49:860–70.
Biering-Sørensen, Jørgensen T and Hilden J (1978) Acta Paediatrica Scandinavica 67:129–137.
Bonser RSA, Knight BH and West RR (1978) International Journal of Epidemiology 7:335–340.
Borhani NO, Rooney PA and Kraus JF (1973) California Medicine 118:12–16.
Fedrick J (1974) British Journal of Preventive and Social Medicine 28:93–97.
Fohlin (1974) in 'SIDS 1974' ed. R.R. Robinson, Canadian Foundation for the Study of Infant Deaths, Toronto.
Froggatt P, Lynas MA and MacKenzie G (1971) British Journal of Preventive and Social Medicine 25:119–134.
Grice AC and McGlashan ND (1978) Medical Journal of Australia 2:177–180.
Hilton JMN and Turner KJ (1976) Medical Journal of Australia 1:427–430.

Lewak N, van den Berg BJ and Beckwith JB (1979) Clinical Pediatrics 18:404-11.

Milligan HC (1973) Public Health London 88:49-61.

Naeye RL et al (1976) Journal of Pediatrics 88:511-515.

Naeye RL, Ladis B and Drage JS (1976) American Journal of Diseases in Childhood 130:1207-10.

Standfast SJ, Jereb S and Janerich DT (1979) Journal of the American Medical Association 241:1121-24.

Standfast SJ et al (1983) in 'Sudden Infant Death Syndrome' Ed. JT Tildon et al. Academic Press, New York. pp. 59-75.

Strimer R, Adelson L and Oseasohn R (1969) Journal of the American Medical Association 209:1493-97.

Sunderland R and Emery JL (1979) British Medical Journal 9:575-576.

Tonkin S (1974) in 'SIDS 1974' Ed. RR Robinson, Foundation for the Study of Sudden Infant Deaths, Toronto.

Valdes-Dapena M et al. (1968) Journal of Pediatrics 73:387-394.

Gestation and Birthweight
Carpenter RG and Gardner A (1979) Archives of Disease in Childhood 54:406-7.

Fedrick J (1974) British Journal of Preventive and Social Medicine 28:164-171.

Jørgensen T, Biering-Sørensen F and Hilden J (1970) Acta Paediatrica Scandinavica 11;22.

Kraus JF (1983), in 'Sudden Infant Death Syndrome' Ed. JT Tildon et al, Academic Press, New York. pp. 43-58.

Protestos CD et al. (1973) Archives of Disease in Childhood 48:835-841.

Steel R, Kraus AS and Langworth JT (1967) Canadian Journal of Public Health 58:359-71.

Head circumference, birth length, blood group
Froggatt P, Lynas MA and Marshall TK (1971) Ulster Medical Journal 40:116-135.

Lewak N, van den Berg BJ and Beckwith JB (1979) Clinical Pediatrics 18:404-411.

Naeye RL, Ladis B and Drage JS (1976) American Journal of Diseases in Childhood 130:1207-10.

Protestos CD et al. (1973) Archives of Disease in Childhood 48:835-841.

Jørgensen T, Biering-Sørensen, F and Hilden J (1982). Acta Paediatrica Scandinavica 71:183-9.

Twins
Beal S (1973) Medical Journal of Australia 1:1146–48.
Beal SM (1983) In 'Sudden Infant Death Syndrome' Ed. JT Tildon et al, Academic Press, New York.
Daily Telegraph; November 19th, 1983.
Fedrick J (1974) British Journal of Preventive and Social Medicine 28:164–171.
Froggatt P, Lynas MA and Marshall TK (1971) Ulster Medical Journal 40:116–135.
Kraus JF (1983) In 'Sudden Infant Death Syndrome' Ed. JT Tildon et al. Academic Press, New York, pp. 43–58.
Kraus JF and Borhani NO (1972) American Journal of Epidemiology 497–510.
Getts A (1981) American Journal of Public Health 71:317–8.
Murphy JF, Newcombe RG and Sibert JR (1982) Journal of Epidemiology and Community Health 36:17–21.
Peterson DR, Chinn NM and Fisher LD (1980) Journal of Pediatrics 97:265–7.
Spiers PS (1974) Americal Journal of Epidemiology 100:1–7.
Standfast SJ et al (1983) In 'Sudden Infant Death Syndrome' Ed. JT Tildon et al. Academic Press, New York. pp. 59–75.

Neonatal disorders
Anderson RB and Rosenblith JF (1971) Biology of the Neonate 18:395–406.
Anderson-Huntingdon RB and Rosenblith JF (1976) Developmental Medicine Child Neurology 18:480–492.
Chamberlain R and Simpson N (1979) The Prevalence of Diseases in Childhood, Pitman Medical Press, London.
Lewak N, van den Berg BJ and Beckwith JB (1979) Clinical Pediatrics 18:404–11.
Lipsitt LP (1978) In 'Early Developmental Hazard: Predictor and Precautions'. Ed. FD Horowitz. pp. 11–28.
Naeye RL, Ladis B and Drage JS (1976) American Journal of Disease in Childhood 130:1207–10.
Standfast SJ et al (1983) In 'Sudden Infant Death Syndrome' Ed. JT Tildon et al. Academic Press, New York. pp. 59–75.

Congenital Malformations
Biering-Sørensen F, Jørgensen T and Hilden J (1978) Acta Paediatrica Scandinavica 67:129–137.
Brereton RJ, Zachary RB and Spitz L (1978) Archives of Disease in Childhood 53:276–283.

Fedrick J (1974) British Journal of Preventive and Social Medicine 28:164–71.
Weinberg SB and Purdy BA (1970) Nature 226:1264–5.

The Placenta
Lewak N, Van Den Berg BJ and Beckwith JB (1979) Clinical Pediatrics 18:404–411.
Naeye RL (1977) Biology of the Neonate 32: 189–192.

Chapter 10: Characteristics of the Older Infant

Housing
Biering-Sørensen F, Jørgensen T and Hilden J (1979) Acta Paedatrica Scandinavica 68:1–9.
Clarke J et al. (1977) Archives of Disease in Childhood 52:828–35.
Eckert EE (1976) Medizinische Klinic. 71:1500–1505.
Kraus AS et al. (1971) Canadian Journal of Public Health 62:210–8.

Clinic attendance
Biering-Sørensen F, Jørgensen T and Hilden J (1978) Acta Paediatrica Scandinavica 67:129–137.
Kraus AS et al. (1971) Canadian Journal of Public Health 62:210–8.
Murphy JF, Newcombe RG and Sibert JR (1982) Journal of Epidemiology and Community Health 36:17–21.
Palmer SR, Wiggins RD and Bewley BR (1980) Community Medicine 2:102–108.
Protestos CD et al. (1973) Archives of Disease in Childhood 48:835–841.

Breast Feeding
Biering-Sørensen F, Jørgensen T and Hilden J (1978) Acta Paediatrica Scandinavica 67:129–137.
Fedrick (1974) British Journal of Preventive and Social Medicine 28:164–171.
Froggatt P, Lynas MA and Mackenzie G (1971) British Journal of Preventive and Social Medicine 25:119–134.
Harris JDC et al (1982) Journal of Epidemiology and Community Health 36:162–166.
Kraus AS et al. (1971) Canadian Journal of Public Health 62:210–8.
Murphy JF, Newcombe RG and Sibert JR (1982) Journal of Epidemiology and Community Health 36:17–21.
Naeye RL, Ladis B and Drage JS (1976) American Journal of Diseases in Childhood 130:1207–10.

Protestos CD et al (1973) Archives of Disease in Childhood 48:835–841.
Rhead WJ, Schrauzer GN and Saltzstein SL (1973) British Medical Journal 4:458–9.

Post-neonatal growth
Froggatt P, Lynas MA and Marshall TK (1971) Ulster Medical Journal 40:116–35.
Jørgensen T, Biering-Sørensen F and Hilden J (1982) Acta Paediatrica Scandinavica.
Ministry of Health Report No. 113 (1964) 1–52.
Naeye RL, Ladis B and Drage JS (1976) American Journal of Diseases in Childhood 130:1207–1210.
Naeye RL et al. (1976) Journal of Pediatrics 88:511–515.
Peterson et al (1974) American Journal of Epidemiology 50:389–94.
Peterson DR (1981) American Journal of Epidemiology 113:583–9.

Passive smoking
Bergman AB and Wiesner BA (1976) Pediatrics 58:665–668.

Postneonatal temperament
Naeye RL et al (1976) Journal of Pediatrics 88:511–515.

Post-neonatal illness
Beal SM (1983) In 'Sudden Infant Death Syndrome' Ed. JT Tildon et al. Academic Press, New York. pp. 15–28.
Benjamin DR (1979) Lancet ii:954.
Carpenter RG and Shaddick CW (1965) British Journal of Preventive and Social Medicine, 19:1–7.
Carpenter RG et al. (1977) Archives of Disease in Childhood 52:606–612.
Fedrick J (1974) British Journal of Preventive and Social Medicine 28:164–71.
Froggatt P, Lynas MA and Marshall TK (1971) Ulster Medical Journal 40:116–135.
Stanton AN et al (1978) British Medical Journal 2:1249–1251.

Bedding and sleeping position
Carpenter RG and Shaddick CW (1965) British Journal of Preventive and Social Medicine 19:1–7.
Valdes-Dapena M (1977) Pathology Annual 12:117–145.

Chapter 11: Medical History of the Siblings and the Mothers

Siblings

Beal SM (1983) in 'Sudden Death Syndrome' Ed. JT Tildon et al. Academic Press, New York. pp. 15–28.

Fedrick J (1974) British Journal of Preventive and Social Medicine. 28:164–171.

Froggatt P, Lynas MA and MacKenzie G (1971) British Journal of Preventive and Social Medicine 25:119–134.

Peterson DR, Chinn NM and Fisher LD (1980) Journal of Pediatrics. 97:265–7.

Steinschneider A (1972) Pediatrics 50:646.

Chapter 12: Summary of Epidemiological Findings

Summary of Epidemiological Findings

Beal SM (1983) In 'Sudden infant death syndrome' Ed. ET Tildon, et al, Academic Press, New York pp. 15–28.

Carpenter RG and Gardner A. (1982) In 'Studies in sudden infant deaths' Studies on Medical and Population Subjects, no. 45 Her Majesty's Stationery Office, London. pp. 23–31.

Fedrick J. (1973) British Journal of Preventive and Social Medicine 27:217–224.

Fedrick J. (1974) British Journal of Preventive and Social Medicine 28:164–71.

Fedrick J. (1974) British Journal of Preventive and Social Medicine 28:93–97.

Chapter 13: Methods of Generating and Testing Hypotheses

Near-Miss

Kelly DH, Shannon DC and O'Connel K (1978) Pediatrics 61:511.

Peterson DR (1983) In 'Sudden Infant Death Syndrome' Ed. JT Tildon, LM Roeder, A Steinschneider, Academic Press, New York. pp. 89–97.

Chapter 14: Excesses and Deficiences

Hypernatraemia

Andrews PS (1975) Medicine, Science & Law 15:47–50.

Department of Health and Social Security (1974) Committee on Children Nutrition: Present Day Practice in Infant Feeding. Her Majesty's Stationery Office, London.

Emery JL, Swift PGF, & Worthy E. (1974) Archives of Disease in Childhood 49:686-692.
Finberg L and Harrison HE (1955) Pediatrics 16:1-14.
Mason JK et al (1980) Journal of Epidemiology and Community Health 34:35-41.
Robertson JS and Parker V. (1978) Lancet ii:1012-6.
Salge B (1911) Zeitschrift für Kinderheilkunde 1:126-138.
Sunderland R and Emery J. (1979) British Medical Journal 3:575-577.
Taitz LS and Byers HD (1972) Archives of Disease in Childhood 47:257-260.

Magnesium Deficiency
Caddell JL, (1972) Lancet, ii:258-262.
Caddell JL, (1977) Journal of Pediatrics 90:1039.
Chipperfield B & Chipperfield JR (1979) Lancet i:220.
Erickson MM et al (1983) Pediatric Research 17:784-7.
Godwin JD & Brown C. (1973) Lancet i: 1178.
Lapin CA et al (1976) Journal of Pediatrics 89:607-8.
Peterson DR & Beckwith JB (1973) Lancet ii:330.
Swift PGF & Emery JL (1972) Lancet ii:871.

Selenium Deficiency
Asher MI (1975) New Zealand Medical Journal 82:369-373.
Money DFL (1970) Journal of Pediatrics 77:165-6.
Rhead WJ (1977) Journal of Pediatrics 90(3):500.
Saltzstein SL (1975) Lancet i:1095.
Schrauzer GN, Rhead WJ & Saltzstein SL (1975) Annals of Clinical and Laboratory Science 5:31-37.

Vitamin E deficiency
Rhead, WJ et al (1972) Journal of Pediatrics 81:415-6.
Schrauzer, GN, Rhead, WJ, and Saltzstein SL (1975) Annals of Clinical and Laboratory Science 5:31-37.
Tapp, E and Anfield, C. (1975) Lancet i:467.

Vitamin C deficiency
Kalokerinos A, (1974) 'Every Second Child' Thomas Nelson (Australia) Ltd, Melbourne.
Kalokerinos A & Dettman G (1976) Medical Journal of Australia 2:31-32.
Phelon P (1979) Medical Journal of Australia 2:696.

Vitamin D deficiency
Geertinger, P (1967) Danish Medical Bulletin 14:109–119.
Hillman LS, Erickson M, & Hoddad JG (1980) Pediatrics 65:1137–39.
Hoff N et al (1979) Journal of Pediatrics 94:460–6.
Hunt SP et al (1976) British Medical Journal 2:1351–4.
Slykes F, Hamil B and Poole M (1937) Proceedings of the Society of Experimental & Biological Medicine 37:499.

Biotin deficiency
Johnson AR, Hood RL & Emery JL (1980) Nature 285:159–160.
Tildon JT & Roeder LM (1983) In 'Sudden Infant Death Syndrome' ed. JT Tildon et al, Academic Press, New York. pp. 211–221, 243–262.

Thiamine deficiency
Davis RE, Icke GC & Hilton JMN (1980) New England of Medicine 303:462.
Davis RE, Icke GC & Hilton JMN (1983) In 'Sudden Infant Death Syndrome'. Ed. JT Tildon et al, Academic Press, New York. pp. 201–210.
Paterson DR et al (1981) American Journal of Clinical Nutrition.
Read DJC (1978) Australia & New Zealand Journal of Medicine 8:322–36.
Tildon JT & Roeder LM (1983) In 'Sudden Infant Death Syndrome' Ed. JT Tildon et al, Academic Press, New York, pp. 243–262.

Hypoglycaemia
Submilla et al (1983) European Journal of Pediatrics 140:276–7.

Thyroid Hormones
Chacon MA and Tildon JT (1981) Journal of Pediatrics 99: 758–760.
Moshang T et al. (1980) Journal of Pediatrics 97:602.
Peterson DR (1983) In 'Sudden Infant Death Syndrome' Ed. JT Tildon. et al. Academic Press, New York.
Root AW (1983) Journal of Pediatrics 102:251–2.
Tildon JT and Roeder LM (1983) In 'Sudden Infant Death Syndrome' Ed. JT Tildon et al, Academic Press. New York. pp. 211–221, and 243–262.

Over-Heating
Bacon C, Scott D and Jones P (1979) Lancet i:422–425.
Dallas RJ (1974) British Medical Journal iii:347.

Stanton AN, Scott DJ and Downham MAPS. (1980) Lancet i:1054–1057.

Febrile Convulsions
Berry AC (1981) Lancet ii:633.
Sunderland R and Emery JL (1981) Lancet ii: 633.

Malignant Hyper-pyrexia
Denborough MA, Galloway GJ, and Hopkinson KC (1982) Lancet ii:1068–9.

Chapter 15: Sleeping, Breathing and Heart Rate

Internal Mechanical Suffocation
Kravitz H, and Scherz RG (1978) Clinical Pediatrics 17:403–408.

External Mechanical Obstruction to Breathing
Berger D (1979) Journal of Pediatrics 95:554–6.
Lynch MA and Roberts J (1977) British Medical Journal 1:624–6.
Roberts J, Lynch MA & Golding J (1980) British Medical Journal 281:102.
Taylor EM & Emery JL. (1982) Archives of Disease in Childhood 56:668–673.

Abnormal Lung Surfactant
Morley CJ et al (1982) Lancet i:1320–1322.

Other Sleeping Problems
Avery ME, and Frantz ID (1983) New England Journal of Medicine 309:107–8.
Schiffman PL et al, (1980) New England Journal of Medicine 302:486–491.

Heart Beat Abnormalities
Southall DP et al (1983) British Medical Journal 286:1092–6.

Chapter 16: Infections and the Immune System

Immunological mechanisms
Clark JW et al, (1979) Journal of Pediatrics 95:85–6.
Clausen CR et al, (1973) Pediatrics 52:45–   .
Coe JI, (1963) Pediatric Digest Sept. pp. 44–53.
Ehrhardt G Von, (1975) Zentralblatt allgemeine Pathologie unt pathologische unt anatomie. 119S:91–99.
Gunther M, (1975) Lancet i:441–2.

Henschel MJ and Coates ME, (1974) Proceedings of the Nutrition Society 33: 112A.
Mulvey PM, (1972) Medical Journal of Australia 2:1240–4.
Raven C et al, (1978) Journal of Forensic Sciences 23:116–128.
Tait BD et al, (1977) Monographs on Allergy 11:55–59.
Turner KJ, Baldo BA and Hilton JMN, (1975) British Medical Journal 1:357–60.
Turner KJ et al, (1975) Medical Journal of Australia 2:855–9.
Warnasuriya N et al, (1980) Archives of Disease in Childhood 55:876–8.

Botulinism
Arnon SS, Damus K and Chinn J, (1981) Epidemiologic Reviews 3:45–66.
Arnon SS, et al, (1978) Lancet i:1273–6.
Leading Article, Lancet i:1295–6.
Urquhart GED and Grist NR, (1972) Journal of Clinical Pathology

Congenital infection
Potencz H, (1974) Journal of Pediatrics 85:281–3.

Postnatal infection
Clarke SKR et al, (1978) British Medical Journal 2:796–8.
Downham MAPS et al, (1975) British Medical Journal 1:235–9.
Ferris JAJ et al, (1973) British Medical Journal 2:439–442.
Foy HM and Ray CG, (1973) American Journal of Epidemiology 98:69–71.
Gardner PS, (1972) Journal of the Forensic Science Society 12:587–9.
Nelson KE, et al, (1975) American Journal of Epidemiology 101:423–430.
Ray CG et al, (1970) Journal of the American Medical Association 211:619–623.
Urquhart GED and Grist NR, (1972) Journal of Clinical Pathology 25:443–6.

Chapter 17: Bereavement

Bluglass K (1981) Journal of Child Psychology and Psychiatry 22:411–421.
Cornwell J, Nurcombe B and Stevens L (1977) Medical Journal of Australia. 1:656–658.
DeFrain J & Ernst (1978) Journal of Family Practice 6:985–989.

DeFrain J, Taylor J, & Ernst L (1982) 'Coping with Sudden Infant Death' Lexington Books, Toronto.
Lewis S (1981) The Health Visitor. 54(8):322-325.
Steele R (1980) Understanding Crib Death, The Canadian Public Health Association, Canada, p. 50.
Gorer G (1965) Death, Grief and Mourning in Contemporary Britain. Doubleday, Garden City, New York.
Watson E (1975) Public Health, London 89:153-5.

Vaccination
Taylor EM and Emery JL (1982) Lancet ii:721.

Chapter 19: The Coroner's Investigation

Emery JL (1972) British Medical Journal 1:612.
Watson E (1981) Medical Science Law 21:99-104.

Chapter 20: Funerals and Administrative Problems

'What do do After a Death' (August 1979) Department of Health and Social Security Leaflets Unit (PO Box 21, Stanmore, Middlesex HA7 1AY).

Chapter 21: Support for Parents

Watson E (1981) Medical Science Law 21:99-104.

Leaflets:
Information for parents following the Sudden and unexpected death of their baby.
Your Next Child.
When to consult a doctor about your baby.
Available from:
   The Foundation for the Study of Infant Deaths
   5th Floor,
   4/5 Grosvenor Place
   London SW1X 7HD.

Chapter 23: Prediction

Carpenter RG et al (1977) Archives of Disease in Childhood 52:606-612.
Madeley RJ (1978) Public Health 92:224-230.

Oakley JR, Tavare CJ and Stanton AN (1978) Archives of Disease in Childhood 53:649–652.

Protestos CD et al (1973) Archives of Disease in Childhood 48:835–841.

Carpenter RG (1983) Journal of the Royal Statistical Society A:146:1–32.

Carpenter RG and Emery JL (1974) In 'Sudden Infant Death Syndrome 1974' Ed. RB Robinson, Foundation for the Study of Infant Deaths. London and Toronto. pp. 91–96.

Carpenter RG, Gardner A and Emery JL (1979) Archives of Disease in Childhood 54:406–7.

Chapter 24: Prevention

Introduction

Southall DP (1983) Archives of Disease in Childhood 58:75.

Taylor EM & Emery JL (1982) Archives of Disease in Childhood 57:668–73.

Symptoms

Pattison CJ, Drinkwater CK & Downham MAPS (1982) Journal of the Royal College of General Practitioners 32:149–162.

Health Visitor Intervention

Carpenter RG & Emery JL (1977) Nature 268:724–5.

Taylor EM, Emery JL & Carpenter RG (1983) Lancet ii:1033–4.

Apnoea Alarms

Simpson H (1983) Archives of Disease in Childhood 58:469–71.

Southall DP (1983) Pediatrics 72:133–138.

Stanton AN (1982) British Medical Journal 285:1441–2.

Stewart-Brown S (1982) British Medical Journal 284:1628.

Chapter 25: Amelioration

Brodrick Report (1971) Interdepartmental Committee on Coroners and Death Certification, Her Majesty's Stationery Office, London.

Chapter 26: The Mystery Unsolved

Introduction

Emery JL (1976) in Recent Advances in Pediatrics no. 5, Edited D. Hull, Churchill-Livingstone p. 203–220.

Season
Bonser RSA, Knight BH & West RR (1978) International Journal of Epidemiology. 7:335–340.
Bull GM (1980) Lancet i:1405–8.
Clarke SKR et al (1978) British Medical Journal 2:796–8.
Davey ML and Reid D (1972) British Journal of Preventive and Social Medicine 26:28–32.
Gupta MM, Round JM and Stamp TCB (1974) Lancet i:568–8.
Hoppenbrouwers T et al. (1981) American Journal of Epidemiology 116:623–635.
Lunn JE, Knowelden J and Handyside AJ (1967) British Journal of Preventive and Social Medicine 21:7–16.
Martin AJ, Gardner PS and McQuillin J (1978) Lancet i:1035–8.
Nelson KE et al. (1975) American Journal of Epidemiology 101:423–430.
Poskitt EME, Cole TJ and Lawson DEM (1979) British Medical Journal 1:221–3.
Robertson WG et al. (1974) British Medical Journal 4:436–7.
Wagnerova M et al. (1979) International Archives of Occupational and Environmental Health 42:325–332.

Age and Sex Differences
Arnon Damus and Chin (1981) Epidemiologic Reviews 3:45–66.
Clarke SKR et al. (1978) British Medical Journal 2:796–8.
Hutt C (1972) Males and Females. Penguin Books. Harmondsworth.
Lind T et al (1977) Acta Paediatrica Scandinavica 66:333–7.
Michaels RH and Rogers KD (1971) Pediatrics 47:120.
Moss H. (1967) Merril-Palmer Quarterly. 13:19–36.

Area differences
Freedman D (1975) British Medical Journal 4:463.
Petersson PO and von Sydow G (1975) British Medical Journal 3:490.
Rantakallio P (1979) Social Science and Medicine 13A 423–9.

Maternal Age, Birth Order, and Social Class
Brown GW, Bhrolchain MM and Harris T. (1975) Sociology 9:225–254.
Crellin E, Pringle MLK and West P (1971). Born Illegitimate: Social and Educational Implications. National Foundation for Educational Research in England and Wales: Slough.
Golding J. Howlett B, Butler NR and Palmer S (1984). In Preparation.
Wolff S. (1981) Children under Stress. Penguin Books, Harmondsworth.

Smoking

Butler NR and Alberman ED (1969) Perinatal Problems: the 2nd Report of the 1958 British Perinatal Mortality Survey. E & S Livingstone, Edinburgh.

Cardozo LD, Gibb DMF, Studd JWN, & Cooper DJ (1982) British Journal of Obstetrics & Gynaecology 89:622–627.

Lyon AJ (1982) Archives of Disease in Childhood 58(5)378–380.

Birthweight and Gestation

Brook CGD (1983) British Medical Journal 286:164–165.

Douglas JWB & Mogford C. (1953) Archives of Disease in Childhood 28:436–445.

Golding J, Butler NR, Howlett B. (1984) In Press.

Index

Page numbers preceded by the letter 'A' refer to Appendix Tables obtainable from Dr. Golding (a charge is made to cover the costs of preparation and postage).

Abuse 90-1, 120-2
  suspected 143
Accident and Emergency Departments
  (see Casualty)
Adenoviruses 133
Aetiology 228
Age
  at death 31, 94-5, 218-9
    & birth order 98-9
    & birthweight 99, 101-2
    & gestation, 32, 99-101
    & infections 131, 133, 219
    & marital status 99
    & season 98-9
    & sex differences 31, A2
    & smoking 99
    & social class 98-9
    & vitamin deficiency 113, 115
  at smiling 84
  of mother 46-7, 94-5, 220
    & age at death A51
    & birth order 47-8, A7
    & child abuse 121
Aims of book 4
Air
  fresh 199
  pollution 41, 217-8, 219
Alcoholism 92
Allergic reaction 128-9
Allergy
  in mother 59, 130, A17
  to cows' milk 8, 80, 129-30, A40
Altitude 30
Ambulance staff 142, 143
  recommendations for 205
Amelioration 204-215
Amniocentesis 61, A23

Anaemia in pregnancy 60, A19
Analgesics in labour A31
Anniversary of death 177
Antenatal care 55
Antibiotics 62, 74
Apgar score 74, 75, 228, A41
Apnoea 228
  alarms 141, 200-3
    false negative 202
    false positive 202
  obstructive 202
Apnoeic attacks 75, 94, 123-5, A40
  in siblings 90
  use of apnoea alarm 201
Appendicectomy 58
Appetite loss 139
Appointments for dead baby 173-4
Area variation 28-30, 94-5, 219-20
Artificial feeds 79-81, 94-5, A48
  & sodium 108-110
  preparation of 109, 198
Asian immigrants 50-1
  & vitamin D 114
Asphyxia 74 (see also Apgar score)
  in siblings 90
Asthma 129, 130
Atelectasis 74
Atopy 130, 228
Attendance
  at infant clinic 79
  for antenatal care 55
  for postnatal checkup 79
Australia
  incidence 22, 26
  seasonal variation 38
  sex differences A34
Autopsy (see post-mortem)

Baptism 144, 145, 162, 206
Barbiturates 62, 65, 94-5, A31
Barometric pressure 41
Beckwith definition 6
Bedding 85-6
Bed-wetting
  in siblings 140
Bereavement 136-40
Beri-beri 115
Berkshire, West 28-9, A1
  (see also ORLS study)
Bilirubin 74, 75, A42
Biotin deficiency 114
Birth order 47-8, 94-5, 220
  & age at death 99, A51
  & age of mother 47-8, 220
  & viral infection 134
Births and Deaths Registration Act
  148, 155
Birthweight 68-70, 94-5, 220-1, A36
  & age at death 99, 101-2, A51
  & child abuse 121
  of twins 71-2
Blackouts in siblings 140
Blood group
  of baby 70, A38, A39
  of mother 51-2, 94-5, A11
Blood pressure, maternal 60, A18
Botulism 105, 131-2
Breast
  engorgement 147
  feeding 79-81, 94-5, A48
    & discomfort following death 147
    & immunity 128
Breathless during feeding 84
Breech delivery 65, A32
Britain
  incidence 22, 25
  sex differences A34
Broderick Report 210
Bronchiolitis 85, 133
Brown fat 125
Burial order 160

Caesarean section 65, A32
Calcium 111
Canada
  incidence 24
  seasonal variation 38
Capillary bronchitis 7
Cardiac triggering 202
Cardiff
  incidence 29

  weather 40
Carotid body abnormalities 125
Casualty staff 142
  recommendations for 204, 205-7, 212
Cause of death 175
Cerebral palsy
  in siblings 89
Chaplain, hospital 206
Child Benefit Book 164-5, 215
Child Guidance Clinic 187, 188
Child Health Clinic 174, 215
Choanal atresia 119
Chronic hypoxia 124-5
City residence 28-9, 94-5, 219-20, A1
  & air pollution 219
  & viral infection 133, 219
Cleft palate 76
Clothes, retrieval of 153
Clothing 199
Clustering
  in hospital of delivery A25
  in space 28
  in time and space 42
  on same day 39-40
Coffee 57
Cola 57
Communication
  between health personnel 206-7
  problems of parents 177
Community Health
  Department 174
  Services 204
Community paediatrician 211
Compassionate Friends, The 213
Conducting system, of heart 126
Confirmation of death 142, 143-4
Congenital
  infection 132
  malformations 75-6, 94-5, A43, A51
    & child abuse 121
    of mother 59-60
    of siblings 89, 91
Contraceptives 55
Controls 228
  in ORLS study 49, A8
Convulsions
  & over-heating 117-8
  in siblings 90, 91
  neonatal A40
Copper 111
Coroner 148-54 160
  recommendations for 204, 209-11, 212
  support from 171

Coroner's
  Act 148
  certificate for cremation 160
  investigation 148-59
  Officer 142, 149-52, 154, 160, 171, 212
  post-mortem 148
  Rules 153, 154-5, 210, 211
Cot death 9
Co-twin 71, 73, 183, 186, 208
Cough 85
Counselling 166-82, 213-4
Counsellor 175
Cows' milk allergy 8, 80
Cremation 160
  cost 163
Crib death 9
Cry
  abnormal 84, A40
  changes in 85
Cyanotic attacks A40
  in siblings 90
Cytomegalovirus (CMV) 132
Czechoslovakia
  incidence 26

Daily risk of death 32-3
Day of death 39, 94-5, A4
Deafness 126
Death Grant 163-4, 215
Deficiency of trace elements 110-2
Deficiency of vitamins 112-6
Delivery, method 65, A32
Denmark, incidence 22, 26
Dental treatment 164-5, 215
Depression 92, 137
Dextran 62
DHSS Leaflet 164, 212
DHSS procedures 163-5
Diabetes, maternal 61
Diarrhoea 85
Distress, maternal in labour A30
Diving reflex 127
Divorce 137
Doctor
  (see General Practitioner,
    Paediatrician, etc)
Drug
  addiction 57-8
  ingestion
    by babies 76, A44
    in labour 65, A31
    in pregnancy 61-2, A50
Drunkenness, as cause 7

Eczema 129, 130
Education of parents 45
Electromagnetic fields 77
Enteroviruses 133
Epidemiological
  evidence for two sub-groups 96-102
  methods 18-20
  results, summarised 94-96, 98-9

Fall in pregnancy 58, 59, A17
Familial recurrence 87-9, 176
Family
  organisation following death 138-9
  Practitioner Committee 174, 215
Feeding problems 122
  neonatal A40
Fertility, subsequent 93
Fever 85
Floor of residence 77
Forceps delivery 65, A32
Foundation for the Study of Infant Deaths
  Leaflets 150, 179-80, 181
    'Information following the Death'
    206, 208, 211
    'When to consult a doctor' 198, 212
    'Your next child' 212
  role 181-2
  study 21, 140, 226-7
    age at death 98-9
    birth order A53
    place of death 141-2
    season of death A54
    sex distribution A55
    social class A52
    time of death 33-5
    twinning A56
Frequency 18
Friends
  of the Foundation 181-2
  support from 171
Funeral
  advice for arranging 160
  cost 161, 162-3
  Directors (see Undertakers)
  service 161-2

Gastroenteritis
  & hypernatraemia 108
  in siblings 90-1
General Practitioners 142-3, 154, 155,
  162
  & suppression of lactation 147
  & surviving children 187

General Practitioners (*Contd*)
  recommendations for 204, 207-9,
    210-1, 212
  support from 167-9, 170, 171
Genetic counselling 212
  (see also Recurrence risk)
Germany, incidence 26
Gestation 67-8, 94-5, 221-2, A35
  & age at death 32, 68, 99-101, A51
  & immaturity 128
  & lung surfactant 122
  definition 67
Glycosuria A19
Grief 136-7, 166, 175-7
  abnormal 176-7
  prolongation with drugs 173
  reactions 208
Gritty placenta 76, A46
Growth
  postnatal 81-3
  retardation 69-70, 101-2, 113, 221-2
Guilt, feelings 137, 138, 167, 171
  & registered cause of death 158

Haemorrhage in pregnancy 60, A19
Happiness, loss of 138-9
Hay fever 129
Head circumference 70, 82, A37
Health
  Authority 211
  prior to death 174-5
  Visitors 162, 166, 167
    & surviving children 187
    recommendations for 204, 211-2
    support from 169-71
Heart beat, abnormalities 126-7
Heating, of home 78
Height of mother 49, A9
Heroin (see Opiate)
Historical perspectives 5, 6
HLA antigens 130
Holding the baby 145-7, 206
Hospital admissions 85
  to mothers 91-2, A49
  to siblings 90-1
Hospital of delivery 63-4, A24
House dust mites 129
Housing 50, 77-8
Humidity 41
Hydramnios 61, A19
Hydrochlorothiazine 62
Hypernatraemia 108-10
Hyperthermia (see Over-heating)

Hypoglycaemia 114, 116
Hypothermia A40
Hypotheses 8-9, 108-34
  generation of 104-5
  testing of 105-7
Hypothyroidism
  in siblings 89
Hypotonia 74
  in siblings 90

Identification of body 151, 206, 209
Illegitimacy (see Marital status)
Immaturity 68
Immigrants 50-1, 94-5
Immunisation 134
  & vitamin C levels 112
Immunoglobin levels 129-30
Immunological mechanisms 128-30, 220,
    221, 222
Incidence 18, 22, 228
  within area 28-30
  world-wide 22-28
Income 45, 50
Incubator 74
Index infant 228
Induction of labour 64, 94-5, A26
Infanticide (see Abuse)
Infarcted placenta 76
Infections 131-4
  & immunity 128
  butulinism 131-2
  CMV 132
  congenital 132
  in pregnancy 58-9, A17
  postnatal 132-4
  viral 132-4
Infertility 54
Influenza
  in infant 133
  in pregnancy 58, A17
Inhalation of vomit 19, 20, 157-9
Inquest 152, 156, 209
Interval
  inter-pregnancy 53-4, 94-5
  since marriage 53, A13
Intervention
  health visitor 199-200
Interview, as therapy 211
Iron 111
Irritability 85
  following death 139
Israel, incidence 27, 28

Japan, incidence 27
Jaundice 74, 75, 94-5, A40
  in siblings 90
Job loss, after death 179

Kaiser Health Plan 45, 54

Labour 63-5
  length of 64, 94-5, A27, A28
Last menstrual period (LMP)
  interval from last delivery 53-4
  interval from marriage 53
  knowledge of 55-6, 94-5, A14, A51
  month of 56
Learnt helplessness 138
Leigh's disease 114
Length
  of baby 70
  of labour 64, 94-5, A27, A28
Literature
  for bereaved parents 145, 164, 179-80,
    182
  for recognition of symptoms 198
Longitude 29-30

Magnesium 110-1
Magnetic fields 77
Malignant hyper-pyrexia 118
Manganese 111
Marital
  disharmony after the death 139, 179
  status 46, 94-5, 221, A6
    & age at death 99, A51
    & child abuse 121
Mattress 86
Mechanical obstruction to breathing
  external 120-2
  internal 119-20
Medical
  Certificate of Cause of Death 148
  history of mother 91-2
Membrane rupture, duration 64, A29
Mental retardation, in siblings 89
Midwife, support from 170, 171
Minister of Religion 211, 212
  & funerals 161-2
  support from 171, 176
Monitor (see Apnoea alarms)
Month (see Season)
Moro reflex 74
Mortuary technicians 146, 212
Moving house, following death 139, 179
Multifactorial 222

Multiple births (see Twins, Triplets) 228
Mumps 58

Nasal obstruction 119
Near-miss 105-6
  & apnoea alarm 201
    results 202
  & apnoeic attacks 124
  & child abuse 121
Neonatal deaths 228
  early 36, 228
  late 228
Neonatal disorders 73-6, A40
  in siblings 89-90
Nervousness after the death 139
New Zealand, incidence 27
Nightmares
  in siblings 140, 184, 185
Non-obstetric disorders in pregnancy
  58-60, 228
North America, incidence 22, 23-4
Notification of death 174

Obesity, maternal 61, A21, A22
Obligatory nose breathers 119
Oculo-cardiac response 127
Oesophageal atresia 75, 76
Onset of labour 64
Opiate
  addiction 58
  in labour 65, A31
  in pregnancy A50
ORLS study 20-21, 25, 28-9, 31-2, 38,
    40-1, 44, 46-7, 49-61 63-4, 68-70,
    74-6, 80, 224-5, A1-A51
  controls 49, A8
Overcrowding 7, 45, 77
Overdose 92
Over-heating 116-8
Overlaying 6-7, 120
Over-protection, of siblings 140
Oxfordshire 28-9, 94-5, A1
  (see also ORLS)
Oxygen to neonates 74

Paediatricians 144, 155, 171
  recommendations for 204, 211-2
Pain in pregnancy 61, A19
Palmar creases, single 75, 76
Parental characteristics 43-52
Parity 228
  (see Birth order)
Passive smoking 83

Past obstetric history
  (see Previous pregnancy loss)
Pathologists 146, 160
  paediatric 210
  recommendations 210-1
Pharmacists 215
Perinatal death 228
Phenobarbitone (see Barbiturates)
Pill, the 55
Pillows 85-6
Place of birth
  of baby 63-4, 94-5
  of mother 50-1, A10, A51
Place of death 35-6
  Foundation Study 141-2
Placenta 76, A45, A46
Planned pregnancies 54-5
Pneumonia, as cause of death 8, 157, 158
Police 142, 144, 145, 149-50, 171
  recommendations for 209, 212
Population 18
Post-mortem
  change in appearance 146
  findings 167
    explanation of 175
    by paediatrician 172
    interpretation 20
  notification
    to General Practitioners 168, 172
    to parents 153-5
    recommendations 204, 210-1, 212
  importance of 6, 19
Postnatal
  growth 81-3
  illness 84-5
  infection 132-4
  temperament 83-4
Post-neonatal death 36, 228
Post-perinatal death 228
Post-term 68, 228
  (see also Gestation)
  by age at death 101
Potassium 111
Prediction 190-5
Pregnancy 53-62
Prescription, free 164-5, 215
Press reports 152-3, 209
Pre-term 68, 228
  (see also Gestation)
  by age at death 100
Prevalence 228
Prevention 196-203
  primary 196-7

  secondary 197-203
Previous pregnancy loss 52, 94-5, A12
Procedural questionnaire 21
Procurator Fiscal 148
Protein deprivation 128
Proteinuria 61, A20
Psychiatric disorder in mother 59, 92, A17
Psychiatrist, support from 176

QT interval 127

Race 49-51
  sex differences 67
Rainfall 41
Rate 228
Recurrence risk 88
Registered cause of death 19, 157-9
  recommendations 211
Registering the death 155-6
Registrar of Births and Deaths 148, 149,
    155-6, 160, 212
Relative risk
  definition 44, 229
  scoring system 192-5
Relatives
  second degree 229
  support from 171
  third degree 229
REM sleep 123, 125
Respiratory
  distress 74, A40
    & lung surfactant 122
    in siblings 90
  syncytial virus 133-4, 218-9
Resuscitation 74
  attempts 141, 159
Retrieval of baby's clothes 153
Rickets 113
Risk assessment
  (see scoring systems)
Rubella 58, 59
  contact A17
Rural-urban differences
  (see urban-rural)

Schizophrenia 92
Scoring systems 190-5
  relative risk method 192-5
  sensitivity and specificity 195
  Sheffield multistage 190-2
Season
  of birth 65-6, 94-5, 218
    & vitamin C 113

of conception 56, 218, A15
of death 38-9, 94-5
  & age at death 98-9, A3, A51
  & biochemical changes 217
  & diet 217
  & infections 132, 217
  & weather 40-2, 217
Secular trends 36-8
Sedatives 62, 65
  after death 172-3
Seeing baby, after death 144, 145-7
Selenium 111-2
Sex differences 67, 94-5, 218
  & age at death 31, A2
    & race 67
    in literature A34
    in RSV 134
    in twins 73
Sibling 87-91, 106-7
  (see also Subsequent sibling)
  behaviour 140
  congenital malformations 89
  definition 229
  hospital admissions 90-1
  mortality 87-9
  neonatal illness 89-90
  reaction to death 183-8
Single mother (see Marital status)
Singleton 229
Sleep
  abnormalities 123-6
  research 123-6
Sleeping
  position 86
  problems
    following death 139
    in siblings 184, 187
Smoking
  of father 57, 83
  of mother 83, 220, 221

  in pregnancy 56-7, 94-5, 221, A16
    & age at death 99, A51
    & immunity 128
    & vitamin C 113
Snow 41
Snuffles 85, A40
Social
  Class 43-5, 94-5, 220-1, A5
    & age at death 99, A51
    & child abuse 121
    & infection 132, 133
    & vitamin deficiencies 113, 115

  conditions 78-9, A47
  worker 168, 171, 176, 206, 211, 212
Society's reaction 177-8
Socio-economic index 45
Sodium (see Hypernatraemia)
Special care admission 74, 75
  to siblings 89-90
Stable union 46
Statistical significance 20, 229
Serilisation reversal 179
Stillbirths 36, 229
Stress
  & biotin deficiency 114
  & hyperpyrexia 118
Stridor A40
Subsequent sibling
  & apnoea alarms 202-3
  & Foundation support 182
  & maternal anxiety 138, 139, 176
Sudden
  infant death
    definition 6, 229
    numbers annually 5
    syndrome 9
  respiratory death 229
Suicide 137
Sulphur dioxide 41
Sunshine 40-1,
  & vitamin D 113
Support
  for parents 166-82
  groups 180-1, 204, 211
Suppression of lactation 147, 207, 208, 214
Surfactant, lung 122-3
Sweden 220
  incidence 22, 25, 28
Symptoms, recognition of 197-8

Tactile adaptive scale 74
Tea 57
Temperament 83-4
Temperature 40-2
  in home 78
Term 67, 229
Thiamine deficiency 114-6
Thymus, enlarged 7-8
Thyroid hormones 116
Thyroxine 116
Time
  of death 33-5, 96
  of delivery 65, A33
  trends 36-8

Tongue causing blockage 119
Toxaemia 60,
TPP 115
Trace element deficiencies 110-2
Tranquilisers 172-3
Tri-iodothyronine 116
Triplets 70-71
Twins 70-3, 89, 94-5
    coping with co-twin 186, 208
    grief of co-twin 183
    risk to co-twin 71, 73
    thiamine deficiency 115
Type of delivery 65, A32

Ultrasound scan 61, A23
Undertaker 146, 160, 161
    & cost of funeral 162-3
    recommendations for 209, 212
    support from 171
Unemployment 45-6
Urban-rural differences 28-9, A1
    in confirming death 143-4
Urea (see Hypernatraemia)
Urinary infection in pregnancy 59, A17
U.S.A.
    incidence 23-4
    seasonal variation 38-9

Vaccination (see Immunisation)
Vagal nerve 127
Vaginal discharge/infection 61, A19

Varicose veins 59
Ventilatory response 126
Ventricular fibrillation 126
Viral antibodies 130
Virus infections 132-4
Vital records 229
Vitamin
    C deficiency 112-3
    D deficiency 113-4
        & season 217
    E deficiency 111, 112
    supplements 76, 112
Vomiting 85
    in pregnancy 61, A19

Water
    calcium 111
    magnesium 111
    softening 109
Weather 40-2
    suitable care for 199
Weekends 39
Weight of mother A21, A22
Wind 41-2
    & diving reflex 127
Window open 78
Winter (see Season)

X-ray in pregnancy 61, A23

Zinc 111